LOSING SLEEP

Losing Sleep

Risk, Responsibility, and Infant Sleep Safety

Laura Harrison

NEW YORK UNIVERSITY PRESS
New York

NEW YORK UNIVERSITY PRESS
New York
www.nyupress.org

References to Internet websites (URLs) were accurate at the time of writing. Neither the author nor New York University Press is responsible for URLs that may have expired or changed since the manuscript was prepared.

Library of Congress Cataloging-in-Publication Data
Names: Harrison, Laura, 1983– author.
Title: Losing sleep : risk, responsibility, and infant sleep safety / Laura Harrison.
Description: New York : New York University Press, [2022] |
Includes bibliographical references and index.
Identifiers: LCCN 2021046819 | ISBN 9781479801145 (hardback ; alk. paper) |
ISBN 9781479801152 (paperback ; alk. paper) | ISBN 9781479801183 (ebook) |
ISBN 9781479801206 (ebook other)
Subjects: LCSH: Infants—Sleep—United States. | Infants—Care—UnitedStates. |
Sleeping customs—United States. | Infants—Mortality—UnitedStates. | Maternal and
infant welfare—United States. | Discrimination in medical care—United States.
Classification: LCC RJ506.S55 H356 2022 | DDC 616.8/4982—dc23
LC record available at https://lccn.loc.gov/2021046819

New York University Press books are printed on acid-free paper, and their binding materials are chosen for strength and durability. We strive to use environmentally responsible suppliers and materials to the greatest extent possible in publishing our books.

Manufactured in the United States of America

10 9 8 7 6 5 4 3 2 1

Also available as an ebook

CONTENTS

Introduction   1

1. "Sleep Like a Baby" and Other Historical Fallacies   25

2. Making and Unmaking a Safe Sleep Environment: From the AAP to the Rock 'n Play Recall   53

3. What's Best for Baby? Co-Sleeping and the Politics of Inequality   82

4. "Everybody Loses": Parents as Perpetrators   120

5. Advertising Infant Safety: Gender, Risk, and the Good Parent   161

Conclusion: Rethinking the Safe Sleep Environment   189

Acknowledgments   201

Notes   203

References   233

Index   257

About the Author   273

Introduction

New parents are inundated with advice and products that purport to keep their baby safe, even beginning pre-conception.[1] Many "baby-proof" their home by installing gates or socket protectors before their newborn can even roll over. Despite these precautions, the question of where and in what position the baby will sleep is much more immediate, and often quite controversial. The specter of Sudden Infant Death Syndrome can cast a shadow over the early days at home with a new baby, keeping parents up at night, pacing back and forth to the nursery or glued to the monitor to check the baby's breathing. Sharing a room, or even a bed, with a new baby could ostensibly offer more immediate assurance. However, one pervasive tenet of safe sleep discourse is that it is risky for parents to co-sleep, or share a bed, with their infant. While co-sleeping is common—more than half of parents surveyed in the United States report doing so—leading pediatric organizations also label it a risk factor for infant death.[2] The messages that parents receive from family members, the media, and even their doctors create a great deal of anxiety about sleep-related infant death, often resulting in one-size-fits-all narratives about how a good parent responsibly manages safe sleep.

This book argues that infant sleep safety is a socially constructed paradigm, and that the neoliberal model of health-as-individual-responsibility has come to permeate our understanding of what constitutes safe sleep. In other words, what is necessary to make infant sleep safe has changed over time and across cultures; what makes infant sleep risky, or how to manage that risk, is a point of contestation. Understanding how neoliberalism shapes messages about infant sleep safety is important because safe sleep rhetoric impacts systems, including public health policy and law, that have the power to stigmatize or even criminalize parenting practices. It also shapes broader cultural beliefs about responsibility and risk that impact individuals at an intimate level, including whether they view themselves as posing as an embodied risk

1

to their child. Unsurprisingly, messages about infant sleep safety affect parents differently based on their social location. At the same time that infant sleep safety (and infant mortality more broadly) is positioned as the responsibility of individual parents, the state is taking an increasingly visible role in policing and surveilling parental decision making, including criminalizing the parents of children who die in their sleep. This book examines how the problem of sleep-related infant death is and historically has been framed in relation to parental decision making and biomedical authority, and argues that "infant sleep safety" is a social construction that has evolved in ways that privilege certain types of parenting practice.

This project brings together scholarship on health, risk, reproductive justice, and neoliberalism. As Anna Kirkland and Jonathan Metzl argue in *Against Health: How Health Became the New Morality*, when a behavior is categorized as a health risk, then those who "choose" to engage in it are viewed as opening the door to a broad condemnation of their morality and ethics.[3] When these "risky" health behaviors are associated with parenting, then individual parents are stigmatized as bad choice-makers who are morally suspect, selfish, and dangers to their children. This ignores the institutional and historical violence experienced by low-income people and people of color, often at the hands of the same systems (medicine, government, police) that are creating, codifying, and enforcing health-related norms. Feminist science studies also inform this analysis; safe sleep guidelines and the policies informed by them are not constructed in a vacuum. Who is authorized to produce knowledge about sleep safety—medical researchers? Pediatricians? Public health officials? Parents? What technologies are created to solve the "problem" of infant sleep safety, who determines what the problem is, and what groups benefit? How are health disparities in infant sleep linked to historical patterns of discrimination and oppression?

Consumer culture also contributes to and reflects the neoliberal emphasis on individual control over health; the infant safety industry is valued at more than $325 million a year in part by creating products that claim to reduce the risk of illness, accidents, and even death, often with an authoritative veneer that belies limited or absent government oversight and regulation.[4] This book will point to neoliberal ideologies and policies as factors that shift attention from the role of the state in maintaining wellness to the responsibility of the individual. Yet as feminist theorist Leela Fernandes argues, the state has not ceded all authority to the market; it continues to utilize policing and surveillance as mechanisms of social control. Indeed, the free market and the state may have similar interests as pertains to infant sleep safety.[5] The message that all "unsafe sleep" deaths are preventable normalizes the criminalization of families who "choose" not to follow safe sleep guidelines, while the market purports to solve the problem through the sale of technology and devices that promise peace of mind for parents.

This narrative is complicated further by the fact that at its core, safe sleep is about preventing infant mortality, and infant mortality rates in the United States differ widely by race and are linked to socioeconomic status. Infant mortality is defined by the Centers for Disease Control and Prevention as the death of an infant before their first birthday, and is assessed as a significant measure of the health of a nation. The United States ranks fifty-first in the world for infant mortality, largely because of racial disparities.[6] While the overall infant mortality rate in the United States is 5.9 deaths per 1,000 live births, major disparities in infant mortality fall along the lines of race, with African Americans experiencing the highest rates (11.3), and Asian Americans/Pacific Islanders the lowest (4.2).[7] Even as overall infant mortality rates are falling across ethnic groups, the disparity in deaths between white and Black infants has more than doubled in the last decade.[8]

The focus on infant sleep safety suggests that individual parents have the agency to protect their own children from unexpected infant death, if only they would make the right choices about safe sleep. However, children's health is interconnected with multiple factors both internal and external, including whether they were born full term, their mother's lifetime exposure to chronic stress, and environmental hazards in their home and community.[9] These are among what are termed the "social determinants of health" or "the conditions in which people live (shaped by the distribution of resources, such as money and political and economic power) at global, national, and local levels."[10] The social determinants of health include access to health care, affordable day care, safe housing, and the broader effects of poverty and structural racism.

Infant sleep safety is not commonly framed as a reproductive justice issue, but this book will demonstrate that safe sleep guidelines are implicitly modeled on a white, middle-/upper-class norm that assumes access to resources without providing the support for safe sleep equity. It also taps into deeply held beliefs about gender, and women's responsibility as primary caretakers. This matters because poor women and women of color are more likely to be implicated as bad decision makers, and to be surveilled, policed, and criminalized. This book demonstrates that infant sleep safety is an intersectional issue, and that creating the conditions for safe sleep for all infants requires starting with the needs and involvement of communities of color. Finally, I will argue that what is conveniently pushed aside in the focus on individual choices is the systemic ill effects of poverty and racism on the health of mothers and babies. Which babies are born with *access* to safe sleep in United States? Who decides?

Safe Sleep, Sudden Infant Death, and Co-Sleeping

In order to examine the social construction of infant sleep safety, it is vital to understand how a safe sleep environment is defined and what it is meant to protect against, namely unexpected infant death. This section will begin to unpack the meaning of safe sleep, a project that will be ongoing throughout this book. It will also introduce key medical terms like Sudden Infant Death Syndrome, Sudden Unexpected Infant Death, and accidental suffocation or asphyxia.[11] The development of these classifications is significant because they play a role in shaping the discourse of infant sleep safety, including the culpability of parents for managing risk. Co-sleeping is also introduced in this section, because co-sleeping is frequently characterized as a violation of safe sleep guidelines and as a risk factor for unexpected infant death.

"Safe sleep" is a loaded term. It is normative in that it implies an idealized environment for children and an approved set of behaviors by caregivers. It is prescriptive in that it implies a singular model of safety that all caregivers should follow, and because its binary opposite ("unsafe sleep") carries the moral weight of potential harm to an infant. And, like a lot of childrearing norms and guidelines, safe sleep is a social construct that has changed significantly over time and continues to vary across cultures. While humans have evolved to sleep, the way that we format and structure sleep is both shaped by and shapes the structure of our lives, including reproductive labor, education, and work responsibilities.[12] Contemporary norms concerning "safe sleep" are inseparable from broader cultural beliefs about the sanctity and importance of uninterrupted sleep, the belief that "good" or "bad" sleep impacts our health, the association between sleep and morality (for example, the belief that "early to bed, early to rise" is a sign of productivity and hard work), and expectations of privacy or companionship during sleep. Many of these social norms transfer to infant sleep: New parents often feel intensely judged by questions about how their baby is sleeping, with the unspoken assumption that a "good baby" sleeps through the night, and that parents are responsible for "training" their baby to sleep alone and for uninterrupted stretches of time. Likewise, parents who do not follow all safe sleep guidelines—such as allowing their infants to nap on their stomachs, or co-sleeping—may hesitate to share this information with pediatricians or peers for fear of negative responses.[13] Judgments about sleep thus travel in multiple directions, implicating "good" (or "bad") babies, and "good" (or "bad") parents.

In this book, safe sleep refers primarily to a set of guidelines that are meant to prevent deaths that occur during sleep to infants under the age of one. As will be discussed further in chapter 2, the most authoritative safe sleep standards in the United States are set by the American Academy of Pediatrics (AAP), a professional organization of pediatricians that creates guidelines for children's health; in addition to safe sleep, the AAP publishes recommended limits on screen time, vaccination schedules, and car seat standards, among other day-to-day parental concerns. The AAP's most recent safe sleep recommendations include that babies should always sleep on their back, on a firm surface, sharing a room (but not a bed) with their parents until at least six months of age, but preferably a year.[14] Chapter 2 will analyze how these recommendations have changed over time and the role of the AAP and other medical professionals in shaping safe sleep discourse.

The Centers for Disease Control and Prevention tracks the number of unexpected infant deaths that occur in the United States each year. As of 2017, roughly 3,600 deaths annually fell under the umbrella category of Sudden Unexpected Infant Death (SUID). SUID encompasses death attributed to SIDS, accidental suffocation and strangulation in bed, and those designated as "unknown cause." Sudden Infant Death Syndrome

(SIDS) was first formally defined in 1969 as "the sudden death of any infant or young child, which is unexpected by history, and in which a thorough postmortem examination fails to demonstrate an adequate cause for death."[15] In 1991, the National Institute of Child Health and Human Development revised the definition to include an age limit (that SIDS is only applicable to children under the age of one) and added that an autopsy and a death scene investigation must be completed. Most recently, the journal *Pediatrics* published an updated definition in 2004 that defines SIDS as "[T]he sudden unexpected death of an infant <1 year of age, with onset of the fatal episode apparently occurring during sleep, that remains unexplained after a thorough investigation, including performance of a complete autopsy and review of the circumstances of death and the clinical history."[16]

Of the 3,600 SUID deaths in 2017, 38 percent (1,400) were attributed to SIDS, while 36 percent (1,300) were classified as "unknown cause." While "unknown cause" may seem like another term for SIDS, given that deaths are categorized as SIDS when no known cause can be identified, they are actually two different classifications. A death can only be classified as SIDS if it meets the relatively stringent criteria discussed above, including the completion of an autopsy and death scene investigation. Some deaths may be categorized as "unknown cause" because these criteria were not met. The remaining 26 percent (900) were attributed to accidental suffocation or strangulation in bed.[17] The National Institutes of Health defines Accidental Suffocation and Strangulation in Bed (ASSB) as occurring when a baby's breathing is restricted by soft bedding, or when an infant gets trapped between objects, like a bed and a wall or couch cushions.[18] Accidental suffocation differs from SIDS in that the cause of death is identified. As later chapters will discuss, accidental suffocation is physiologically indistinguishable from SIDS—in other words, an autopsy cannot differentiate the two causes of death.[19] Thus, a death is categorized as accidental suffocation based on evidence gathered at the death scene and reports from parents or other caregivers. If a deceased infant is discovered on a sleep surface other than a crib, the cause of death may be attributed to accidental suffocation rather than SIDS because of the location of the death.[20]

The root cause of SIDS remains poorly understood and greatly debated. Historically, unexpected deaths during sleep have been documented in the Bible, in medieval writings, and in laws and statutes from the thirteenth century onward; they were often attributed to mothers rolling over on their babies during the night.[21] These deaths were frequently blamed on the immorality and vice of poor women, which is a theme that has remained relatively consistent over time.[22] In the early twentieth century, theories included that affected infants were born with an enlarged thymus gland, or that the deaths were attributed to "accidental mechanical suffocation." By mid-century, researchers began to take seriously the idea that sleep-related infant deaths were truly unexplained, and SIDS was medicalized as a confounding disease with no known cause. The second half of the twentieth century saw the rise of the apnea theory of SIDS, that infants suffered from respiratory and breathing difficulties. As Brittany Cowgill argues in *Rest Uneasy*, her detailed history of SIDS in the United States, by the 1980s researchers had returned to theories that often directed the focus back on parents, in part because studies revealed that low-income families and people of color experienced far higher rates of SIDS deaths than did middle-income white families.[23]

In 1994, the Triple Risk model was introduced, which held that SIDS deaths are caused by the convergence of three factors: a critical development period (meaning the age of the infant); an external stressor (such as the presence of soft bedding, prone sleep, or overheating); and an underlying vulnerability (such as prematurity or low birth weight).[24] This theory is tied to research that has consistently revealed commonalities in infants who die of SIDS. The vast majority die between two to four months of age, and 90 percent of cases occur by the time an infant is six months old. Other "intrinsic risk factors" include prematurity, male sex, low birth weight, and prenatal exposure to cigarette smoke and alcohol, while "extrinsic risk factors" include sleep position or soft bedding.[25] As further chapters will discuss in detail, co-sleeping is also considered an extrinsic risk factor for sleep-related infant death. The Back to Sleep Campaign (later renamed Safe to Sleep) was initiated in 1994 by a coalition of pediatric, public health, and SIDS organizations, with a focus on retraining parents and caregivers to put babies to sleep on their backs instead of their stomachs. This initiative is credited with a major decrease in unexpected infant deaths that eventually plateaued, but major disparities in SUID deaths remain.[26]

As I discuss at length in chapter 4, "Everybody Loses," a diagnostic shift has impacted the way unexpected infant deaths are categorized and counted. As a result of this shift, deaths that at one time would have been labeled SIDS are increasingly recorded as accidental suffocation or "unexplained." In other words, SIDS rates may appear artificially low because many deaths that were once labeled SIDS are now categorized in a different way. As researchers have learned more about risk factors for SUID, such as soft bedding and co-sleeping, medical examiners are increasingly uncomfortable calling a death SIDS if these risk factors are present.[27] This is significant because "accidental" deaths are viewed as preventable, resulting from modifiable risk factors. The result is an increased public health focus on safe sleep education, which later chapters will argue is disproportionately aimed at communities of color and low-income communities, at times with calamitous results. Communities of color are often the focus of safe sleep campaigns because rates of SIDS did not drop evenly across racial groups after Back to Sleep; while Native American and Black populations had the highest initial declines, infants in those populations are still roughly twice as likely to succumb to SIDS.[28] Native Americans have the highest number of SUID deaths (205.8 deaths per 100,000 live births), followed by non–Hispanic Black infants (181 deaths per 100,000 live births). According to Cowgill, the Back to Sleep campaign in the United States did not adequately reach minority communities, and some were resistant to its message because it did not fully address cultural differences in sleep norms.[29] Similar disparities are found internationally, with indigenous populations in Canada, Australia, and New Zealand facing higher SUID rates than other racial/ethnic groups in those countries.

Another factor that affects whether an infant death is categorized as SIDS is if the infant was found to be sleeping in an adult bed. What to call this—when an infant shares a sleep surface with an adult—is both controversial and important. It impacts how statistics are collected regarding the safety of shared sleep, which then influences recommendations by doctors and public health experts that are taken up by hospitals, daycare providers, and parents, and even used by the criminal justice system to assess parental negligence. Most proponents of shared sleep use the term co-sleeping to describe a parent sharing an adult bed with their child. However, when researchers have defined "co-sleeping" in some significant studies of sleep-related infant death, they used it as an umbrella term for any shared sleep surface between children and adults, including couches and chairs. This matters because couches and chairs are more dangerous for shared sleep than are adult beds; if researchers lump all surfaces together as "co-sleeping," then the practice looks significantly more dangerous than when "co-sleeping" refers only to sharing an adult bed.[30] Co-sleeping has also at times been used to describe both bed- and room-sharing, further muddying the waters. As a result, some use the term "bed-sharing" to refer to a more specific shared sleep location. I use both bed-sharing and co-sleeping throughout the book; when I use the term co-sleeping, I am referring to the sharing of an adult bed (not a couch or chair).

While parents co-sleep with children well past infancy for a variety of reasons, and children of various ages may share a sleep surface, this book focuses on co-sleeping between adult caregivers and children under the age of one. Research indicates that co-sleeping is very common in the United States, and the practice has increased in the last several decades. A 2010 study found that more than 60 percent of parents reported co-sleeping with their infants at least once,[31] and an analysis of the National Infant Sleep Position study found that 45 percent of parents reported bed-sharing at least some of the time.[32] Co-sleeping between adults and infants is significant for this project; leading organizations like the AAP contend that there is no safe way to co-sleep, and that co-sleeping is a risk factor for SUID deaths. However, in recent years the AAP has begun to acknowledge (if perhaps reluctantly) the frequency of co-sleeping, and to inform caregivers that should they fall asleep with their baby, it is safer to do so in an adult bed than on other surfaces.[33]

Co-sleeping is a key tenet of attachment-based parenting philosophies that valorize parent-child bonding through physical contact. This type of co-sleeping is sometimes referred to as "intentional," and as previously mentioned, intentional co-sleepers may be selective about disclosure, knowing that pediatricians or family members may disagree with their decision.[34] Low-income parents, and especially poor parents of color who co-sleep, are often assumed to be "reactive" co-sleepers, meaning that they intend for their infant to sleep separately, but end up sharing a bed because the baby is ill, fussy, or the parents are tired.[35] Research consistently demonstrates that African Americans and Hispanics co-sleep at higher rates in the United States than do white parents.[36] A qualitative study of African American mothers found that safety was the top consideration for where an infant would sleep—whether mothers chose to have their infants sleep in their beds or in a crib, they did so based on the belief that they were making the safest choice for their child.[37] As discussed later in this book, public health campaigns that aim to eliminate co-sleeping may directly acknowledge "traditions" of co-sleeping in communities of color, but situate them as risky and dangerous.

To be clear, the purpose of this book is not to adjudicate whether or not co-sleeping is a significant risk factor for unexpected infant death—even most vocal proponents of co-sleeping acknowledge that there is huge variation in how people co-sleep, with attendant variations in safety. What I do argue is that the primary drivers of racial disparities in infant mortality are structural and systemic, and are intimately tied to living in a white supremacist society. The historical injustices that contribute to contemporary health inequalities have deep roots in the American legal system, public policy, politics, and medicine. They include the legacies of scientific racism, residential segregation, employment discrimination, mass incarceration, and unequal access to quality education and health care. However, much of the discourse surrounding infant sleep safety, and particularly co-sleeping, implicates the choices of individual parents in determining whether an infant lives to their first birthday. These choices—about where a baby will sleep, with whom, and in what environment—are presented as equally available to parents, and as somehow separable from the multifactorial risks for infant mortality like premature birth, low birth weight, and the chronic stress of racism. In this neoliberal paradigm, individuals are responsible for managing risk, and the state will intervene if they fail to do so.

Risk and Neoliberalism

Infant sleep safety in all of its guises, including guidelines, recommendations, policy, and marketing, centers around notions of risk. The American Academy of Pediatrics, in one of its policy statements concerning sudden infant death, defines risk as an epidemiological term that refers to "the probability that an outcome will occur given the presence of a particular factor or set of factors."[38] Risk *factors*, then, can be modifiable or non-modifiable; the role of an organization like the AAP is in part to educate patients about modifiable risk factors, and change their behavior or environment (or both) in ways that reduce the probability that a negative outcome will occur. Sociologist Ulrich Beck argues that we now live in a "risk society"; as industrial development has led to seemingly ever-present yet invisible hazards in our environment (such as air pollution and global warming), citizens become increasingly skeptical and anxious about the role of government in protecting them from these dangers.[39] Individuals are pressured to take personal responsibility for ensuring their own health and that of their families, and thus attempt to manage risk independently in order to maintain a sense of agency and self-control.[40] Risk is a key element within the ideology of neoliberalism, which centralizes privatization, free trade, and deregulation, and transfers political, economic, and social responsibility from the state to the individual.[41] Feminist theorist Leela Fernandes argues that "state regulation of poor and socioeconomically marginalized communities expands" at the same time that neoliberal policies privatize responsibility for structural inequalities.[42] In other words, individuals are held increasingly accountable for outcomes such as the health of their children while being denied access to necessities like affordable day care, parental leave, and safe housing. And, as Fernandes points out, this agenda aligns with neoliberalism but predates it in the history of the US "racial state."[43]

While neoliberalism is often linked to economics, it has also become embedded in social policy and approaches to health. The rhetoric of personal responsibility is particularly salient for health discourse, because the "responsibility framework" sidesteps explicit mention of identity categories like race, class, or sexuality, while contending that individuals are less deserving of assistance and protection if they "choose" unhealthy lifestyles or risky behaviors.[44] In relation to health, neoliberal ideology emphasizes the moral responsibility of individuals to avoid risk for themselves and their families and downplays the structural inequalities that locate certain groups in riskier environments while also disproportionately surveilling and policing them. As David Harvey argues, "individual success or failure are interpreted in terms of entrepreneurial or personal failings . . . rather than being attributed to any systemic property (such as the class exclusions usually attributed to capitalism)."[45]

As Beck's definition suggests, risk has extended beyond its original, neutral usage "referring to probability, or the mathematical likelihood of an event occurring."[46] While Beck focuses primarily on external risks (like those posed by environmental hazards), Deborah Lupton adds that many risks today are considered "lifestyle risks," or risks that individuals incur based on their own choices and behaviors. Co-sleeping, for example, would be considered a "lifestyle risk," and thus public health officials and pediatric organizations contend that unsafe sleep deaths are entirely preventable. Lupton argues, however, that all risk is socially constructed, and behaviors that are deemed "risky" are determined within a given cultural context—"the risks which are selected by society as requiring attention may therefore have no relation to 'real' danger but are culturally identified as important."[47] In safe sleep education, the parental bed has taken on outsized cultural significance as a site of risk; as I discuss at length in chapter 3, the City of Milwaukee, Wisconsin's public health campaign in the early 2000s compared an adult bed to a grave in order to get this message across. One unintended consequence of such messaging is that some parents have switched from feeding their infants in bed to feeding them on a couch or armchair—locations that pose a significantly higher risk of suffocation should the parent fall asleep.[48]

Lupton also clarifies that individuals may assess risk far differently than experts; parents who refuse to vaccinate, for example, rarely do so because of ignorance or lack of concern for their children. Rather, their own assessment of risk leads them to conclude that vaccination is more dangerous than potential exposure to illness.[49] Parents who co-sleep, especially poor parents, are also often assumed to be selfish or ignorant at best, or careless at worst. However, many mothers assess their environment, their child's health, and their own histories and determine that keeping their child close during the night reduces their risk of a host of ills, including environmental threats like violence or pests.[50] Dorothy Nelkin also finds that the way risk is defined is always in relation to social and political issues, like fears about immigration, poverty, or corporate greed.[51] Co-sleeping is perceived to be differentially risky when done by low-income parents versus middle- and upper-class parents. The social stigma surrounding parenting while poor impacts assessments about whether low-income parents can learn to co-sleep safely.

Of course, co-sleeping is not the only sleep-related risk that infants face. The ideology that characterizes infant sleep safety is one in which all sleeping infants are at risk, even healthy infants with no significant "risk factors" for unexpected infant death. Parents are framed as both vectors of risk (because they may make bad choices that put infants in danger) and also personally responsible for mitigating risk, regardless of structural factors that may limit them or their access to resources that could mitigate these factors. The underlying assumption is that all individuals are inherently at risk, even when asymptomatic, and thus require professional intervention and assessment.[52] Worry and anxiety are normalized as the expected state for new parents; clinically diagnosed postpartum anxiety affects 10 percent of new mothers, often triggered by "the awareness of how fragile a baby is," according to reproductive psychiatrist Alexandra Sacks.[53] While this anxiety is very real, it is not necessarily a result of greater risk for infants and children,[54] even specifically for sleep-related risk like Sudden Infant Death Syndrome, which is lower for most infants today than it was 30 years ago.[55] Anxiety may stem in fact from the nebulous and ever-growing category of risk: as Jan Macvarish argues, "a defining feature of contemporary parenting culture is the exponential expansion of apparent risks to the child that a parent is obliged to take account of and avoid."[56] The privatization of risk means that parents of infants are "responsibilized" for ensuring that their babies appropriately bond, that they are breastfed, that their brains are developing, that they sleep alone but without feeling abandoned or relying on "crying it out."

Parents, and mothers in particular, are expected to operate in a perpetual state of anxiety; Brenda Cossman terms this "anxiety governance," arguing that anxiety is constitutive of risk and encourages parents to focus exclusively on how to limit risk to their own children, at the expense of organizing collectively for social change.[57] Anxiety governance also necessitates what has been termed the "anticipatory nature of risk,"[58] the "logic of preemption,"[59] and the "precautionary principle"[60]—essentially, the responsible neoliberal citizen ascertains the potential for risk prior to ill health and manages it preemptively, perhaps by consuming the right products or engaging the services of experts. Should the individual fail to manage risk appropriately, her social location will likely (but not always) determine the level of surveillance she is under, and thus the threat of state intervention. As Natalie Fixmer-Oraiz argues, "surveillance and policing are two sides of the same coin—one cultivates self-discipline and lateral observation; the other ensures strict sovereign enforcement when neoliberal governmentality fails to induce compliance."[61] Later chapters will demonstrate how self-discipline is centralized in messages about infant sleep safety that are crafted by public health officials and also will examine how surveillance and policing disproportionately impact certain groups of parents. A hegemonic notion of good parenting is fundamental to the rhetoric of safe sleep, replete with gendered ideologies of a mother's role in ensuring infant well-being and classed and racialized assumptions about parenting behaviors.

Gender, Race, and "Good Parenting"

Stereotypes about parenting (and specifically mothering) are gendered, racialized, and inflected by beliefs about class. Recent political trends demonstrate a growing—or at least increasingly overt—distrust of women's decision making concerning their bodies, reproductive health, and parenting decisions. What has been termed the "War on Women" has resulted in expanded restrictions in access to contraceptives, abortion, and women's health resources, which have dire effects on women's ability to parent the children that they have.[62] Feminist theorists have analyzed the cases of women like Regina McKnight, who was convicted of homicide by child abuse in South Carolina for using crack during her pregnancy and experiencing a stillbirth; Bei Bei Shuai, charged with homicide in Indiana after she attempted suicide while pregnant and the baby, born seven weeks premature, died shortly after birth; Purvi Patel, sentenced to 20 years in prison in Indiana for feticide for what she reported as a miscarriage; or Alicia Beltran in Wisconsin, who was detained against her will for months after acknowledging a history of past substance abuse to a prenatal counselor.[63] All are indicative of the criminalization of women's conduct during pregnancy, as are laws passed in states like Alabama, George, Louisiana, Missouri, Ohio, and Texas, sometimes called "heartbeat bills." These bills outlaw abortion as early as a fetal heartbeat is detected (or, in Alabama's legislation, at any stage of pregnancy), some without exceptions for rape or incest, some proposing criminal prosecutions of doctors who perform abortions, or restrictions on women's ability to leave the state to seek an abortion.[64]

Alicia Beltran's case starkly reveals how a woman who has been identified as a risk to her child is vulnerable to extensive state intervention and surveillance. Beltran had not been using drugs during her pregnancy, but a social worker recommended that she begin taking anti-addiction medication due to her history of substance use. Beltran refused, triggering Wisconsin's Unborn Child Protection Act (commonly referred to as the "Cocaine Mom Act") of 1998,[65] which gave the state the authority to detain pregnant women suspected of using drugs.[66] Her fetus was appointed a legal guardian, and in 2013 Beltran was committed to a drug treatment center for 78 days.[67] Beltran's case was used as evidence in a federal suit contesting Wisconsin's law, which in 2018 was found unconstitutional by a federal judge. However, the Wisconsin Attorney General appealed the ruling, and the US Supreme Court ruled in favor of the state, allowing the law to stay in place. It was used similarly in 2014 against Wisconsin woman Tammy Loertscher, who was jailed for almost 20 days after she tested positive for methamphetamine while pregnant and refused drug treatment. Loertscher was tested weekly throughout her pregnancy, and did not test positive for drugs again.[68] The cases of Loertscher and Beltran demonstrate the state's readiness to intervene upon pregnant women and mothers, even without evidence of harm to a fetus or infant.

As Linda Fentiman argues, mothers are increasingly viewed as vectors of risk, tasked with carefully self-disciplining their minds and bodies to produce a "good pregnancy." A supporter of the Wisconsin law, for example, stated to Wisconsin Public Radio that the legislation was necessary because "there's so much risk"[69]—while she was referring in part to the opioid epidemic, the law frames mothers as embodied conduits of that risk. The risk posed by drugs is inseparable from the risk posed by mothers, because it is through mothers that fetuses are potentially exposed. While this may seem logical, it is in fact quite complicated to determine what type of drug exposure at what point during pregnancy poses a measurable risk to a fetus. However, because socially constructed and hegemonic ideologies of parenting unequivocally associate any illegal substance abuse by mothers as a sign of maternal failure, a mother with a history of drug use is an embodied risk to her child. This logical chain is relevant to the discussion of co-sleeping that will follow in this book, in which poor or "bad" mothers who co-sleep are assumed to do so out of laziness or carelessness. In contrast, "good" mothers may still face judgment for co-sleeping but are understood to do so in order to bond and breastfeed, based on a philosophy of childrearing that signifies love, care, and middle-class parenting mores.

Despite these gradations in how parents are assessed, medical and public health gatekeepers often utilize a "lowest common denominator" approach to women's and children's health. For example, while extensive research demonstrates that moderate alcohol use during pregnancy does not harm a fetus, medical authorities recommend that all women abstain from alcohol use entirely, in part because women are not trusted to understand and maintain moderation.[70] Similarly, mainstream safe sleep guidelines insist that there is no safe way to co-sleep, for the most part refraining from providing guidance on how to co-sleep more safely. This distrust cannot be separated from stereotypes about low-income mothers and mothers of color as uneducable and irresponsible. Like other advice given to pregnant women and mothers, guidelines concerning infant sleep safety err on the side of blanket prohibitions and "thou shalt not"-style commandments. Safe co-sleeping is framed as an oxymoron, despite the reality that most parents at times share a bed with their children, whether "intentionally" or "reactively."

"Intentional" co-sleeping can be understood as a form of what Sharon Hays terms "intensive motherhood." Hays coined this term in her 1998 book *The Cultural Contradictions of Motherhood*, arguing that despite women's increased presence in the workforce and resulting economic responsibility and time deficits, the "emotionally demanding, financially draining, labor-consuming childrearing" model remains central to the ideology of motherhood.[71] Hays describes intensive motherhood as fraught with contradictions; women are expected to devote themselves fully to the project of childrearing, while also maintaining a career outside of the home. Feminist scholars have written extensively about the barriers facing working mothers in the United States and globally; Caitlyn Collins's book *Making Motherhood Work* compares the environment and experiences of working moms in the United States to those in Italy, Sweden, and Germany. She concludes that women in the United States are the most stressed and the least supported, "caught between the competing devotions of ideal worker norms and intensive mothering norms."[72] Mothers of young children in the United States continue to lack social and structural support for parenting, while being held to standards of "breast is best," tummy time, brain enrichment, screen-time limits, and "nighttime parenting" that seem to require a time investment that exceeds 24 hours in a day.

Despite the pervasive messages about individualism and personal fulfillment, moms are directed to set aside their own wants or needs, channeling those passions into orchestrating their children's futures. Hays's model of intensive motherhood has instigated research and social commentary from academic and popular authors who have further mapped out the terrain of "concerted cultivation," "the new momism," "total motherhood," and "parenting out of control."[73] Co-sleeping and attachment parenting, the parenting philosophy it is most frequently associated with, have garnered some feminist critique as yet another demand upon women to centralize motherhood as their primary role, regardless of their other commitments. Attachment parenting, while still popular today, arguably reached its zenith in the early 2010s; its originator, pediatrician William Sears, upheld the three main tenets of breastfeeding, sharing a family bed (co-sleeping), and baby wearing (carrying your baby next to your body). While attachment parenting is in theory practiced by both mothers and fathers, its commitment to exclusive breastfeeding and baby wearing are likely to require greater physical and emotional labor from mothers based on the cultural and structural realities of parenting in the United States.

The idea that women should devote themselves physically and emotionally to their children above all else is reflected in what Susan Douglas and Meredith Michaels term the "new momism" and the "mommy myth"—ideologies that "seem on the surface to celebrate motherhood, but which in reality promulgate standards of perfection that are beyond your reach."[74] Douglas and Michaels note how risk, and a sense that children are in ever-present danger, have been used to sell women on the idea that protecting their children requires heightened vigilance and effort. Mothers must develop what Ana Villalobos terms "security strategies" for their families in order to mitigate risk in an insecure global world.[75] However, these impossible-to-achieve standards of ideal motherhood, including the ability to buffer children from physical and environmental risk through economic security, fail to account for the massive structural disparities that privilege some parents and create barriers for others. This "stratified reproduction" describes "the power relations by which some people are empowered to nurture and reproduce, while others are disempowered."[76] Although this is not to say that more privileged mothers are immune from the discourse of "bad motherhood," it does mean that marginalized social identities intersect with motherhood in ways that normalize the additional scrutiny experienced by poor mothers, substance-using mothers, mothers of color, and others.[77]

In *Governed Through Choice*, Jennifer Denbow compellingly argues that the concept of autonomy is used in contemporary reproductive rights debates in order to justify the surveillance of and intervention into women's reproductive lives. If women are assumed to have the capacity for autonomy and self-governance, then any decisions they make that do not align with what is deemed rational by those in power is evidence that they require intervention. Indeed, Denbow argues, even restrictive interventions like mandatory waiting periods prior to abortion are framed as offering women *greater* autonomy, because they are afforded the potential to conduct themselves more rationally. "Crucially," Denbow notes, "race, class, and ability all affect how an individual's conduct is managed."[78]

Parents, and especially mothers, are expected to be capable of providing a safe sleep environment for their children regardless of access to resources. According to this logic, parents who are unable to secure a safe sleep environment, or choose options that do not align with safe sleep guidelines (like co-sleeping, or placing a baby in the prone position), are failing to properly self-govern. While as of this writing anti–co-sleeping legislation has failed to become law, some cities have mandated safe sleep education in hospitals and birth centers and rolled out public health campaigns aimed at eradicating what is deemed unsafe sleep. The increased focus on individual behavior change has been noted by scholars of both public health and women's health.[79] According to sociologist Miranda Waggoner, "maternal and child health as a field has moved away from broader social policy interventions toward individualized medical interventions to address child health and well-being."[80] As later chapters will demonstrate, some of these initiatives have unforeseen consequences like demonizing parents of color or creating a safe sleep education paper trail that is later used against parents whose children die unexpectedly during sleep.

While debates surrounding the safety of co-sleeping are ongoing, most health professionals agree that some proportion of unexpected infant death is unexplained, and thus impossible to fully prevent. But this conclusion is difficult to align with the pressure that mothers are under to identify and mitigate all potential risks to their children. Women are taught that self-discipline is essential to becoming a "good mother," including what food, drink, and medications are consumed during pregnancy, disciplining the body and environment to overcome any barriers to breastfeeding, or subsuming their own preferences concerning sleeping arrangements. Given that women are framed as having a "double responsibility" for risk—every action and choice (often even pre-conception) either creates risk or mitigates risk for both themselves and their fetus/future fetus—the pressure to self-discipline is unsurprising.[81] Indeed, "bad outcomes in children are a sign that the woman did not subvert her needs to those of her child."[82]

The type of combative relationship that this paradigm implies is known as maternal-fetal conflict, or the idea that a woman and fetus are separable entities with divergent interests. Sociologist Elizabeth Armstrong argues that public health's growing focus on personal responsibility highlights maternal-fetal conflict because it centers women's supposed obligation and capacity to minimize risk.[83] While infant sleep safety concerns babies rather than fetuses, there are similarities in the rhetoric surrounding both. For one, women are advised on the safest sleep position for their child before the baby is born; during pregnancy, women are often warned that sleeping on their backs could interrupt blood flow to the fetus. Moreover, the rhetoric of safe sleep education frames newborns as helpless and vulnerable, in many ways similar to fetuses. The sense that women are at odds with their pregnancies (or even their children) is reflected in legislation surrounding reproductive rights; as feminist theorist Laury Oaks argues, at the same time that states are passing legislation that supposedly protects the rights of fetuses and children, they are also approving laws that restrict the rights of pregnant women and mothers.[84]

Losing Sleep will take up some of the questions that are raised by this political reality: How is "safe sleep" determined, and by whom?

How does the idea of sleep-related risk evolve over time, and attach to different objects (cribs, beds, blankets), people, and parenting philosophies? How is the neoliberal governance of safe sleep (by public health officials, politicians, the criminal justice system) inflected by racialized, class-based, and gendered notions of parenting? And finally, what can we learn about risk and responsibility from the safety products that we are sold?

Overview of the Book

This project applies an interdisciplinary feminist methodology to analyze messages about infant sleep safety in US culture. I utilize a reproductive justice framework for understanding how these diverse sources interact, reinforce, and contradict one another to create a discourse about infant sleep safety. Reproductive justice is a framework created by women of color that demands a holistic, human rights approach to the issues surrounding reproductive health. From a reproductive justice perspective, the social determinants of health are inseparable from women's reproductive decision making, as well as their ability to raise and nurture healthy children. Reproductive justice "disrupts the dehumanizing status quo of reproductive politics," using "creative inquiry to illuminate connections of resistance to specific means of domination."[85] Reproductive justice activism likewise disrupts and denaturalizes neoliberal discourse that pathologizes those in most need of support.[86] The theory and activism that animate reproductive justice are important to this project because they reveal what it would look like to trust women of color, to support community decision making and knowledge production, and to insist that reproductive rights do not begin and end with the ability to prevent pregnancy, or with birth.[87] A reproductive justice approach to infant sleep safety asks who determines safe sleep guidelines, who benefits from the child safety industry, and what groups are likely to be targeted by safe sleep programs and policies.

In addition to feminist theory, feminist science studies, and reproductive justice, I also draw upon medical literature on Sudden Unexpected Infant Death, feminist and sociological analyses of risk, the work of historians of women's and children's health and parenting, anthropological analyses of co-sleeping, and pediatric and public health research on infant sleep safety. As the chapter descriptions below will make clear, different methods are used throughout the book in ways that cannot always be neatly categorized. The project is multi-sited, with an archive that includes a thorough analysis of public health materials such as billboards, bus shelter advertisements, and radio spots, news media coverage of prosecutions of parents for co-sleeping deaths, court records, parenting advice books, interviews, safe sleep guidelines and reports, and marketing materials for sleep safety products. Utilizing an interdisciplinary methodology that includes thematic analysis of legal cases, feminist analysis of news media and marketing, selected interviews and more allows me to rely on methods that are best suited to my research questions, and that adapt to my multi-sited archive. Together, the archive and methods offer different avenues for approaching this topic because infant sleep safety is a matter of public policy, of public health, of consumer culture, of historical record, and of parenting philosophy.

Chapter 1, "'Sleep Like a Baby' and Other Historical Fallacies," will provide a historical context for infant sleep safety, with a focus on events that have shaped safe sleep practices in the United States. This chapter will consider who the "experts" on sleep safety have been over time, from infant care manuals in the seventeenth and eighteenth centuries, to religious institutions excommunicating women for "overlay," to domestic education uplifting the responsibility (and potential blame) leveled at mothers in the nineteenth century, public health reform and the rise of pediatric and psychological expertise in the twentieth century. Chapter 1 considers how social institutions have regulated women, the poor, and various "Others" through intervention into infant care, including enslaved women, immigrants, and those whose babies died in their sleep. Even public health initiatives aimed at alleviating the high rates of infant mortality in the United States, such as the Back to Sleep campaign launched in the mid-1990s, have not affected all communities equally, which speaks in part to the impact of histories of medical and scientific racism. Mother-blame also remains a consistent theme throughout, reinforcing the focus on the individual's responsibility for infant sleep safety over time.

Chapter 2, "Making and Unmaking a Safe Sleep Environment: From the AAP to the Rock 'n Play Recall," considers the role of this prominent professional organization in shaping policy around infant sleep safety in the United States. This chapter uses AAP policy statements from 1992 to 2016 to trace how the parameters of safe sleep shifted from SIDS prevention to the management of the safe sleep environment. Chapter 2 also considers how anthropological research on co-sleeping as well as work by breastfeeding advocates has pushed back against the relatively hard line the AAP took for many years in opposition to bed-sharing, and how the AAP's messaging has recently softened in this regard. Finally, chapter 2 introduces the recall of Fisher-Price's Rock 'n Play sleeper after the device was linked to the death of many infants, and argues that this incident reveals how a lack of oversight in the infant safety industry and the broader acceptance of personal responsibility narratives allow corporations to scapegoat parents when their flawed products harm children.

Chapter 3, "What's Best for Baby? Co-Sleeping and the Politics of Inequality," centralizes a case study of a campaign to eliminate co-sleeping in Milwaukee, Wisconsin. The City of Milwaukee's Safe Sleep Campaign was intended to reduce the risk of SIDS by eradicating bed-sharing among low-income people of color. The anti–co-sleeping campaign in Milwaukee took aim at an implicitly racialized and class-based stereotype of "bad parents" without addressing the much more pervasive and structural factors that lead to infant mortality. The chapter addresses how Milwaukee's campaign utilized a "risk elimination" approach that attempted to end all forms of bed-sharing. I contrast the city's initiative with an alternative outreach campaign that emerged in Milwaukee and was created and informed by communities of color. This chapter will also compare Milwaukee's approach to bed-sharing with that of the city of Baltimore.

Chapter 4, "Everybody Loses: Parents as Perpetrators," considers what happens when the worst possible outcome occurs; namely, what consequences do parents face if a child dies while co-sleeping? This chapter analyzes a data set of 29 cases in which caretakers were prosecuted for co-sleeping deaths by compiling news reports from LexisNexis and US Newsstream from the year 2011 to the present. Several themes emerge, including that the vast majority of parents who face criminal prosecution were using drugs or alcohol at the time of the infant's death, that a high proportion of parents had lost more than one child to sudden unexpected infant death, and that many had been previously counseled about the dangers of co-sleeping. This chapter explores these themes through narratives about specific cases. I argue that contemporary research on SIDS has led to a diagnostic shift in which infant deaths that would previously have been categorized as SIDS are now attributed to accidental suffocation. As a result, individuals who do not meet the class, gender, and racialized standards of "good" parenting are increasingly likely to be investigated and even prosecuted when their children die while co-sleeping.

Chapter 5, "Advertising Infant Safety," turns to an analysis of how safe sleep technology is marketed in ways that eclipse the traditional baby monitor, including a wearable "smart sock" and app that (controversially) promise parents safety, security, and risk avoidance through biometric surveillance. This chapter builds on the book's argument that the contemporary discourse concerning safe sleep is primarily a neoliberal one; in other words, safe sleep rhetoric from medical experts, public health, commercial interests, and the media frequently espouse an individual (as opposed to collective) risk management strategy, holding parents wholly responsible for infant health outcomes. They reflect a privatized, data-driven approach to health that explicitly focuses parental concern on the internal, such as baby's heart rate and oxygen level. Doing so isolates the individual family unit from the broader social factors that impact health, such as access to health care, affordable day care, safe housing, clean air and water, and the broader effects of poverty and structural racism. At the same time that these products privatize and individualize infant health, they also appropriate the language of social justice by urging parents to "join the movement" for safe sleep.

The conclusion acknowledges how the ongoing COVID-19 pandemic is exacerbating the existing race- and class-based health inequalities in the United States. The conclusion reinforces the importance of challenging neoliberal trends in health policy that hold individuals responsible for structural failures in health care. I use a reproductive justice framework to rethink the traditional definition of the safe sleep environment, and argue that it must be extended beyond the crib or the bedroom to consider structural and systemic factors that influence disparities in infant mortality. Finally, the conclusion returns to the Black Health Coalition of Wisconsin's community-based education around infant sleep safety as an example of the agency of communities of color in addressing safe sleep.

While this book analyzes certain parenting practices like co-sleeping, room-sharing, or the use of devices like wearable monitors, my intention is not to provide parenting advice or guidance. For caregivers of any kind who do read this book, I hope you feel more informed about infant sleep safety and perhaps better able to navigate the complex and at times contradictory advice you will receive from a plethora of other sources. This book is also not meant to suggest that all safe sleep education is inherently racist or classist, or that pediatricians, professional organizations, or public health officials do not play a valuable role in promoting infant health. If anything, this research has reinforced to me that the vast majority of parents are deeply invested in ensuring the safety of their infants, and many are open to learning more about how to do so when the reasoning behind the "rules" is explained, is relevant to their circumstances, and comes from a trusted source. Rather, I hope that this book challenges readers to consider how parents make choices within an often increasingly narrow range of viable or livable options, how the flexibility of options within that range is shaped by historical and ongoing practices that stratify the access to resources that could encourage or inhibit safe and healthy childrearing, and to value the agency and determination of those who continue to fight for the safety of their families every day.

1

"Sleep Like a Baby" and Other Historical Fallacies

Stories of infant death and maternal responsibility are rich in pathos, lending themselves to mythologization and allegory. The story of the Judgment of Solomon from Hebrew scripture—in which two women claim maternity of the same child, leading Solomon to propose cutting the baby in half—transpired because the baby of one woman "died in the night, because she lay on him."[1] Solomon determined that the infant's true mother was the one willing to forgo her claim in order to save the baby from the gruesome fate he had proposed; a true mother, we learn, is selfless and does not put her infant at risk. As this tale suggests, infant death during sleep has not always been viewed as natural or inevitable, but potentially a by-product of maternal failure. Tracing how the safety of sleeping infants has been defined and managed is thus also the story of how parents have navigated the competing information, resources, and authorities on infant sleep.

While sleep itself is a biological necessity, the way that we organize it, schedule it, and assign responsibility for it is determined by social pressures.[2] These include proscribed gender roles concerning maternal responsibility for feeding, comforting, socializing, and otherwise training infants to meet the needs of the household. Women, whether in their familial role (mothers, sisters, grandmothers), as domestic servants (nannies and nurses), or coerced or enslaved caregivers, have frequently been assigned the primary day-to-day responsibility for managing infant sleep, including the expectation that babies will sleep safely. Expectations of how they will manage this responsibility and whether they require external intervention are predictably mediated by factors like gender, age, citizenship status, race, class, and ability. As ideas about women's role, character, and autonomy have changed over time, so has the guidance about parenting practice.

This chapter will trace the messages Western parents have historically received about infant sleep, with a focus on who has been authorized to provide such instruction and how mothers have been expected to follow it. The biopolitical project of managing the population through assigning responsibility and blame for infant sleep safety has remained consistent in certain ways, such as the through line of mother blame and class and race bias. However, the form that authority takes and the discursive framework in which it is communicated are flexible; infant death during sleep has been a sin punished by religious institutions, a symptom of the carelessness of the poor and the wickedness of women, a burgeoning public health crisis to be managed by a new field of experts, a tragedy to be avoided through proper scientific motherhood, an outcome to be governed through neoliberal risk management, and a niche target of consumer technologies.

To a certain extent the story of infant sleep safety as described by historians is buried within other trends in infant health, like infant feeding, the medicalization of infant care, and the struggles over the authority of pediatricians and psychologists versus mothers.[3] As historians Peter Stearns, Perrin Rowland, and Lori Giarnella write in the *Journal of Social History*, "sleep is not a conventional historical topic. It is after all a normally silent and unrecorded activity, which means that records of past sleep patterns are hardly abundant."[4] This creates some limitations on what we can know about how parents have managed sleep safety over time, and is a reminder that the records we have are often of exceptional sleep events—in other words, while most children do not die in their sleep, we mark the uncommon instances in which they do, thus increasing the likelihood that sleep is viewed through the lens of risk. In addition, sources such as infant care manuals, newspapers, magazines, advice from physicians, clergymen, elite mothers, or domestic education texts may reveal what certain "experts" advised, but not necessarily what the average mother enacted. Most mothers have historically received the majority of their childrearing advice through "informal" channels from other women, including family members and neighbors, rather than from experts via printed material.[5] Further, access to expert advice in the form of written texts or interaction with healthcare workers has varied over time, both by geographic location (urban versus rural) and among different racial and ethnic communities. Much of the written advice is filtered through an unmarked racial lens of whiteness, reinforcing the hegemonic normativity of medicalized, middle-class, white cultural sleep customs. As Bethany Johnson and Margaret Quinlan point out in *You're Doing It Wrong: Mothering, Media, and Medical Expertise*, the boundaries between what constitutes lay and expert advice have also shifted and blurred over time, and cannot be truly understood as a binary when it comes to what they call "the life cycle of early motherhood."[6] In effect, it is not always obvious whether parents received or adopted advice about where and with whom a baby should sleep from a pediatrician, an authoritative text, a family or community member, or a combination of these sources.[7] However, these texts do reflect changing discourses about infant care advice more broadly, and how authoritative sources of knowledge production framed motherhood, childhood, and the value of expert knowledge in different time periods.

This chapter will examine how the history of infant sleep safety in Western Europe, and later in the United States, taps into shifting cultural beliefs about maternal responsibility for health, and asks to what degree mothers can be trusted to manage infant safety. It will explore changing patterns in knowledge production and dissemination about infant sleep safety historically. This chapter is not, however, a history of Sudden Infant Death Syndrome; this work has already been admirably undertaken by other scholars, with a focus on how the "syndrome" was informed by changing medical understandings of infant death as well as advocacy by parents of the victims.[8] While some parts of this narrative will be interwoven throughout chapter 1, I focus on how the notion of safe sleep has developed over time, mapping the influence of various social institutions in relation to perceptions about the capacity of different mothers to understand and act upon the ever-changing advice that they receive.

Sleep Advice Before the Twentieth Century

In examining childrearing advice before the twentieth century, infant care manuals provide a record of how advice and expertise changed over time. The content, authorship, and intended audience of infant care manuals has evolved, with early guidance often written in a prescriptive manner, and without the direct address to mothers that would be seen in later years. Advice books in the seventeenth century were frequently authored by members of the clergy, male medical practitioners, and midwives. Such manuals were written in a tone "promising disaster if the advice was not followed," including guidance on appropriate clothing, breastfeeding, and weaning.[9] In the eighteenth century, it became more common for those practicing medicine to write childrearing manuals to be read by parents in addition to doctors and nurses. Childrearing manuals were also authored by apothecaries, whose services were more affordable than doctors, and philosophers like Locke and Rousseau also contributed influential theories of how to raise a healthy child.[10] Rousseau, for example, critically emphasized the role of nursing mothers in the moral upbringing of the infant, and thus the status of the nation.[11]

Advice pertaining to infant sleep was clearly motivated in part by religious and social concern about sleep-related infant deaths. These deaths were often attributed to either infanticide or overlay, although these categories were not entirely mutually exclusive. Overlay refers to an infant that is "laid over" and suffocated by someone with whom they shared a bed, or that has suffocated in blankets or other bedding.[12] As the name suggests, overlay points to suffocation from an external source (as compared to contemporary explanations of Sudden Infant Death Syndrome, which may also implicate internal factors like brain structure or genetics). The persistence of overlay as an explanation for unexpected infant death is significant, because it reflects a core component of infant sleep safety more broadly, which is that unexpected infant death during sleep has always been haunted by its association with infanticide and parental neglect.

Overlay was viewed as a persistent social problem in Western Europe, and was written about by doctors, philosophers, religious authorities, and even poets. While overlay could be deemed as accidental, it was frequently attributed to the carelessness of mothers or other female caregivers, or even intentional infanticide. Religious institutions utilized a punitive approach to overlay that reflects how mother blame has adhered to infant sleep deaths across centuries. The Irish Church recognized overlaying as a sin in the sixth century, and punished the accused accordingly.[13] The Catholic Church declared suffocation akin to infanticide, and in the ninth century marked it as a violation of the Fifth Commandment.[14] The Catholic Church was still grappling with overlay in 1576, when it threatened the excommunication of mothers whose babies died in their beds or who failed to utilize a proscribed wooden box devised to protect infants from suffocation. Early technologies like the wooden "arcuccio" suggest attempts to mediate the risk that the maternal body posed to infants, and in the case of the Catholic Church, the perceived role of religious institutions in overseeing the management of risk.[15]

Other sleep safety guidelines included specific (though often contradictory) advice concerning what a baby should wear, and the surface on which they should sleep. Swaddling infants was recommended by some in the seventeenth and eighteenth centuries, in part because it could increase an infant's hours of sleep, and thus allow caregivers to take care of other tasks.[16] Swaddling was also a matter of risk management; an infant's bones and overall physical alignment were considered to be quite malleable and prone to disfigurement if they should have too great a range of movement.[17] Other texts, such as William Cadogan's 1748 *Essay Upon Nursing and the Management of Children* advised against the practice of swaddling because it did not "follow nature."[18] Swaddled babies could be placed to rest in a variety of locations, including cradles, which date as far back as the thirteenth century. Like the arcuccio, cradles were a device intended to physically separate sleeping mothers from their babies.[19]

Decisions about how and where a baby would sleep were significant because infant care was more than a personal matter; according to feminist philosopher Rebecca Kukla, maternal behavior and the maternal body became increasingly public in the late eighteenth century, in the sense that even "mundane practices" were seen to be "performed for the public benefit and open to public scrutiny" from institutions like law, medicine, and public health.[20] This notion of "republican" or "moral" motherhood emphasized the role of mothers in shaping future citizens of a nation; as feminist historian Rickie Solinger notes, this "venerated" mother was white, as "the prescription described an exclusionary, racialized ideal."[21] Parents were encouraged to consider the emotional safety of their children in addition to physical concerns like smothering due to excessive pillows, overheating from feather mattresses, or lockjaw from a supine sleeping position.[22] The rocking of cradles, for example, was discouraged not only because it could be done too strenuously and injure the child, but also because it could encourage them to demand repetitive motion during the night.[23] The fear of spoiling a baby speaks to the growing belief that motherhood was an emotional task as well as a physical one; mothers had to manage their own responses to infants, and shape the developing nature of the child.[24]

The nineteenth century saw an influx of books about childrearing in the United States and in Britain, reflecting the growing view of childhood as a precious and innocent period of life.[25] According to feminist historian Nancy Cott, advice books were part of a "new popular literature" in the early nineteenth century that emphasized domesticity, "advocating and reiterating women's certain, limited role," which was "to be wives and mothers, to nurture and maintain their families, to provide religious example and inspiration, and to affect the world around by exercising private moral influence."[26] White, middle-class mothers who were part of the private sphere of home and family were expected to devote themselves to a romanticized version of mothering that was glorified but also excluded from the arenas of political and economic life.[27] This exclusion was justified by valorizing a femininity that elevated motherhood, piety, and the haloed space of domesticity.[28] These guidebooks, written for an audience of mothers, advised women on issues both medical and moral, and portrayed infant care as a personal responsibility as well as a social obligation. They offered mothers advice on day-to-day care including sleep routines, as well as what an infant should be fed and how they should be dressed.[29]

By the nineteenth century, parenting advice reflected changing views of the baby, and increasingly suggested that parents could shape the habits of their baby, or that infants could develop "bad habits" such as refusing to sleep alone.[30] The authors of "domestic education" books declared that parents (not extended family or communities) had sole responsibility for the raising of children, and that mothers "could decide their child's fate" and "produce misery or joy for themselves through their own parental acts."[31] Again, mothers had to carefully regulate their own emotions, which could directly influence the character of the infant; should a child display an ill temper, it was the mother who was at fault.[32] According to Cott, this elevation of maternal responsibility in the first few decades of the 1800s reflected a shift from prior periods in which mothers were responsible for the physical duties of childrearing, but the weighty moral, educational, and spiritual guidance was more suitable for fathers. Instead, "childrearing had become a specialized domestic process carried on by mothers."[33] The value of the child was also changing; children, as sociologist Viviana Zelizer argues, were "sacralized" during this time period, and attributed sentimental rather than economic value.[34]

The extent to which parents are thought to value and protect their children has of course always been shaped by the perception that "good" or caring mothers are white, married, and economically secure. This is reflected in the public response to unexpected infant death; by the nineteenth century, the idea that unexpected infant death during sleep was caused by suffocation or overlay was so thoroughly entrenched that it was often assumed to be the cause of death even with very little evidence to the contrary.[35] Poor mothers and nurses (who were typically from the lower classes) were accused of suffocating infants because they were intoxicated, or to rid themselves of an unwanted charge.[36] Suffocations were said to peak on Saturday nights; one physician wrote in a letter to the *English Women's Journal* in 1862 that society must not ignore "a lamentable but frequent cause of death, that in which the infant is 'overlaid' in its slumbers by a careless, perhaps drunken nurse or mother."[37] The belief that inebriated mothers and nurses were to blame for infant suffocation was widely held in Europe, but also made its way to the United States and informed educational outreach efforts and legal responses to prohibit mothers from sleeping with their babies.

As the nineteenth century progressed, however, evidence began to accumulate that children were dying in their sleep in circumstances that did not involve bed-sharing. This led physicians to propose alternative explanations that would be debated, dismissed, and replaced for decades before the classification of Sudden Infant Death Syndrome was widely adopted.[38] The introduction of new theories did not put overlay to rest, however, and the question of whether such deaths were intentional or accidental, and whether they should be treated as a crime, was fraught with tensions about class, gender, and power.

As Silvia Federici argues in *Caliban and the Witch*, determining what is considered a reproductive "crime" has historically been a tool of state control, thus deeming suffocation deaths to be infanticide was a means of "breaking the control they [women] had exercised over their bodies and reproduction."[39] Doing so had greater consequences for some women than for others. In the United States, it was not uncommon for enslaved women to be accused of infanticide when their infants died during sleep. When infant mortality rates were first compiled in the 1850s, the Black infant mortality rate was one and a half times higher than that of white babies.[40] Nearly 10 percent of infant deaths among slave populations were attributed to suffocation in 1850, whereas white infant suffocation deaths fell at 1.2 percent.[41] They were also clustered geographically, with 94 percent of suffocation deaths in 1860 reported in slave states.[42] White slave owners and others at the time attributed these deaths to the carelessness of Black mothers; such fatalities actually share common characteristics with what is now called Sudden Infant Death Syndrome, as well as underreporting of suffocation deaths in white populations, and over-classification of Black infant deaths as suffocations rather than other causes like illness or infection.[43] Infant mortality rates reflect the overall health of a population; as such, Black babies in the South born to enslaved women were vulnerable to conditions like low birth weight that are now known risk factors for SIDS.[44] Blaming enslaved mothers for the death of their infants aligned with their dehumanizing treatment as reproductive property and the devaluation of mothers' relationships to their children.[45] In reality, terrible working conditions for pregnant women, poor diet, and inferior living conditions were likely contributors to high infant mortality.[46] The conditions of enslaved women are perhaps the most explicit articulation of a common theme throughout this book, which is that women are blamed for childhood health outcomes despite the lack of sufficient conditions for healthy pregnancy and infancy.

The maternal capabilities of poor women and women of color were deemed to be suspect by those in positions of authority, such that the deaths of their infants were more likely to be investigated than those of wealthier white women. In a study of deaths attributed to infanticide in Baltimore from 1835 to 1860, historian Katie Hemphill found that most women indicted for their infants' deaths were racially and/or economically marginalized. Poor women experienced higher infant mortality rates in part because of their often squalid living and working conditions, and their lack of privacy meant that they were more closely surveilled and less able to properly dispose of their children's bodies. However, this does not solely account for their disproportionate criminalization, Hemphill argues. Black and poor women were excluded from standards of respectability and good motherhood, such that they were already assumed to have criminal tendencies and to care less about their children than other mothers.

As Hemphill writes, "that such deaths were so frequently blamed on poor women is indicative of the tendency, especially on the part of the middle class, to see them as neglectful or even malicious mothers."[47] This assertion is echoed by historian Ariane Kemkes, who concludes that "class-cultural biases" likely influenced the way that authorities perceived sleep-related infant death in the mid-nineteenth century, even outweighing the forensic evidence.[48] This historical analysis aligns with the work of Black feminist theorists who have analyzed how "controlling images" of Black women as mothers have been used to justify their subordination in a white supremacist society.[49] Black women have been categorically excluded from ideal motherhood, and then, in the words of Dorothy Roberts, "stigmatized for violating the dominant norm and considered deviant or criminals."[50] The criminalization of Black and poor motherhood seeps into the way in which social institutions respond to sleep-related infant death, as will be demonstrated throughout this book.

Infant sleep practices have always been impacted by the spatial layout of the home, and in the nineteenth century the physical arrangement of houses reflected the increased value placed on privacy, with public houses and then private homes increasingly designed with private bedrooms.[51] Bed- and even room-sharing would decrease in popularity as it became more common for homes to have internal heating, and as the value granted to marital privacy grew.[52] Stand-alone sleep options for infants were also changing. By the end of the nineteenth century, cradles—which may have been located in the parents' bedroom—were being replaced by cribs, which were stationary and often placed in a separate room from adults. Moreover, as Matthew Wolf-Meyer argues in *The Slumbering Masses*, the nineteenth century saw the consolidation of a "hegemonic spatiotemporal formation" that assigned normative periods of work, school recreation, and rest. "Training children to sleep alone," he argues, "and parents to want to sleep apart from their children, lays the basis for a particular desire for sleep and wakefulness."[53]

By the 1890s, it was common for babies to sleep alone, which reflected guidance from both mainstream and alternative sources.[54] For example, in Luther Emmet Holt's influential 1894 text, *The Care and Feeding of*

Children: A Catechism for the Use of Mother's and Children's Nurses, Holt contends that children should never sleep with their mother, nurse, or older siblings because "bad habits are contracted by children sleeping together."[55] According to Hilary Hinds in *A Cultural History of Twin Beds*, mid- to late nineteenth-century practitioners of "fringe" or alternative medicine also warned that co-sleeping could cause a loss of "vitality" in the young, particularly if they shared a bed with an elderly person. Hinds describes these claims as "widely held and frequently rehearsed," and lingering into the twentieth century as an argument against infants or children sharing beds with older adults or even one another.[56] Solitary sleep for children also aligned with ideologies about marriage, including that the bond between husband and wife is primary, and that sexual relationships happen at night, in the marital bed.[57]

Holt's advice was representative of the "American style of sleep," in which the path to a self-sufficient and independent adulthood began with solitary infant sleep.[58] As the title of Holt's book suggests, this text was written with mothers as an intended audience, and was penned by a physician who specialized in the new field of pediatrics, which was extending medical expertise beyond sickness and into the realm of health. This book would come to be known as "the infant bible of the nation" and was reflective of many of the changing attitudes about infancy that the twentieth century would bring.[59] Holt was also a proponent of another ideology that Americans enthusiastically embraced, and one that was influential among infant welfare reformers, namely eugenics. Holt and others believed that infant death during the first month of life was primarily a result of hereditary deficiency and could only be reduced by preventing the marriage and procreation of the "unfit," including criminals and the diseased.[60] His interest in eugenics aligns with his advice on childrearing, in that both assume that scientific knowledge holds the promise for social improvement.

The expansion of pediatric expertise would have implications for the kind of advice parents received about infant sleep, as doctors laid out medicalized guidelines for what made sleep "healthy," including its duration, location, and other minutiae that twentieth-century mothers would be expected to learn from experts, and then follow with scientific rigor. The medicalization of sleep would also create sleep norms that individuals could compare themselves (or their babies) to, and see how they measured up.[61] These sleep norms and notions of safety would evolve as the twentieth century ushered in the growing influence of science, psychology, and medical expertise, followed by an eventual backlash from those espousing the "natural" connections between mother and child.

The Century of the Child

Between the mid-nineteenth to the early twentieth century, infant mortality was recognized as a distinct and alarming problem, and also one that could enhance the legitimacy of workers in the field of public health. As historian Richard Meckel argues, the development of public health as a field in the United States was intimately tied to the issue of infant mortality.[62] As public health officials were better able to calculate infant mortality rates in the United States and compare them (unfavorably) to rates in other industrialized nations, the problem was seen as increasingly acute.[63] American parents were having fewer children than they had in the past, and were more likely to expect that their children would survive.[64] To increase the likelihood that this would happen, health reformers focused on the abysmal conditions in urban environments, including unsafe milk sources and the need to educate mothers on proper childrearing and hygiene. According to Meckel, infant mortality reforms happened in three overlapping stages, which started with environmental reform (sanitizing the environment), followed by improving the quality of the urban milk supply, and then addressing maternal ignorance as a key factor.[65]

The push-pull among public health reformers regarding the need to address environmental factors that lead to infant mortality *and* the need to educate mothers on proper caregiving and hygiene was ongoing, with mother-blame as a consistent thread.[66] A physician in 1918, for example, claimed that the mothers, grandmothers, and sisters were to blame for high rates of infant mortality, noting both feeding practices and those associated with sleep environment. He wrote, they "killed by feeding them with dirty, uncooked cow's milk or some other improper food, killed by weakening them with heavy clothing and then exposing them to a sudden draft."[67] Such screeds were frequently aimed at the urban immigrant poor, who were believed to be "wasting" child life with the highest rate of infant mortality and thus requiring intensive intervention.[68] Infant mortality was pigeonholed as an urban immigrant problem, despite the reality that Black infants were dying at higher rates. Black infant mortality was thought to be caused in part by negative racial characteristics, and because of these racist stereotypes, Black infants were largely excluded from early campaigns to reduce infant mortality in the United States.[69]

Indeed, much Progressive-era education attempted to influence individual households or the parenting choices of individual mothers.[70] This attention to "domestic hygiene" was significant in its role of reducing deaths due to conditions like diarrheal diseases, but the emphasis on maternal responsibility for some health reformers "refocused attention away from the environment and toward the individual, away from external conditions and toward personal behavior and health."[71] This means that while environment and individual behavior were both considered important factors in theory, in practice the strategies that aimed to fix mothers at times took precedence over structural and institutional factors like unsafe and crowded tenement housing, poor plumbing, a lack of access to clean milk, or other poverty-related conditions, which contributed to disparities in infant mortality based on class, race, and national origin.[72] The end result was a decrease in infant mortality, but without an attendant structural shift in conditions for women and people of color that contributed to the initial problem.[73] This approach is strikingly familiar to the twenty-first-century public health response to unexpected infant death in Milwaukee, Wisconsin, which is the focus of chapter 3. Public health officials in that state chose to focus their efforts on educational campaigns aimed at reducing rates of bed-sharing to reduce infant mortality, drawing attention and potentially resources away from structural factors contributing to racialized health disparities in infant mortality. This strategy is akin to Meckel's description of early twentieth-century interventions into infant mortality, in that "the appeal of maternal education was the relatively simple antidote it offered for what was in reality a very complex problem."[74] In both instances the inadvertent consequence is the individualization of a social, structural problem, and the consistency of this approach over time is symptomatic of broader failures at addressing the effects of structural racism and poverty.

As the nineteenth century advanced, advice to mothers about infant care became increasingly regimented, specific, and "scientific." This change has been attributed by some to the rise in bureaucratization in society, which for mothers translated into the need to utilize reason, rationality, and the modern tools of science to manage their infants.[75] Women in the United States learned the new tenets of "scientific motherhood" from different sources than they had historically, including home economics courses, exhibits in department store windows, magazines, and advice columns in addition to physicians and childcare manuals.[76] While many of these sources were directed to middle-class mothers, Black and immigrant women received scientific parenting advice from newspapers targeting their specific communities, as well as public health nurses and campaigns.[77]

According to historian Rima Apple, a key tenet of scientific motherhood was that mothers need not merely evaluate the information available to them about how to raise their children, but rather to seek out and accept expert guidance and direction. Scientific motherhood, according to Apple, "made them responsible for the health and welfare of their families, but it denied them control over child rearing."[78] Mothers could not rely solely on their own maternal instincts or "mother love" to raise children, but rather required the modernization and standardization of medical management.[79] Mothers must be disciplined and attentive to the measurements and timetables of feeding, sleeping, and eating proscribed by medical experts, and to abandon the "traditions" passed on from family or friends.[80] The care of children was viewed as imperative to the improvement of humanity, which meant that mothers were taking on an essential task. Were they capable of such responsibility? As Ehrenreich and English note, "if children must be left with their mothers, they must not be left *alone* with them," hence the rise of the scientific expert.[81] Experts emerged to parent the parents: "the experts would be as intently observant of the mothers as mothers were to be of their children."[82] Advice pertaining to sleep became increasingly detailed in kind, including that sleep should happen on a schedule, and that babies should sleep in a sunny room with fresh air, and when necessary, warmed with dry heat.[83] Mothers continued to be warned against sharing a bed with their babies, even if it was what the infant preferred.[84]

Mothers learned these methods of childcare from infant care manuals, magazines, childcare journals, and even home economics classes, with urban women continuing to have greater access to pediatricians than those in rural communities.[85] Apple argues, however, that the insistence on a scientific approach to childrearing would have had a far more limited impact on American society had it not also been taken up by popular culture (including eventually film and television), advertising, baby contests, and educational programming.[86] The government also took on a growing role during the Progressive era. For example, the high infant mortality rate of Native American babies on reservations was targeted by the Save the Babies campaign, initiated by the Office of Indian Affairs in 1912. The campaign involved intensive surveillance of Native American women with the stated goal of improving infant and maternal mortality, but also promoting assimilationist goals such as medicalizing childbirth.[87] While some Native American women welcomed physician-attended birth or hospital deliveries, most resisted these pressures despite knowing that their reproductive lives were under "constant inspection." This demonstrates the dangers in assuming that women passively accepted expert advice on pregnancy or childrearing that was offered to them; rather, they may have selectively and creatively combined such guidance with their own traditions and practices, or resisted them altogether.[88]

With the advent of the Children's Bureau in 1912, government pamphlets also became an increasing source of information about scientific motherhood. According to historian Janet Golden, historians have theorized the Children's Bureau as a method of social control because it promoted middle-class and white models of parenting, but also a feminist effort that at least in part recognized the social determinants of health.[89] One way the Children's Bureau spread its public health messaging was through pamphlets, the most widely read of which was titled *Infant Care*.[90] The original *Infant Care* was written by the primarily female staff of the Children's Bureau, which was one factor that differentiated it from the majority of parenting advice literature of the time. It was very popular, and by 1929 more than half of all parents in the United States had received the pamphlet, which was distributed by well-baby clinics, health departments, and government agencies.[91] *Infant Care* provided parents with very specific instructions on infant sleep, including the number of hours a baby should sleep based on their age, when the evening meal should be served, how far open the window in "his" room should be, and that the door to the room should remain closed. This text also demonstrates that proper parenting was not only a middle-class concern in the twentieth century, as *Infant Care* had a wide geographic distribution and made it into the hands of mothers of all social classes.[92]

The pamphlet included some guidelines about sleep location, including that "he should always sleep in a bed by himself, and whenever possible in a room by himself"; with the 1914 edition of *Infant Care* explicitly stating that "not a few young babies are smothered while lying in the bed with an older person, some part of whose body is thrown over the baby's face during sleep."[93] This aligns with the writings of Dr. Richard Bolt, pamphlet author and president of the American Child Health Association, who advised that "it is dangerous for it [the infant] to go to sleep in the same bed with her [the mother]. A number of instances have been reported where a mother has unknowingly rolled over on the baby during a sound sleep."[94] These warnings reiterate the notion that unexpected infant death was attributed to suffocation, and that parents (and primarily mothers) were held responsible.

While these sections directly outline safety precautions, most advice did not include a rationale, largely because mothers were expected to follow directions without explanation. Also congruent with the strict and scheduled expectations of the time period, parents were advised not to pick the baby up if "he" was crying during the night, except in cases of emergency or a soiled diaper, lest he become a "tyrant" who "ruthlessly spoils the comfort of the entire household."[95] *Infant Care* was an important source of detailed advice for parents, and extended this guidance to mothers in remote and rural areas even when some of the middle-class expectations that babies have their own rooms or a non-working mother were not feasible, and representations of parents of color were non-existent. As historian V. Sue Atkinson notes, through the Children's Bureau and with the support of government policies like the Smith-Lever Act and the Sheppard-Towner Act, the role of "Uncle Sam" as a source of parenting advice grew alongside that of physicians.[96]

Medical professionals had much to gain from the perception that mothers need rely on them to parent correctly. As with the struggle to wrest authority over birth from female midwives, pediatricians sought to consolidate expertise on childrearing in order to maintain their own professional ground.[97] The development of pediatrics was part of the growing specialization of medicine, but unlike other specialties, pediatrics was defined by the age of the patient rather than focused knowledge about a body part or system. Pediatrics solidified as a specialty between 1880 and 1935, along with a rapid rise in newly minted doctors specializing in the care of infants and children, as well as an influx of pediatric societies, journals, and opportunities for pediatric training in medical school. By the 1930s, the problem of infant feeding had become less acute with the advent of safe commercial baby food, which led some physicians to predict the end of pediatrics as a field. Instead, "the growth of primary care pediatrics was made possible largely by a demand that pediatricians themselves created."[98] This was the rise of "infant and child management," which involved repeating the long-standing refrain that mothers could not adequately raise children without professional (male) supervision.[99] Pediatricians joined with developmental psychologists to advise parents on what constituted normal and abnormal behavior in children, and in parenting, including infant sleep.[100] As medical expertise on childrearing gained in standing, infant sleep shifted from a topic of little concern to one that preoccupied American parents.[101] Parents were urged by physicians to put their infants to sleep in a crib in a separate room, and to limit contact with their babies during the night.[102]

This more rigid approach to infant care, including infant sleep, is closely linked to the dissemination of the work of psychologist John B. Watson. Watson, a behaviorist, held that the emotional responses of babies could be conditioned. He did not trust mothers to manage this process on their own, however; they required expert instruction to avoid problem behaviors like kissing or hugging their children.[103] Behaviorism reinforced the growing consensus that motherhood was learned, rather than innate, and that babies must be molded by precise and dispassionate care to ensure both physical and psychological health.[104] Watson's *Psychological Care of Infant and Child*, ominously dedicated to "the first mother who brings up a happy child," includes a chapter titled "The Dangers of Too Much Mother Love"; the "over-conditioning of love," according to Watson, stems from a deviant sex-seeking response in mothers, and leads to lifelong problems of invalidism and dependency that weaken the nation.[105] As for sleep, Watson applauded the decline in the habit of rocking infants to sleep, and suggested a "regime" in which the baby is put to bed with a pat on the head—after that, "if he howls, let him howl."[106]

Watson's hands-off approach was not widely adopted by mothers, but the belief that the "coddling" of infants would negatively shape their personalities did gain traction.[107] It reflected "the conviction that personal mastery and consequent personal responsibility are first among the goals of childrearing," and that mothers are primarily to blame for any flaws in a child's development.[108] Historian Rebecca Jo Plant situates this trend in infant care within the broader political and social context of the time period; as male experts like Watson and other professionals took over the reins from the "maternalist" woman reformers of the Children's Bureau, "new and more psychologically oriented critiques of motherhood emerged, and mother-blaming expanded to encompass middle-class as well as poor mothers."[109] If mothers wanted more rights within the public sphere, Plant says, then many men believed they must abandon their claims to moral superiority within the home.

As the 1930s and '40s progressed, parents were increasingly exposed to media and education promoting the value of science and medicine, and the prestige of these fields continued to grow.[110] Advice about childrearing slowly shifted from strict timetables and detailed record keeping to an embrace of the cognitive, emotional, and psychological development of infants.[111] By the 1940s, experts concluded that affection and maternal closeness were in fact essential to an infant's well-being, and in a significant shift, mothers were encouraged to return to their maternal instincts.[112] This expansion of what mothering could look like was particularly appealing to middle-class mothers, with Dr. Benjamin Spock's *Baby and Child Care* offering a "confiding companion whom suburbanizing mothers yearned for."[113] The quality of instincts and "common sense," however, were always to be verified by a physician; even the "permissive" Dr. Spock gave mothers detailed instructions on low-tech tasks like bathing the baby, and reminded women to follow the directions of their pediatrician rather than their mothers or neighbors.[114] Despite Spock's comparable flexibility, he maintained relatively strict advice regarding infant sleep, including a moratorium on co-sleeping, a strict bedtime, and that babies should be allowed to cry rather than be comforted during the night.[115] While Spock is remembered for his progressive shift in thinking about the relationship between parents and infants, anthropologists who study sleep would later point to the similarities between the approaches of Spock, Watson, and late twentieth-century sleep training philosophies that utilize the moral authority of expert knowledge to enforce culturally specific norms about infant sleep.[116]

Spock was influenced by psychoanalytic theories of development; Freudian theories also contributed to research on mother-infant bonding in the 1940s and '50s. Bonding research was grounded in studies that found devastating consequences for infants who were separated from their mothers early in life, including children who were orphaned and raised in institutions. Psychologist John Bowlby took this research a step further, claiming that even children raised in average homes could be developmentally stunted by the conscious and unconscious attitudes and care practices of mothers.[117] This research "lent scientific credibility to the notion that continuous and solicitous maternal attention in the early years of a child's life was crucial to the healthy emotional and psychological development of children."[118] Bowlby viewed bonding as instinctual, and evolutionarily adaptive, but also something that mothers could get wrong if they lacked the proper knowledge to identify their child's needs.[119] Bowlby compared the effects of full-time working mothers to that of war or parental death, thus his work was taken up by many to warn against women's employment or use of day care.[120] Psychoanalytic theorists also traced problems in infant development to maternal failure, from the ill effects of working mothers to pathological personality traits; psychoanalyst René Spitz described the habit of rocking infants to sleep as a reflection of mothers' "Oscillation Between Pampering and Hostility."[121] As this phrase suggests, mothers could err on the side of overprotection (the destructive effects of which were labeled "momism" by Philip Wylie in his 1942 *Generation of Vipers*) or on the side of absenteeism, but err they would.[122] While not directly linked to sleep safety, bonding theories and psychoanalytic theories do speak to the turn toward "child centeredness" that seemingly required uninterrupted (but not domineering or "overprotective") maternal attention, tempered by expert guidance.[123]

As previously noted, mothers also received infant care advice from popular sources like women's magazines, which often suggested that "traditional" sleep advice could be dangerous.[124] Mothers were seemingly cognizant that sleep position might matter for their babies, as this question was included in a "Q&A"-style article in a 1949 issue of *Good*

Housekeeping. The female pediatric expert who authored the responses wrote that "doctors differ about this" and that the mother could experiment with different positions to determine what the baby preferred. A follow-up question asked, "might a baby smother if he slept on his stomach?" The doctor responded that stomach sleeping posed little danger with a firm mattress and limited bedding. Another question asks whether a crying child may be taken into his mother's bed. The answer:

> No. The child will become too dependent on her. Also, the habit will be hard to break. Go to him, find out what he needs, and give him the help he wants. Let him know you love him and are not leaving him alone. But it is better for him to learn to go to sleep by himself.[125]

Another article titled "Your Baby After Dark" in *McCall's* magazine from 1953 relies on advice from pediatricians including Dr. Spock to warn mothers of the trouble co-sleeping could cause:

> Fear of touchy neighbors who knock on the wall every time the baby cries often leads parents into the trap of bribing their child with an extra feeding at night, or, worse still, taking him into bed with them. This gives even a very young child an idea that he has come upon a powerful weapon to hold over his father and mother.[126]

Safety is not noted as a concern in either; rather, the response reflects the era's attention to baby's emotions with a continued adherence to forming "good habits" of independence. That such advice was published in popular women's magazines suggests that sleep safety was a gendered preoccupation of mothers during the time period, but that a standard definition of what constitutes a safe sleep position and environment had not yet been determined. According to Cowgill, the threat of what was called accidental mechanical suffocation was raised in newspapers and magazines in the mid-twentieth century. Pediatric literature and advice sources like *Infant Care* largely dismissed mothers' fears of suffocation as it pertained to stomach sleeping, but did say that such risks could be reduced by having babies sleep alone.[127]

Alternative perspectives to scientific motherhood did emerge during the mid-twentieth century. "Natural motherhood," as Jessica Martucci terms it in *Back to the Breast*, was promoted by psychologists, psychiatrists, anthropologists (or "psy-entists") who held that women instinctually had the knowledge and skills to mother, which "could be unlocked through 'natural' behaviors like childbirth and breastfeeding."[128] In *The Rights of Infants*, published in 1944, psychologist Margaret Ribble argued that mothers should sleep with their infants because physical proximity ensured stimulation, which would deliver oxygen to their developing brains.[129] Martucci argues that Ribble's research, while often critiqued and resisted by her male peers, offered an alternative model for American mothers to follow.[130] Her obituary in the *New York Times* in 1971 states that Ribble "warned that the natural impulses of an infant cannot be summarily dammed up or snuffed out when their expression becomes inconvenient for adults."[131]

Women were also turning to one another as sources of information and support, as demonstrated by the formation of La Leche League in 1956, and the Boston Women's Health Collective in 1969. The League was created by a group of women in a wealthy Chicago suburb as a way to support breastfeeding, a practice that had declined in the 1940s and '50s.[132] La Leche League celebrated so-called female traits and argued that breastfeeding was natural and best for babies. As the League continued on into the 1960s and '70s, its popularity grew, due in part to the group's resistance to the patriarchal authority of medical professionals, although without rejecting scientific and medical evidence that supported their own cause.[133] The stance of La Leche League was that women had authority in childrearing that need not be secondary to that of a physician, and that practices like breastfeeding empowered mothers to trust their own bodies.[134] Historians and other feminist scholars have analyzed the philosophy of Le Leche League and debated whether or to what extent it reflects feminist values, re-inscribes determinist women's roles, or both.[135] In contrast, the Boston Women's Health Collective explicitly emerged from feminist organizing, and its first books published in the early 1970s included *Our Bodies Ourselves* and *Ourselves and Our Children*. These texts were meant to empower women to assess medical information themselves, and take back medical authority from the experts.[136]

As these examples suggest, the relationship between women, infants, and experts was changing. According to Apple, by the mid-twentieth century, doctors were more likely to collaborate with mothers, who had their own ideas about parenting practices, even though the medical provider was still the final authority.[137] American women were also encouraged to take some measure of control over their birth experiences by the "prepared childbirth movement" and the writings of Fernand Lamaze, as well as Grantly Dick-Read's *Childbirth Without Fear*.[138] Presumably these more egalitarian relationships were most available to women with race and class privilege and the access to pick and choose healthcare providers. Much of the "expert" childrearing advice during this period was aimed at and consumed primarily by the white middle class, but is arguably relevant to consider within this project because hegemonic ideals of motherhood in the United States have always shaped the expectations of mothers from diverse economic and racial backgrounds. We will see throughout this book the ways in which parents are individually held to standards that do not account for the systemic and structural barriers they experience, and these standards are at least partially shaped by the vision of what motherhood should look like according to those whose expertise and knowledge production are valued.

As the women's movement and other countercultural and civil rights movements swept the American landscape in the 1960s and '70s, women's reliance on medical authorities to tell them how to rear their children lost even more of its appeal. Medical intervention was contrasted with what was "natural," innocent, and positioned as morally pure; while these were not new ideas, broader social changes meant that the time was right for some women to assert their demands for a different type of birth and parenting experience. Women's magazines of the 1970s promoted natural childbirth, including the Lamaze method, and more hospitals, forced to compete for clients, began to embrace family-centered births. While some obstetricians feared that this new direction would strip them of their authority, others like the well-known T. Berry Brazelton argued that natural childbirth gave women a sense of control (even if final authority remained with the doctor).[139]

This appealed to women with a growing awareness of feminism, who believed that "to be free, a woman had to make her own rules about her reproductive capacity."[140] The feminist women's health movement insisted that women had the capacity to become experts on their own health and bodies, and resisted the notion that women required the guidance of a male-dominated medical system to make decisions about their bodies or their babies.[141] As Jennifer Nelson argues in *More Than Medicine*, the women's liberation movement began to "define health care delivery for themselves in ways that challenged sexed and gendered hierarchical power relations."[142] Black feminists and other women of color were simultaneously demanding attention to the lack of healthcare access for poor and marginalized groups in the United States, which they argued were prerequisites to true reproductive control.

SIDS researchers, however, were continuing to grapple with how to explain racial disparities in sleep-related deaths. In the 1980s, Cowgill argues, thinking about SIDS began to shift. Those who had initially created the SIDS diagnosis had viewed babies with the condition as physiologically normal infants; this changed in the '70s and '80s. Researchers began to investigate SIDS as multifactorial, linking demographics like race and class to the factors associated with the syndrome.[143] In addition to the factors that researchers had already identified in the 1960s (sleep-related, male sex, winter birth, and having a cold), a more in-depth profile of "risky babies" emerged; SIDS was more common in infants born to young mothers with lower education and socioeconomic status. It was linked to prematurity, low birth weight, and drug use, which were also proxies for class. This linkage was problematic, Cowgill argued, because it resurrected the shadow of preventable overlay and infanticide that had been haunting SIDS for generations.[144] This view of SIDS as linked to modifiable risk factors and race is also reminiscent of how Progressive health reformers viewed Black infant mortality in the early twentieth century. As Meckel argues, the high rates of Black infant mortality at the time were interpreted by many as a reflection of the degeneracy of the African American family and destructive cultural norms surrounding parenting rather than poverty or the effects of structural racism.[145] "Culture" can stand in for race and become just as essentialized and biologized; according to anthropologist Khiara Bridges, healthcare providers' belief in culture contributes to racial healthcare disparities when it is viewed as fixed or unalterable.[146] Accounts of Cowgill, Bridges, and Meckel all underscore how the recurrent theme of mother-blame intersects with classism and racism to normalize infant mortality among marginalized groups, and privatize responsibility for it.

As SIDS risk became increasingly associated with low-income and non-white families, a slippage or elision also occurred between associating certain demographics with risk factors for SIDS, and associating certain types of parents as risky. In other words, low-income mothers of color came to embody a risk to their children, rather than the structural and systemic conditions of poverty and racism. Cowgill supports this argument via the types of evidence that researchers collected about parents whose children died of SIDS, including their marital status, intelligence levels, quality of their homes, and perceived sorrow at the death of their child. As we will see in chapter 4, "Everybody Loses," many of these factors continue to be assessed in contemporary legal proceedings that aim to prosecute parents for sleep-related infant death. Cowgill also cites unambiguous statements from medical professionals, such as that of a physician at the 1974 International Symposium on SIDS, who said that "those people with a better background take better care of their children, and they take them seriously and give them better care."[147] This bias extended beyond physicians; it was reflected in clear disparities in how unexpected infant death was classified, with Black families in the 1970s four times more likely to have their infants' death categorized as suffocation as compared to white families.[148]

The disparate treatment of Black families who were experiencing the tragedy of SIDS aligns with the broader state response to the reproductive lives of women of color in the United States historically. As Dorothy Roberts argues in *Killing the Black Body*, the state has systemically blamed the poor health outcomes in Black communities on the behavior of Black mothers, and then used evidence of these outcomes to justify the surveillance, policing, and reproductive control of Black communities.[149] While SIDS was being increasingly attributed to the poor parenting of low-income families and people of color, sources including the media and lawmakers in the 1980s were making unsupported and eventually invalidated claims that drug- addicted Black mothers were birthing a permanent underclass of "crack babies." Such racially biased claims, even after being thoroughly debunked, would later contribute to the development of fetal protection laws across the country. Such laws are used today to disproportionately ensnare poor women and women of color into the criminal justice system, appropriating the discourse of fetal personhood to allege harms against "the unborn."[150]

During the same era in which mothers of color were increasingly surveilled for their reproductive decision making, a parenting philosophy that would reject many mainstream safe sleep guidelines was growing in popularity. The *Book of Child Care* published in 1980 by Dr. Hugh Jolly took up anthropological evidence of cross-cultural bed-sharing to promote the concept of a "family bed," downplaying suffocation risk for babies who slept in bed with their parents.[151] Jean Liedloff's *The Continuum Concept* likewise focused on the parenting practices of non-Western families (in her case, based on her time spent in what she terms the "Stone Age" jungles of South America) and evolutionary arguments to support shared sleep among other practices "appropriate to the ancient continuum of our species."[152] According to Hardyment, these books and Deborah Jackson's 1989 *Three in a Bed* were early forays into parenting literature promoting co-sleeping, but would all be overshadowed by Martha and William Sears's 1993 *The Baby Book* (and later *The Attachment Parenting Book*) which codified what would become known as "attachment parenting."

The Baby Book, described on Amazon.com as a "million copy best-seller," and Sears's others name what he calls "sharing sleep" as among the three key criteria to instill attachment and bonding between parent and infant. Sears acknowedges that co-sleeping is the most popular term, but says that it "sounds like something adults do,"[153] while bed-sharing "appears in medical writings."[154] Attachment parenting philosophy is premised on psychological theories such as the aforementioned work of John Bowlby, which contend that a sense of secure attachment is crucial for the emotional well-being and development of infants. Attachment parenting builds on this to argue that secure attachment is achieved through specific practices by parents (primarily mothers).[155] Attachment parenting practices are meant to create in children a secure attachment style, which will benefit them behaviorally and emotionally throughout their lives.[156] The most important of these practices are exclusive breastfeeding, baby-wearing (carrying a child in a sling attached to the body whenever possible), and sharing a family bed, or co-sleeping.

The Baby Book also refers specifically to Dr. James McKenna's anthropological research, which will be discussed at greater length in chapter 2; McKenna's studies focus on the benefits of sleep-sharing, with significant findings concerning arousal, breastfeeding, and SIDS reduction. Sears cites this work before provocatively asking the reader to "draw your own conclusion: if there were fewer cribs, would there be fewer crib deaths?"[157] Attachment parenting has been critiqued as anti-feminist, given its reliance on intensive mothering practices that many argue would be difficult for a working parent to accomplish, but also applauded for some of the same reasons as other maternalist ideologies: for valorizing motherhood and taking mothers seriously as experts in their own right. Attachment parenting was still such a phenomenon in 2012 that it earned a controversial cover in *Time* magazine titled "Are You Mom Enough?" featuring a young, conventionally attractive white mother staring defiantly at the camera while her three-year-old son breastfed, standing on a chair in order to reach her chest.[158] The sustainability of a parenting philosophy that unabashedly promotes co-sleeping and utilizes reputable anthropological evidence to do so suggests that the divide over what constitutes safe sleep is a pernicious one.

Meanwhile in 1994, the United States launched the Back to Sleep Campaign; researchers in the United States had by then accepted the significance of sleep positioning in reducing unexpected infant death, but a large-scale public health effort was necessary to convince American parents to change the way they put their babies to sleep. The Back to Sleep Campaign was endorsed by national health organizations including the National Institute of Child Health and Human Development, the AAP Task force, and SIDS advocacy organizations. The primary message, as stated by then US Surgeon General Joycelyn Elders, was that all infants should be put to sleep on their back to reduce the risk of SIDS.[159] The campaign utilized widespread messaging that included public service announcements, education in hospitals and clinics, and the support of spokeswoman Tipper Gore (wife of then Vice President Al Gore). These tactics were successful in many communities; prone sleep position for infants dropped from 70 percent to 24 percent between 1992 and 1996, and SIDS rates fell roughly 50 percent.[160] By 2006, SIDS rates had leveled off and were no longer decreasing, which leads researchers to conclude that prone sleep is but one of the extrinsic factors that contribute to unexpected infant death. This is in part why the Back to Sleep Campaign was re-named Safe to Sleep in 2012—in addition to sleep position, Safe to Sleep emphasizes both breastfeeding and a solitary "safe sleep environment" to minimize the risk of entrapment, suffocation, or strangulation in bed.[161]

Although Back to Sleep was credited with widespread success, it did not have the same impact across all racial and ethnic groups. While groups with the highest SIDS rates (African Americans and Native Americans) had the most significant initial declines, from 2010 to 2013 the SIDS mortality rate of Black infants was 83 percent higher than that of white infants, and the mortality rate of Native American infants was 95 percent higher.[162] Research demonstrates that most contemporary SIDS cases occur in families considered "high risk" based on socioeconomic status or race, which include Native Americans and African Americans in the United States, and groups like the Maori in New Zealand.[163] Again, this conceptualization of "high-risk" families is problematic because it creates a potential slippage between types of people (Black, Native American, poor) and "risky" behaviors, such that the negative behavior is assumed to be an inevitable attribute of that group of people, rather than an outcome that is influenced by a complex array of economic, social, and historical factors. For example, some researchers argue that disparities in SIDS rates between countries like the United States, which has one of the highest SIDS rates in the world, and a country like the Netherlands, which saw a consistent decline after promoting prone sleep, can be partially explained by the latter's system of universal health care.[164]

Public health information also may not be equitably distributed. A study comparing infants born in a three-year period before the Back to Sleep campaign (1989–1991) with those born after the rollout of the campaign (1996–1998) found that racial disparities and social class disparities in infant mortality increased after Back to Sleep. The researchers concluded that either safe sleep information was not being equally disseminated to these groups, or was not being followed. To support the theory that educational materials were not equally distributed, these researchers cite a study in Louisville, Kentucky that found 72 percent of families who attended a private practice medical clinic and were mostly upper-middle-class and white received advice about sleep position, while only 48 percent of families at a clinic serving primarily low-income Black populations received the same advice.[165] This research suggests that low-income people of color may not be receiving the same safe sleep education as their higher income and white counterparts; other studies indicate that Black mothers of varying socioeconomic backgrounds are skeptical of the safe sleep messaging they do receive. A sample of such mothers, interviewed individually or in focus groups between 2006 and 2008, reported that the shifting recommendations on sleep position and SIDS felt arbitrary, and handed down without sufficient proof or evidence.[166] Another piece of this picture is whether mothers trust physician recommendations. A study of 671 mothers who attended Women, Infants, and Children (WIC) Program Centers around the country, 64 percent of whom were Black, found that only 60 percent trusted recommendations on sleep position that were made by a doctor or nurse. Mothers reported that they were more likely to trust advice from a family member or friend.[167] In summary, low-income women and women of color are less likely to have received information about the link between sleep position and SIDS, less likely to be convinced by the quality of evidence provided to them, and less likely to trust the advice of medical professionals.

The mistrust of medical authorities revealed in these studies is a product of the unfinished history of medical racism in the United States. African Americans have been abused, mistreated, and experimented on by the medical community in the United States since this country's founding.[168] History of medicine scholar Vanessa Northington Gamble notes that the notorious Tuskegee Syphilis Study, in which treatment was withheld from 399 Black men with syphilis in order to study the disease, is often cited as a reference point for African American mistrust of medical authorities. However, it is imperative to look further back to the history of coerced and forced medical experimentation on enslaved populations, including in the origins of American gynecology. In effect, Gamble argues, "there is a collective memory among African Americans about their exploitation by the medical establishment."[169] The ongoing problem of racism in health care is one that happens at both the individual level and the structural level; as Bridges argues in *Reproducing Race*, "physicians harboring racist beliefs (and physicians not harboring racist beliefs) practice medicine within institutions that function to both reiterate racial and racist discourses and to maintain racial inequality."[170] Black Americans continue to receive disparate treatment in healthcare settings, exacerbated by the view of some medical professionals that African Americans are "bad patients" who cannot or will not follow medical advice.[171]

This history also impacts the success or failure of public health campaigns, which may be affected by the targeted population's reluctance at being negatively judged by categories such as race or age, also known as stereotype threat.[172] When Black women are aware that they are being stereotyped as irresponsible mothers or as unable or unwilling to follow safe sleep guidelines, they may be less receptive to public health efforts to change their behavior. Dána-Ain Davis builds on the research on healthcare stereotype threats (HCSTs) in *Reproductive Injustice: Racism, Pregnancy, and Premature Birth* to argue that HCSTs are frequently used in public health education campaigns, which may negatively impact the utilization of these resources.[173] Davis's contention is supported by the results of a 2006 study; after mothers were told that Black infants are more likely to die of SIDS, only 43 percent reported that they believed sleep position is connected to SIDS for Black babies. Mothers may have been responding to a healthcare stereotype threat; in other words, if marginalized mothers conclude that their race or class status is being conflated with a risk factor for SIDS, they may reject related guidance. In effect, it is critical to consider how the history of gendered and racialized oppression impacts contemporary parents when assessing the efficacy of public health programs that attempt to reduce rates of unexpected infant death in communities of color, as will be discussed in detail in chapter 3.

As this chapter demonstrates, infant care and sleep safety have been increasingly medicalized over time. Health reformers have identified environmental and structural factors that contributed to infant mortality, but also intensified the surveillance of mothers and confirmed their responsibility for child health and safety. Women were tasked with adopting the exacting and regimented style of scientific motherhood, while remaining under the watchful eye of medical professionals. As pediatrics and psychology gained stature in American society, advice about infant safety, including sleep safety, became increasingly pedantic and remained quite inflexible. Class and race have stratified parents' access to sources of information about sleep safety, and have shaped researchers' and healthcare providers' perception of their parenting capabilities. The second half of the twentieth century saw challenges to medical authority, but also the advent of "sleep safety" as a set of authoritative rules mandated by an increasingly powerful authority that is discussed in depth in the next chapter—the American Academy of Pediatrics.

2

Making and Unmaking a Safe Sleep Environment

From the AAP to the Rock 'n Play Recall

The late nineteenth and early twentieth centuries saw the growth and professionalization of pediatrics as a medical specialty. The development of pediatrics is significant in the context of infant sleep safety because the field recognizes infants and children as a unique population requiring specialized treatment for disease prevention as well as "optimal health." In other words, pediatrics as a field was organized around the assertion that "infants and children themselves, rather than the diseases they suffered, were special";[1] it follows from this perspective that infants could be uniquely at risk from an activity like sleep that is not a disease or pathology, and that does not impact other populations in the same way. Sleep instruction may have garnered less attention when public health workers and doctors were primarily battling illnesses related to infant feeding practices. However, some of the most common questions parents ask pediatricians today center around sleep and sleep safety, like whether a baby should be swaddled, how long they should sleep without eating, whether they are old enough to sleep through the night, and why they should sleep on their backs.[2] To varying degrees, parents rely on pediatricians as a source of authoritative information on sleep safety. The leading pediatric organization in the United States today, which represents 67,000 pediatricians nationwide and sets widely recognized guidelines for infant sleep safety, is the American Academy of Pediatrics (AAP).

The AAP was founded in 1930, reflecting the demand for pediatric services among an increasingly middle-class clientele;[3] it differed from its forerunner, the American Pediatric Society (founded in 1888) in that the AAP had a specific focus on "political and social issues" like public health and education.[4] In addition to offering professional development and educational opportunities for its approximately 60,000 members, the organization today also publishes the monthly journal *Pediatrics*, disseminates research, informs policymaking through advocacy and lobbying, and conducts public education outreach in the form of brochures and childcare books for patients.[5] The AAP disseminates policy statements on a wide range of issues, including bariatric surgery, emergency contraception, and nonnutritive sweeteners; while most of their policies are largely non-controversial, some, such as their 2012 statement concluding that the benefits of newborn male circumcision outweigh the risk, do inspire debate among medical professionals and the general public. That is in part because recommendations made by the AAP carry significant weight in the American medical community; in the case of male newborn circumcision, for example, critics concluded that the guidelines released by the AAP were not in line with those of other international medical bodies, and could increase the overall number of circumcisions in the United States.[6] In other words, AAP guidelines have the potential to shape the advice that parents receive from medical professionals, and even how pediatricians practice medicine; they are also impacted by the cultural norms of the members of the task force that writes each policy, which likely change over time.

The AAP is a significant organization for the history of infant sleep safety because of its policies regarding SIDS and safe sleep. These include recommendations on sleep position and sleep environment and are utilized by a host of sources, including pediatricians, public health officials, researchers, policymakers, and the Centers for Disease Control and Prevention, and the standards that they create are implemented to mandate safety in institutions ranging from hospitals to daycare centers, and through public health outreach campaigns. This chapter will first unpack the evolution of the AAP's policies regarding infant sleep from 1992 to 2016, which are written by a group of medical doctors who make up the Task Force on Sudden Infant Death Syndrome.[7]

I focus primarily on the gradual shift in these policies from SIDS prevention to the prevention of all sleep-related infant deaths, which centralizes adherence to a safe sleep environment. This shift is significant because it broadens the scope of infant sleep safety, which impacts a range of issues covered in this book, from bed-sharing and room-sharing guidelines, to the prosecution of parents for bed-sharing deaths, to the type of safety equipment that parents are urged to purchase by the baby safety industry. Next, this chapter will address how the AAP's definition of a safe sleep environment compares with the stance of those who advocate for the bonding and breastfeeding benefits of co-sleeping. Finally, I consider the AAP's guidelines in relation to the 2019 recall of the Fisher-Price Rock 'n Play sleeper. Taken together, this chapter presents the evolution of infant sleep safety guidelines from a biomedical perspective, how other stakeholders affiliated with women's and children's health have responded to the guidelines, and argues that despite consistent and widely disseminated AAP guidance, the case of the Rock 'n Play sleeper reveals that weak federal regulation and oversight fail to hold corporations responsible for infant sleep safety.

AAP Safe Sleep Guidelines

The AAP's first policy statement regarding infant sleep safety was published in 1992 when the AAP Task Force on Infant Positioning and SIDS released guidelines recommending that infants sleep on their side or back rather than prone.[8] This recommendation was based on epidemiological research on infant death in Australia and Europe, which indicated that certain sleep positions reduced the risk of Sudden Infant Death Syndrome.[9] Parents of children who had died of SIDS had been pushing the AAP and other bodies like the Children's Bureau to raise parental awareness about the condition since the 1960s, but these organizations had been hesitant to do so, concluding that it would create unnecessary fear regarding a condition that was not understood, let alone preventable.[10] As American SIDS researchers eventually accepted the international consensus that sleep position was linked to SIDS, the Back to Sleep campaign was launched in 1994 with the goal of changing the behavioral norm in the United States. Up until that point, most parents put their babies to sleep on their stomachs rather than their backs.[11] While the AAP's initial 1992 statement endorsed both side and supine sleep position, subsequent guidelines revised the advisement to recommend only supine sleep, with the latest 2016 report stating that "side sleeping is not safe and is not advised."[12]

The task force revised its SIDS recommendations in 1996,[13] and then again in 2000, this time with the title "Changing Concepts of Sudden Infant Death Syndrome: Implications for Infant Sleeping Environment and

Sleep Position," indicating an added emphasis on hazards in the sleep environment in addition to sleep position. This shift in focus foreshadowed the later disaggregation of the syndrome SIDS into the broader category of Sudden Unexpected Infant Death, in which accidental suffocation is delineated as its own category of death within the umbrella of SUID. This was not, however, the first time that researchers had linked accidental suffocation with SIDS. Accidental Mechanical Suffocation (AMS) was proposed as an explanation for sudden infant death as early as the 1930s. Accidental mechanical suffocation encompassed what had been called overlay as well as suffocation by bedding or while in bed, and some researchers connected suffocation with stomach sleeping. By the end of the 1940s, AMS was rejected by most researchers as an explanation for sudden infant death, and sleep position was not taken seriously in the United States until the 1980s. As Cowgill notes, American SIDS researchers found explanations regarding bedding or sleep position "strikingly elementary in comparison to detailed medical investigations into particular aspects of sleep," especially because stomach sleeping was the norm in the United States.[14] The conclusion that unexpected infant deaths during sleep were "unexplained" or "inexplicable" eventually led to the adoption of the term Sudden Death Syndrome in 1963, and the first formal definition of Sudden Infant Death in 1969.[15] While Cowgill adds that concerns about stomach sleeping were repeatedly debated by physicians and raised by parents throughout the twentieth century,[16] the 2000 recommendations identify soft bedding and covered airways as hazards to infants that had been demonstrated "only recently."[17] The emphasis on hazards in the sleep environment demonstrate how ideas about unexpected infant death were already beginning to shift from the "unexplained" to the seemingly modifiable.

By 2005, the AAP recommendations were taking a clearer anti–bedsharing stance than they had in the past, in several ways.[18] In 2000, the guidelines did not explicitly advise against all bed-sharing, but rather stated that if a mother shares a bed with her infant in order to breastfeed, she should follow all the other guidance about supine sleep, soft bedding, and avoiding entrapment. The same policy also balanced studies on the dangers of bed-sharing with other research suggesting that bed-sharing infants may have lighter sleep and more arousals (which are protective factors for SIDS) before concluding that "no epidemiological evidence exists that bed-sharing is protective against SIDS."[19] In the 2005 update, the AAP's language surrounding bed-sharing becomes increasingly definitive in its opposition to the practice. The statement notes that bed-sharing is "controversial"; it enhances bonding and breastfeeding, but "can be hazardous under certain conditions."[20] By 2005, bed-sharing was more definitively cast on the side of risk, as exemplified by the guidance that "infants not bed share during sleep."[21]

The AAP guidelines were revised next in 2011, with a new title, "SIDS and Other Sleep-Related Infant Deaths: Expansion of Recommendations for a Safe Infant Sleeping Environment." As the revised title suggests, the statement notes the shift in the AAP's focus for preventing unexpected infant death, asserting "the AAP is expanding its recommendations from focusing only on SIDS to focusing on a safe sleep environment that can reduce the risk of all sleep-related infant deaths, including SIDS."[22] Because of this, the policy statement uses the term Sudden Unexpected Infant Death (SUID), which encompasses deaths that are explained (by factors like accidental suffocation, infection, entrapment, other forms of asphyxia, or trauma) and unexplained (SIDS). The statement focuses on SUID that occurs during sleep, which would include SIDS, accidental suffocation, and entrapment.[23] The 2011 guidelines also mark the first time that the AAP uses the phrase "safe sleep environment" as part of these recommendations, which indicates a continued broadening of the scope from risk factors associated with the physiology and placement of the infant to the modifiable environment that surrounds the baby. By the release of the ensuing (and, as of this writing, latest) guidelines in 2016, a safe sleep environment is explicitly defined as "supine positioning, the use of a firm sleep surface, room-sharing without bed-sharing, and the avoidance of soft bedding and overheating."[24] I will discuss the AAP's room-sharing recommendations later in this chapter, as the recommendation in these guidelines that infants room-share until their first birthday was met with dismay and criticism by some parties.

The other item that garnered attention in the 2016 recommendations was the revised section on bed-sharing, which included the statement that "the AAP acknowledges that parents frequently fall asleep while feeding the infant."[25] It noted that if parents are to fall asleep, a bed is significantly safer than a couch or chair, and thus beds should be kept free of pillows, sheets, and blankets. Some interpreted this addition as a long-awaited acknowledgment that parents *are* bed-sharing, and thus it is prudent to teach them how to do so more safely. Others, such as Kathleen Kendall-Tackett, a health psychologist and pediatrics professor, note that as early as 2011 the AAP had begun to address the concern that strict anti–bed-sharing guidelines were leading parents to feed their infants on couches or armchairs instead of in bed. In a study of 4,789 US mothers who completed the Survey of Mothers' Sleep and Fatigue in 2008–2009, Kendall-Tackett and colleagues found that 44 percent of mothers who fed their infants in a chair, recliner, or sofa at night reported that they sometimes fell asleep with their babies in that location.[26] This is troubling because chairs and couches are much riskier places for infants to sleep with adults due to the higher likelihood of entrapment and suffocation. The 2011 AAP guidelines, Kendall-Tackett says, acknowledge that couch and chair deaths have been included in statistics about bed-sharing (a problem that has "dogged the bedsharing debate for more than a decade") which can create "heterogeneity" in the analysis.[27] The 2011 guidelines recommend explicitly against feeding infants on a couch or armchair because of the likelihood that parents may fall asleep, and Kendall-Tackett says, "acknowledge—and seem to affirm—*feeding* babies in bed, but putting them in their own cribs for sleep."[28] The 2016 guidelines moved further in this direction by expressly acknowledging that parents may fall asleep while feeding and by making suggestions for a safer sleep environment in the event that bed-sharing occurs.

Bed-sharing is clearly a growing preoccupation of the organization; by 2016, bed-sharing is mentioned 13 times in the body of the AAP's recommendations, as compared to once in 2005. In part, this reflects the trends in bed-sharing in the country. In the years 1992–2016, which mark the span of the AAP guidelines, SIDS rates drastically declined, while the number of families who reported co-sleeping continued to climb.[29] The AAP's National Infant Sleep Position study found an increase in infants sharing an adult bed from 5.5 percent in 1993 to 13.5 percent in 2010. Bed-sharing among white parents leveled off between 2000 and 2010, but continued to rise among Black and Hispanic parents.[30] In a CDC analysis of data from the 2009–2015 Pregnancy Risk Assessment Monitoring System, which assesses the self-reported behaviors of women before, during, and after pregnancy, 61.4 percent of respondents in 14 states reported any bed-sharing with their infant.[31] Bed-sharing rates were highest among Native American and Alaskan Natives (78.9 percent of mothers in Alaska reported some bed-sharing) and those who identified as Black or Asian/Pacific Islander.

It may be difficult to find consistent levels of bed-sharing in studies of mothers' self-reported behavior in part because some parents hide the practice to avoid negative judgment from medical practitioners. Knowing this, the AAP's most recent set of guidelines may have made the calculated choice that in order to reach bed-sharing parents, they must acknowledge the prevalence of sharing a bed. Lori Feldman-Winter, a pediatrician and member of the task force, told news media that the APP stands by research that bed-sharing can be hazardous but acknowledges that "we don't want to put our heads in the sand," even suggesting that the organization might publish recommendations that include safe bed-sharing in the future. Healthcare providers should have open and non-judgmental conversations about infant sleep with parents, Feldman-Winter asserts, and the change to the guidelines is meant to promote that dialogue.[32]

Were the AAP to do so, they would be moving in the direction that some Western European countries are now taking. UNICEF in the United Kingdom, for example, has chosen to "acknowledge that bed-sharing is a common practice and specifically target hazardous circumstances" rather than adopt a strict anti–bed-sharing stance.[33] This follows case control research on bed-sharing deaths in the UK that concludes that bed-sharing in the absence of additional hazards does not increase the risk of SIDS. As previously mentioned, it also reflects reports that strict anti–bed-sharing messaging has led some parents to feed and fall asleep with their babies on couches or armchairs, resulting in infant death. The authors of this research conclude that "giving across the board advice simply to not do it [bed-share] negates the option of highlighting the specific and highly significant risks we have found," such as the use of alcohol and tobacco, and the danger of sleeping with an infant on a chair or couch.[34] Whether the AAP will fully trust parents, and particularly women, with nuanced information about infant sleep safety is yet to be seen.

AAP's Room-Sharing Guidelines

Another aspect of the 2016 guidelines that caused some public controversy was the recommendation that parents room-share with their infants on a separate sleep surface for at least the first six months of life, and ideally up to one year. While the AAP had been recommending room-sharing in their guidelines since at least 2005, the wording of the 2016 guidelines was interpreted by many as more definitive in its guidance to room-share well past the "newborn" stage. The AAP makes this recommendation because room-sharing is understood to have multiple benefits for infant health. First, room-sharing keeps babies "within view and reach" to promote ease of feeding and the ability to comfort an infant during the night. The CDC's website and the AAP's healthy-children.org site both visually represent this messaging with images of a woman in an adult bed leaning over and touching a baby in a portable crib that is positioned next to the bed. In both images, the presumed mother is making physical and visual contact with the infant.[35] Theoretically, room-sharing is also a potential alternative to bed-sharing, and can encourage parents to put their baby back into a separate surface after feeding, but before the caregiver falls asleep. Finally, these organizations recommend room-sharing because of research suggesting that it can reduce the risk of SIDS by up to 50 percent.[36]

If room-sharing is a SIDS-reduction strategy, it takes on the weight of a moral imperative to reduce risk, which is why it is worth considering the strength of this research in assessing how room-sharing recommendations contribute to an overall climate of intensive motherhood. In an article in the *New York Times* titled "Should Your Baby Really Sleep in the Same Bed as You?" *Times* correspondent Claire Cain Miller and professor of pediatrics Aaron E. Carroll assess the sources cited in the AAP's recommendations. They note that because of the infrequency with which SIDS occurs, the design of the three studies cited in the 2016 AAP guidelines were all case-control. Case-control means that:

> researchers compiled records of babies who died of SIDS and matched them as closely as possible, based on things like age or geography. Then, by comparing the groups, they tried to identify factors that might place babies at higher risk.[37]

Case-control studies, Miller and Carroll note, are only able to demonstrate association as opposed to causation, and run the risk of "recall bias," meaning that individuals are likely to remember things differently if they experience a traumatic outcome such as the death of a child than they would otherwise. Data collection also occurred in European countries, where room-sharing is more common, and in the 1990s, when SIDS rates were higher and prone sleep was more often practiced. Thus, the assertion that room-sharing could reduce the likelihood of SIDS as much as 50 percent may be over-inflated based on current SIDS data. The authors conclude that efforts to reduce SIDS should be made in ways that are likely to be effective and unlikely to increase harm. By "harm," they are referring to harm to both children and parents (and arguably that these two harms cannot be separated from one another). Harm to parents could be caused by increasing the pressure to constantly monitor infants while they are asleep.[38]

A 2017 study published in *Pediatrics* confirmed what many parents suspected, which is that room-sharing leads to less uninterrupted sleep for babies and parents. Ian Paul and colleagues found that babies who were room-sharing with their parents at four and nine months of age slept less overall during the night and had lower sleep consolidation (consecutive minutes of uninterrupted sleep).[39] They found that infants who were room-sharing were more likely to have an "unapproved object" in their sleep surface (such as a blanket) and were more likely to be brought into the parental bed to sleep after night waking. They conclude that the recommendation to room-share for up to one year is not evidence-based, in part because of the aforementioned weakness in case-control studies; in addition, 90 percent of SIDS deaths occur before six months of age, which points to a limitation of the efficacy of room-sharing from six months to one year.

While Paul and colleagues use the gender-neutral "parents" at times in the article, they also cite evidence that "room-sharing is associated with more sleep disruption for *mothers*" (emphasis added).[40] The unexamined assumption is that it is mothers who take on the reproductive labor of caring for infants at night, and thus would be more significantly impacted by room-sharing if this type of sleep arrangement negatively impacts parental sleep.

Another study of the sleeping arrangements of 167 families with infants in the United States confirmed that responsibility for infants during the night is deeply gendered. The study compared parents who co-slept with infants (with co-sleeping encompassing both room-sharing and bed-sharing) with those whose infants slept in a separate room to analyze how sleep arrangements impacted infant-parent sleep and family functioning. The researchers found that the sleep of mothers (but not infants) was disrupted by "persistent" co-sleeping arrangements (meaning those lasting longer than six months). In contrast, infant sleep arrangements had little impact on fathers' sleep. Evidence including video data showed that "mothers in this study were almost exclusively the primary caregivers for their infants, and much more likely than fathers to take primary responsibility for putting their infants to bed."[41] They concluded that fathers' sleep quality would likely be impacted by sleep arrangements if fathers were more involved in nighttime routines. This evidence suggests that recommendations guiding parents to room-share for longer than six months is contested in its ability to reduce SIDS rates, and will have a greater impact on mothers than fathers due to gendered disparities in reproductive labor.

Again, this is not to say that room-sharing is in reality unequivocally worse for mothers than sleeping in separate rooms; regardless of what a study might report about average sleep disruption, many parents who sleep with their children report doing so *because* of their self-assessment that they get more sleep.[42] What is troubling about the implication that the AAP's recommendation may be built on evidence that is partial or not particularly strong is that the decision of whether to follow them carries an outsized moral significance. Because the decision to room-share is tied to SIDS reduction, choosing whether or not to do it carries much more emotional valence than, say, whether to follow other medicalized childrearing guidelines like whether to use fluoride in children's toothpaste. The ideology of intensive parenting includes the message that good parents accept expert intervention; if pediatric experts recommend one year of room-sharing to reduce SIDS rates, then parents are morally obligated to reduce the risk of SIDS by complying. While guidelines are framed as advice rather than obligations—particularly in this case, where room-sharing is recommended for *at least* six months but *ideally* one year—they implicitly rest on the assumption that the knowledge produced by experts is indisputably superior to the experiential evidence gathered by parents.[43] Consolidated sleep is framed as a parental "want," whereas room-sharing is an infant "need," and the needs of infants necessarily outweigh the wants of parents.[44] As Ellie Lee argues in "Experts and Parenting Culture," what is often posited as "information" or "evidence" is really a push for parents to accept expert advice.[45]

However, parents are receiving these guidelines as part of a tidal wave of expert guidance that indicates that intensive parenting with limitless resources (including both time and money) is the best way to reflect love for one's child.[46] This guidance aligns with the privatization of responsibility for infant health and increased surveillance of women's reproductive decision making. The effect is that measures to protect infants are framed as a necessary sacrifice without a transparent gendered analysis of how such guidelines could disproportionately impact mothers. Room-sharing and bed-sharing guidelines implicitly promote the narrative that infants are always at risk; a later section of this chapter demonstrates how that risk is expected to be shouldered and foreseen by parents, even if corporations and the state fail to uphold safe sleep standards.

Anthropology and Breastfeeding Advocacy

While the AAP was producing and refining a biomedical approach to safe sleep guidelines, research from other disciplines continued to develop in ways that "instigated an unanticipated collision between anthropologists and epidemiologists over the role of parent-infant sleep proximity in preventing or promoting sudden infant death."[47] Best known in this field is anthropologist James McKenna, who conducts studies of infant sleep behavior at the Mother-Baby Behavioral Sleep Laboratory at the University of Notre Dame. McKenna had been researching the connections between what he terms sleep proximity (where a baby sleeps in relationship to a caregiver) and unexpected infant death since the 1980s. In 1986, McKenna first published a study suggesting SIDS should be approached in an interdisciplinary manner, and that the field of anthropology offers an evolutionary perspective on sleep that is cross-cultural and cross-species.[48] Anthropologist Helen Ball, director of Durham University's Durham Infancy and Sleep Centre, is another leading expert in the biosocial study of parent-infant sleep. Her research likewise contends that bed-sharing promotes breastfeeding, and thus guidelines should be tailored to address the circumstances in which bed-sharing occurs.[49]

This group of researchers that I will call the "anthropological school" argue that breastfeeding mothers and infants have evolved to sleep in close proximity, and that several components of this arrangement can actually protect against unexpected infant death. Bed-sharing increases arousal in infants, meaning that they have fewer periods of deep and uninterrupted sleep, and it regulates their breathing, because of their proximity to an adult caregiver (usually the mother).[50] Breastfeeding mothers who co-sleep are likely to place infants to sleep on their backs as this position is necessary for nursing, and SIDS rates are lower in breastfed infants.[51] The anthropological school of research links SIDS deaths that occurred before the initiation of the Back to Sleep/Safe to Sleep campaigns with anti-breastfeeding and anti–bed-sharing medical advice. During the time period in the United States when parents were encouraged to formula-feed, they were also advised to put babies to sleep alone and on their stomachs to increase sleep duration, which these researchers contend led to the SIDS deaths of thousands of infants.[52] McKenna argues that cultural beliefs, including the significance of marital privacy, infant self-sufficiency, and the importance of consolidated sleep, have led Western cultures to embrace, at various times, practices that have contributed to infant death such as stomach sleeping, formula feeding, and solitary infant sleep, which he argues are all independent risk factors for SIDS and SUID.[53] In other words, these researchers conclude that the move away from the evolutionarily adaptive model of mother-infant bed-sharing and breastfeeding was what historically increased SIDS rates, and that bed-sharing is not an independent risk factor for SIDS.

Others who follow the anthropological school of thought on infant sleep, like Thomas Anders and Teresa Taylor, echo the assertion that babies evolved to have close contact with adults during sleep, and that the "Western" model of solitary sleep is an aberration from that norm.[54] Melissa Bartick, Cecília Tomori, and Helen Ball note that generations of medical advice about sleeping and feeding infants (such as that they should sleep alone, and be formula-fed on a schedule) has reinforced what they argue "are recent Euro-American historical inventions."[55] Such anthropologists use an evolutionary perspective to argue that the contemporary ideology about solitary and uninterrupted sleep "seems to reflect far more about what societies want parents to be and infants to become (self-sufficient and independent) rather than what infants actually are—exceedingly dependent, and unfinished."[56] From this angle, the expectation that infants will sleep alone as is recommended by the AAP is not responsive to the needs of newborn infants, and instead reflects the values of an industrialized and capitalist society that privileges efficiency and autonomy.

This ideology is not consistent across all industrialized nations; the norms of infant sleep in the United States differ when compared to countries like Japan and Italy, where co-sleeping is more common. This comparison suggests that "the decision to share the parental bed may also be influenced by cultural values regarding interrelatedness and interdependence."[57] McKenna and colleagues contend that the normalization of solitary sleep is a social construction that reflects more than 100 years of ethnocentrism and biased ideology in sleep science.[58] For example, mainstream research on infant sleep has been conducted primarily on solitary sleeping formula-fed infants, then used to assess "problems" in the sleep of breastfed infants. This pathologizes what the anthropological school terms a biologically normal sleep environment.[59] Former Academy of Breastfeeding Medicine president Nancy Wight was likewise quoted after the release of the 2005 AAP recommendations that they "represent a truly astounding triumph of ethnocentric assumptions over common sense and medical research."[60] Research by McKenna, Ball, and others offers an evidence-based alternative to anti–bed-sharing arguments; their work is influencing policy and practice, including with organizations like UNICEF United Kingdom, which offers a guide for health professionals on how to discuss safer co-sleeping with parents.

Advocacy groups and individuals that promote breastfeeding have also critiqued the AAP's guidelines. Lactation and midwifery experts Catherine Fetherston and J. Shaughn Leach describe public health–style guidelines like the AAP's as a "utilitarian" approach, which "sets out to achieve the best outcomes possible for the greatest number of people," as compared to bioethics, which "focuses more on the issues of the individual, such as autonomy."[61] One problem with the utilitarian approach,

Fetherston and Leach conclude, is that a one-size-fits-all message doesn't account for groups for whom co-sleeping may be protective against SIDS, like low-risk (non-smoking, non–substance-using) breastfeeding mothers. If breastfeeding protects against SIDS, and bed-sharing and breastfeeding are "interdependent," then guidelines that make blanket statements against bed-sharing for all populations regardless of risk are not "ethical or practical."[62]

A 2014 exchange between Dr. Ruth Lawrence, a pioneering breast-feeding expert, and the members of the AAP Task Force on Sudden Infant Death Syndrome is further indicative of the divide between these groups. Lawrence, the founder of the Academy of Breastfeeding Medicine and first editor-in-chief of that organization's journal, portrays co-sleeping as "the source of the disagreement between the SIDS Task Force and the breastfeeding community" in a 2014 editorial titled "Solomon's Wisdom."[63] Lawrence describes a meeting between breastfeeding advocates and the SIDS Task Force in 2014, in which she contends that task force members presented "selected data" on breastfeeding, co-sleeping, and SIDS without inviting any advocates to speak. According to Lawrence, the task force described their position at that meeting as "vigorously against co-sleeping" and without plans to support breastfeeding.[64]

Members of the task force responded to Lawrence's claims in a letter to the editor in the same journal, contesting almost all aspects of her original statement, including who had organized the event, who spoke at the event (they contend that breastfeeding advocates were represented), and whether the task force supports breastfeeding (they refer to the recommendations that mothers breastfeed in the 2011 SIDS policy document). Tellingly, the task force even challenges Lawrence's use of the term co-sleeping to describe what they would term bed-sharing. The task force, its members argue, fully supports co-sleeping when that term refers to sharing a room but not a bed. They reiterate the stance that bed-sharing increases the risk of SIDS even for breastfed infants of non-smoking mothers, and conclude that it would be "irresponsible" not to share this information with parents.[65] While the letter concludes with the stated desire that breastfeeding advocates can work together with safe sleep advocates, the highly contested nature of the exchange demonstrates that even an agreement on what constitutes co-sleeping could not be reached at that time.

The breastfeeding advocacy organization La Leche League also takes issue with the AAP's approach to co-sleeping; in a book titled *Sweet Sleep: Nighttime and Naptime Strategies for the Breastfeeding Family*, the authors argue that the AAP is unrealistic if it expects parents to consistently return their infants to a crib after nighttime feedings. Instead the book and La Leche League website offer tips for how to co-sleep more safely in formats such as a checklist, an infographic, and a safe sleep bed-sharing song set to the tune of the nursery song "Row, Row, Row Your Boat."[66] Rather than dissuading parents from bed-sharing, they urge parents to prepare their beds for safe infant sleep even if they don't intend to co-sleep, comparing it to other preventative measures that most parents would never question: "life is risky, no matter how you live it. A safe bed, like a seat belt, can greatly reduce that risk."[67] La Leche League's stance on co-sleeping overlaps with the philosophy of attachment parenting (and likely has many of the same adherents); as discussed in chapter 1, attachment parenting guru William Sears names breastfeeding and co-sleeping as two of its three main tenets.[68]

That being said, those who promote a family bed do share some perspectives with the AAP. For example, there is near universal agreement that "clearly there are inappropriate circumstances or environments in which co-sleeping occurs,"[69] such as when parents smoke cigarettes, or are under the influence of alcohol, drugs, or sleep aids. Most co-sleeping proponents also offer clear guidelines on what a safe bed-sharing environment looks like, including a firm mattress without pillows or bedding. However, bed-sharing and breastfeeding proponents (who sometimes refer to this combination as "breastsleeping") fear that strict anti–bed-sharing guidelines will reduce the duration of breastfeeding, and thus potentially increase post-neonatal infant mortality.[70] The divergent perspectives of these stakeholders can prove elusive for parents searching for a definitive answer on whether bed-sharing is ever safe, often resulting in competing perspectives from pediatricians, friends, and online groups where mothers (in particular) seek out support, advice, and community. As the history of infant sleep safety in the first half of this chapter demonstrates, infant sleep is complicated in part because it has been embedded within contests over the shifting authority of religion, medicine, and government to manage the health of the nation, and to determine women's roles within it.

Thus far, this chapter has laid out several decades' worth of guidelines and recommendations regarding infant sleep safety, including guidance on bed-sharing and room-sharing, from biomedical, anthropological, and breastfeeding advocacy perspectives. The evidence-based research that these sources produce and disseminate is a resource for medical professionals, public health experts, childcare providers, and parents. While the messaging is not entirely unified, many sleep safety tenets are shared across disciplines and are widely recognized as best practices (for example, that babies should sleep on their backs, and on firm surfaces). Parents are expected to stay abreast of this body of knowledge about infant sleep safety, and as chapter 4, "Everybody Loses," demonstrates, may be held criminally liable if they fail to adhere to sleep safety standards. According to contemporary logics of individual responsibility for health, parental choice-making is paramount in ensuring infant safety. The same logics dictate that corporations will utilize evidence-based best practices to create infant sleep safety products—they will do so voluntarily because it is in their best financial interest to produce safe and effective goods. Following this reasoning, regulation over these corporations should be minimal to ensure maximum profits. The next section gives one example of how the infant sleep safety guidelines that are crafted by the AAP, debated and revised by other stakeholders, and passed on to parents as essential rules to follow are utilized (or ignored) by the corporations that create infant sleep safety products. The Rock 'n Play sleeper recall, I argue, is a clear example of neoliberal health logic that holds individuals responsible for health outcomes while corporations profit from a lack of regulation.

The Rock 'n Play Recall

On April 12, 2019, the Fisher-Price company voluntary recalled 4.7 million of its Rock 'n Play sleepers; these padded infant seats reclined to a 30-degree angle, purportedly to reduce reflux in babies and promote longer lasting sleep. The ten-year-old product was marketed in the United States as the first to safely allow infants to sleep throughout the night at such an incline (rather than flat on their backs, as is recommended by pediatricians). The Rock 'n Play was eventually linked to more than 50 infant deaths,[71] and the broader category of inclined sleepers was linked to 94 infant fatalities by 2021.[72] Most deaths occurred when an infant had rolled from their back to their stomach and then suffocated in the inclined sleeper's soft padding.[73] Before the recall, the Rock 'n Play was the best-selling infant sleeper sold on Amazon.com, earning Fisher-Price over $200 million in revenues;[74] parents by the thousands bought it for their newborns, listed it on their gift registries, and happily accepted a second-hand Rock 'n Play from family or friends.

Fisher-Price initially resisted the recall, releasing a warning that reminded parents to stop using the Rock 'n Play once a baby is old enough to roll over, and to follow all of the safety instructions that come with the product. In other words, the company insisted that its product was safe, and that the risk to infants was introduced by parents.[75] In reality, the company had been aware of links between its product and suffocation for years—countries like Canada and Australia had already prevented Fisher-Price from marketing its device as a sleeper, and the UK Royal College of Midwives had presented the company with a report detailing major safety concerns.[76]

The circumstances surrounding the recall are noteworthy; on April 1, the Consumer Product Safety Commission sent a letter to Fisher-Price to notify the company that they would issue a press alert in 24 hours warning consumers not to use the product. That the CPSC decided to act with such alacrity was in part because the agency had accidentally released unredacted data to *Consumer Reports* that identified the name of manufacturers and products linked to infant deaths. *Consumer Reports* refused to destroy the data, and planned to publish a story; the day after they notified the CPSC about their intentions, the CPSC informed Fisher-Price that their own press release was forthcoming. This series of events is significant, because it reveals the limitations of the CPSC's oversight; it is the only federal safety agency that is hamstrung by a statute requiring extensive back-and-forth with the manufacturer of a dangerous product before publicly releasing any identifying information about that product to consumers.[77] Even when the recall statement was made, Fisher-Price did not admit fault, concluding that "incidents" had occurred when "the product was used contrary to the safety warnings and instructions."[78] This was despite the company's knowledge of infant deaths in the sleeper since at least 2016; at minimum, half of the infant deaths transpired between the time Fisher-Price conceded that it knew of these deaths and when it eventually recalled the product.[79] In addition to the nearly five million Rock 'n Play sleepers, 700,000 reclining infant sleepers under other brand names were recalled shortly after, some of which had also been linked to suffocation deaths.[80]

After this safety record was made public, the testing and marketing of the Rock 'n Play garnered extensive media attention. The story was covered widely by national news media outlets, some with a focus on parenting or general interest, others addressing the business and financial aspects of such a massive recall. The *New York Times* published multiple articles concerning the Rock 'n Play, one noting the "dubious marketing" that Fisher-Price used to gain a cult following for the product among parents. This marketing included the company's use of social media influencers on platforms like Instagram—they commissioned moms with thousands of followers to post pictures of their babies in the Rock 'n Play, sharing stories of this low-price product that was affording them extra hours of sleep.[81] This is known as "native advertising," or advertising funded by a sponsor that may appear similar to or interchangeable with non-sponsored content. Research suggests that consumers trust the advice of mother-influencers on social media, and that mothers often turn to Instagram for product recommendations and inspiration.[82] Combining a product from a trusted company (Fisher-Price) with the power of the most significant platform for influencer marketing likely introduced the Rock 'n Play to many eager consumers.

Investigative reports also concluded that Fisher-Price failed to have the Rock 'n Play thoroughly tested for safety by a third party before it was introduced to the market. While the Fisher-Price website's "Design Story" claimed that the design and engineering team "put a lot of thought" into exactly the right angle, range of rocking motion, and fabric, later depositions and testimony of employees including the product's designer, the integrity engineer, and director of product safety revealed that no independent testing was conducted, nor did employees review the medical literature or contact medical experts.[83] Fisher-Price's own internal Safety Committee had warned the company three times between 2008 and 2009 that research was needed to confirm the safety of infant positioning in the sleeper, and that without this research the product was "unacceptable," but this research was not conducted.[84] In fact, the lone doctor who was consulted on the product was not a pediatrician, and would eventually be found practicing medicine without a license.[85] The physician was also not hired by Fisher-Price to evaluate the Rock 'n Play until the company faced a product liability suit. This information was revealed by the director of Public Safety for Fisher-Price during a deposition in the case *Goodrich et al v. Fisher-Price Inc.*[86] That case was brought after a seven-week-old baby was injured while napping in the sleeper. When the baby's grandmother checked on him during his nap, she found his head turned to the side, his arms gray, and his face and lips turning blue. The baby was revived by a family member, but a pediatrician attributed the asphyxia near miss to the "ill-design" of the sleeper.[87]

Such negligence was systemic; Fisher-Price had known for years that its sleeper was connected to infant suffocations, but had settled for releasing revised warnings, which are unlikely to be taken as seriously by parents as an actual recall.[88] Moreover, the company continued to market the Rock 'n Play as a device that babies could sleep in all night long (one class action suit notes that the word "sleeper" or "sleep" was used five times on the product packaging),[89] even though an inclined and padded rocker does not meet the AAP's guidelines for a safe sleep surface when an infant is not attended by an awake adult.[90] The company considered changing the marketing of the product to a "Soother" rather than a "Sleeper," but when market research revealed that mothers were more likely to purchase a "Sleeper," Fisher-Price opted to protect its sales by retaining the name.[91]

That this product was able to make it to the market without adequate testing raises significant questions about how infant safety products are regulated in the United States, and who is considered ultimately responsible for ensuring children's health. The agency that creates federal safety rules for infant products in the United States is the Consumer Product Safety Commission (CPSC). The CPSC was created as an independent federal regulatory agency by Congress in 1972 as part of the Consumer Product Safety Act. Its stated mission is to create voluntary and mandatory safety standards, obtain recalls of products deemed dangerous, conduct research, and educate the public.[92] After its passage, the CPSC was critiqued for its lack of sufficient oversight of product safety, particularly concerning children's products, for example, regulating lead in toys and unsafe cribs. The Consumer Product Safety Improvement Act was passed in 2008 to strengthen the CPSC's mandate, including the power to enact mandatory standards for "durable infant sleep products." Yet, because the creation of mandatory standards is a lengthy process, infant sleep products can be approved with only voluntary standards, like those attached to the Rock 'n Play.[93] Moreover, the chairperson of the CPSC is nominated by the president of the United States and confirmed by the Senate; their stance toward the regulation of industry is therefore considered by many to be potentially influenced by partisan politics. Consumer watchdog groups have also warned that the agency continues to lack the funding and staffing to adequately monitor the high volume of products it is meant to regulate.[94]

Manufacturers also have significant influence over decisions about the safety of infant products. The CPSC authorizes another organization, ASTM International, to create voluntary safety standards for this industry, which has permitted manufacturers to sell infant sleepers with a recline angle of 10–30 degrees.[95] The 30-degree angle, which allowed infants' heads to tilt to a degree that cut off their breathing, was determined to be an acceptable voluntary safety standard not based on research but because products utilizing that angle were already on the market.[96] The AAP and other consumer groups fought the standard as unsafe, but more than half of the ASTM's board is made up of industry members. This includes representatives from Fisher-Price and other industry leaders who pushed ASTM to create standards for infant sleepers that were separate from those for cribs or bassinets—standards that allowed the Rock 'n Play to be manufactured at an incline that is banned for bassinets.[97]

According to the class action suit against Fisher-Price and Mattel, the corporation "actively manipulated safety standards" in order to ensure the continued sale of the Rock 'n Play by lobbying for an exception when the CPSC proposed regulations for cribs and bassinets in 2010 (eventually passed in 2013) that were stricter than the voluntary ASTM standards. The proposed regulations would have limited the incline on sleepers to no more than five degrees to reduce the risk of fatalities, which was supported by then-president of the AAP. However, the class action suit claims that successful lobbying efforts resulted in the exclusion of inclined sleepers from this enhanced regulation. In addition to this exclusion, the regulation of sleepers with an incline of more than ten degrees was given over to an ASTM subcommittee, which was chaired by Fisher-Price's senior manager for Quality Engineering. The class action suit goes on to cite numerous appeals to Fisher-Price to reconsider the safety of the sleeper in the years leading up to the recall from the leaders in the AAP, outside pediatricians, parents, and even a member of Congress.[98]

In 2017, five consumer groups representing infant and child safety co-authored a letter to the CSPC raising concerns about inclined sleepers and their exclusion from standards regulating cribs and bassinets, which require a flat surface. The letter noted that inclined sleepers are meant to be used with infants, many of whom have not yet differentiated their sleep and wake cycles between night and day, and are thus likely to nap throughout a 24-hour period. Because the product is marketed for all-night sleep, and parents are urged to nap while their baby is napping, the letter notes, infants are likely to sleep unattended in this device. Given this, they contend, the same standards that regulate full-size cribs and bassinets should apply to reclined infant sleepers. Rather than taking this approach, manufacturers can take advantage of the loophole such that "products that cannot meet the bassinet standard simply may now fall under the scope of another category of product which allows the potentially hazardous conditions of an incline and a restraint."[99]

Such reliance on businesses to institute appropriate safety standards is a key tenet of neoliberalism, which embraces the deregulation of corporations in the name of capitalist free enterprise. As sociologist Norah MacKendrick argues, the neoliberal state encourages industry self-monitoring and consumer educational campaigns over regulation and federal oversight, all of which transfer the management of risk to individual families, and the gendered labor of mothers in particular.[100] This process is particularly insidious as it relates to infant sleep safety because most parents assume that a product like the Rock 'n Play is thoroughly vetted before it reaches the market; consumers are more likely to have positive associations with a company like Fisher-Price than, say, Big Tobacco, and assume that it puts infant safety before profits. Fisher-Price marketing promotes a narrative that the company can be trusted; its website promises "it all starts with safety," and assures parents that "there's an entire team of quality engineers who work closely with design groups to make sure every product not only meets U.S. safety regulations and international standards, but lives up to the traditionally high Fisher-Price standards of quality, as well as consumer expectations."[101] While few parents are likely to read a company's "safety story" on their website before purchasing a product, Fisher-Price and parent company Mattel appear to have successfully incorporated safety into their brand. As one grieving mother told the *Washington Post*, "It never crossed our minds it [the Rock 'n Play] could be dangerous."[102] Another said, "Had I been aware of the danger, I never would have opted for the inclined sleeper, and I would have strictly used the crib. I trusted the company, and that's a mistake I'll never make again."[103] In a press release urging the recall of the Rock 'n Play, the president of the AAP similarly noted that "when parents purchase a product for their baby or child, many assume that if it's being sold in a store, it must be safe to use. Tragically, that is not the case."[104]

Even parents who were concerned about safety because of reported deaths were reassured by Fisher-Price employees. Two months prior to the recall, one mother emailed the company, asking for a refund. A consumer services representative responded, writing:

> We can assure you that the Rock 'n Play Sleeper is safe for inclined sleep, including overnight sleep, when used according to the instructions. And we understand it can be confusing to hear an American Academy of Pediatrics recommendation that may seem to conflict with a product designed for inclined sleep. But maybe this will help clarify: what the AAP states is that sitting devices—car seats, strollers, swings, infant carriers and infant slings—are not recommended for routine sleep in the hospital or at home. The Rock 'n Play Sleeper is not a sitting device—it is a product specifically designed for inclined sleep. As such, it meets all applicable industry safety standards, including those of the international standards organization known as the ASTM. We hope that clears up any confusion you may have had.[105]

The email not only contradicts the actual guidance of the AAP, but again turns the responsibility back to the parent, indicating that she was "confused" and had failed to understand the nuances of infant sleep safety. At the time that this email was written, Fisher-Price and Mattel had already been sued in 2015 and 2016 by parents whose infants died or were injured in the sleeper.[106] They had also received and dismissed concerns about sleep safety from mothers during market research, including statements like "it's unsafe for babies to sleep in it, it could lead to positional asphyxia," and "it's not safe and it can actually cause SIDS." The mothers who made these portentous warnings were echoing the ABCs of safe sleep (babies should sleep *alone*, on their *backs*, and in a *crib*) that the AAP had been promoting for decades, but no action was taken based on their feedback.[107]

Despite the ways that this product eluded regulators, with risks that were downplayed and even hidden from parents for years, the takeaway in some popular news sources was that parents need more education on safe sleep from experts. One such article in *USA Today* chastises parents, saying "first things first, parents need to understand how babies sleep." If parents understood that babies should not be expected to sleep through the night without waking or being fed, the article implies, then they might not rely on devices that seem to promise uninterrupted sleep. After acknowledging all the ways that parents are over-extended, over-tired, and likely to assume that products sold in stores meet safety standards, the article concludes that "unsafe sleep deaths among babies are 100% preventable."[108] In light of the Rock 'n Play recall, the assertion that unsafe sleep deaths are 100 percent preventable assigns to parents both the power and responsibility to foresee corporate malfeasance that even federal oversight committees were unable to prevent.

This expectation that parents can and should foresee all risk was highlighted in the public response to one family who lost their child in a Rock 'n Play. Keenan and Evan Overton's five-month-old died while sleeping in the device; in an interview with CNN, the parents were read Fisher-Price's statement contending that it was the responsibility of parents to follow all safety guidelines when using the product. Father Keenan Overton told the anchor, "It's so frustrating to see the blame placed on the parents who've lost their bundles of joy, their whole future, their whole life, their parenthood."[109] When he and his wife Evan shared their story on CNN, the viewer comments on the video-sharing website YouTube included notes of sympathy as well as persistent parent blame. As Linda Fentiman argues in *Blaming Mothers*, psychological constructions of risk lead individuals to blame those who are "nearest" to a tragedy (in this case, the parents) rather than those "farther away" (such as the corporation). This "if only" thinking leads people, like those on juries, to blame whomever was the last actor for failing to foresee the risk, rather than the company that marketed a faulty product. She finds that individuals also prefer monocausal explanations—parents should never let their baby sleep unattended—than more complicated ones, that in this case may involve the partisan oversight of regulatory agencies and its effects on consumer safety. Because we do not want to believe that our trusted products may be unsafe and kill our children, it is easier to blame individual parents for these deaths.[110]

In the case of the Overtons, commentators insisted that the infant should not have been left unattended in the device, was not the right age to use the Rock 'n Play, or that the parents should never have let their baby sleep in anything other than a crib. While cruel comments abound on unmoderated internet spaces, these do highlight the cultural embeddedness of the neoliberal narrative that shifts responsibility from corporations and institutions—even when these entities are demonstrably at fault—and onto individual families. Many of the comments were also explicitly racist. Parents who are young, single, poor, non-citizens, substance-using, and non-white are not only more rhetorically and discursively likely to be positioned as "bad parents," but also face greater surveillance, stigmatization, and criminalization for their pregnancy and parenting practices. Just like these categories influence perceptions of "good" and "bad" parenting, they also undergird the way infant sleep safety is understood and its parameters are policed. At the time of this writing, the Overtons' wrongful death and personal injury lawsuit against Fisher-Price and Mattel was still pending.

While the product and others like it have been recalled, the ability of a recall to fully eliminate these sleepers from households and daycare centers is limited. Parents were told they could receive a full cash refund if they owned the product for less than six months, disassembled the sleeper, and shipped two small parts back to the company in a prepaid envelope. Parents who had owned the product longer than six months would receive a voucher for an amount commensurate with the age of the sleeper, and refunds would be processed within 12–16 weeks.[111] These requirements create barriers to the successful return of the products, many of which are still available for purchase on social media marketplaces, or at garage sales. Separate investigations by two consumer groups found that one in ten daycare centers surveyed in three states were still using the Rock 'n Play sleeper after the recall.[112] According to the *New York Times*, the CSPC is also increasingly moving toward warnings instead of recalls, which former executive director Pamela Gilbert described as "a very dangerous trend" because warnings are not taken as seriously by consumers as are recalls. "This is a discretionary product," Gilbert told the *Times*, "if consumers knew their babies could die, they wouldn't buy it."[113]

The Rock 'n Play scandal has also drawn attention to the political appointment of the CPSC chair. Ann Marie Buerkle, who had led the Consumer Product Safety Commission as chair during the Rock 'n Play recall, withdrew her nomination to renew her seven-year appointment as chair in light of criticism over her handling of the case. She had also been condemned for a lack of transparency in an investigation of the popular Britax BOB jogging stroller, including her role in closing a case seeking to recall the product. Then President Donald Trump next nominated former chemical industry executive Nancy Beck to lead the Commission, whose history at the Environmental Protection Agency includes clawing back regulations on chemicals linked to birth defects and limiting restrictions on asbestos and other dangerous compounds.[114] The story behind the Rock 'n Play sleeper recall suggests that decisions about infant sleep safety products at all levels—from design to testing to whether or not a recall will be issued—are influenced by the voluntary nature of many industry standards, a blurry boundary between regulators and corporations, and the shifting politics at the very top.

This chapter has contextualized how infant sleep safety guidelines by the leading pediatric organization, the American Academy of Pediatrics, have taken shape over a period of several decades in the United States. They have shifted from a focus on the prevention of Sudden Infant Death Syndrome through education and outreach about sleep positioning, to a broader consideration of the sleep environment. Strict anti–bed-sharing messaging emerged from the AAP in order to address risks in the sleep environment, which lately have grown to acknowledge the reality that many parents do share a bed and require advice on how to do so more safely. This acknowledgment is likely influenced by research and organizing on the part of breastfeeding advocates, anthropologists who study infant sleep, and individuals who promote parenting philosophies that centralize a family bed. This dissent suggests that the AAP's biomedical perspective is not the only discourse influencing sleep safety, even though many tenets of safe sleep are consistent across these different stakeholders.

The Rock 'n Play sleeper recall, however, reveals that even in the face of a widely held medical and academic consensus about certain tenets of sleep safety—that infants should sleep on a flat surface, for example—parents continue to be held to a higher standard for ensuring infant safety than do the corporations who manufacture infant sleep safety products. That being said, there has been some political and regulatory response to the egregious misconduct by Fisher-Price. In June 2019, the US House of Representatives passed the Safe Sleep for Babies Act, which would ban the sale of inclined sleepers and crib bumpers as hazardous products. The Act defined inclined sleepers as those with an incline of more than ten degrees that were "intended, marketed, or designed for sleep accommodations for an infant up to one year old."[115] The bill was not approved by the Senate, but was reintroduced to the House in 2021 and endorsed by the nonprofit group Consumer Reports.[116] Banning inclined sleepers would put the United States in closer alignment with other countries like Canada, Australia, and the United Kingdom that have already acted,[117] but would not address the systemic failures in oversight that led to the manufacture of the product.

In June 2021, the US House of Representative's Committee on Oversight and Reform released a 38-page report titled "Infant Deaths in Inclined Sleepers: Fisher-Price's Rock 'n Play Sleeper Reveals Dangerous Flaws in US Product Safety." The Committee gathered and analyzed thousands of documents from five manufacturers of inclined infant sleep products, and interviewed Fisher-Price and CPSC officials. They concluded not only that the inclined sleepers were unsafe and that the company had recklessly put infants in danger, but also that oversight was inadequate, and the CPSC lacks authority to ensure infant safety. The CPSC, the committee argued, is "unique among federal safety agencies for the limited power it holds to disclose safety information without manufacturer consent."[118] The House Oversight Committee also met to discuss the report, and bipartisan Committee members questioned company executives regarding their safety failures. Parent company Mattel's chief executive argued in the hearing that, despite the recall, the product is safe when used properly, rejecting one representative's assertion that Fisher-Price saw infant death as "the price of doing business."[119]

Earlier in the same month, the Consumer Product Safety Commission voted 3 to 1 to approve a new federal safety standard that would replace the voluntary ASTM standards and require that infant sleep products must have an angle ten degrees or lower. The new rule states that products must meet these standards if they use words like sleep, snooze, nap, or dream on their packaging, or include images of sleeping infants. It also closes the previously existing loophole that allowed infant sleepers to utilize different incline standards than those set for bassinets and cribs, which had essentially paved the way for the Rock 'n Play deaths. The CPSC estimates that Americans spend $125 million annually on products that will be impacted by this ruling, and that such products are owned by at least a third of families with infants.[120]

While this action would on its surface appear to be a victory for parents, the debate over the new standards was complicated by an unexpected resistance from bed-sharing parents. CPSC Commissioner Dana Baiocco, who placed the lone vote against the new standard, wrote in a statement that she received a "measurable number of pleas" from bed-sharing parents who viewed the ruling as a limitation on their parenting choices.[121] The new standards, it seems, would ban some products popular among bed-sharing parents, like in-bed sleepers and baby boxes. According to *Consumer Reports* investigations, in-bed sleepers have been tied to 12 infant deaths, and the broader category of "unregulated flat sleepers" has been linked to an additional 11 fatalities. These products, which are meant to allow infants to safely sleep in bed with their parents, do not always meet AAP guidelines for having a flat, non-padded surface with sides high enough to prevent the infant from rolling out.[122] Baiocco warns, however, that banning such products will create a "black market" among the bed-sharing community. The commissioner concludes that the CPSC's decision failed to consider the impacts on "diverse cultures, alternative parenting practices, and the socioeconomic needs of all consumers." One individual who wrote to Baiocco described bed-sharers as "amongst the largest, most underserved population in the US."[123]

Baiocco's statement and this framing of the issue are both complex and fascinating. The commissioner's resistance to the new standard is framed in terms of support for co-sleeping or bed-sharing parents, described as "diverse," "underserved," and having "socioeconomic needs." Although she does not explicitly identify the race or class background of those who reached out to her, this coded language suggests that these parents are marginalized, perhaps by race and class. As we know, co-sleeping is common among families of all racial and class backgrounds, with higher rates of co-sleeping reported among those with lower socio-economic status.[124] At the same time, "intentional" co-sleeping of the type that would involve the purchase of specific products like in-bed sleepers or baby boxes, which are threatened by these new standards, is arguably indicative of socioeconomic security.[125] Baiocco's statement also describes bed-sharing as "a mother's choice," and a "choice" that is being threatened by this regulation. In sum, the opposition to the new standards rests on the assertion that limiting consumer choice is a form of oppression against intentional co-sleepers.

While the regulatory tug-of-war over infant sleep devices is typically framed as being fought between child safety advocates and industry representatives, the child safety interests of parents are also divided here, according to CPSC documents. The CPSC faced pressured from one side to ban dangerous products by parents who lost their infants in Rock 'n Play and other sleepers, and pressured on the other by co-sleeping parents who are resistant to the limitations on their consumer choices that the new regulations would initiate. This division emerges in various contexts throughout this book, in situations in which grieving parents who lost their children during sleep are at odds with other parents who are framed as less risky, more responsible, or better choice-makers. In this instance, some parents are advocating that they are able to recognize and mitigate the potential risk of infant sleep products, and thus deserving of access to the products of their choice, while others are demanding accountability for infant injury or death that could have been prevented by higher standards of product safety. These rifts, I argue, may unintentionally reinforce the blame and stigmatization of grieving parents and miss an opportunity for parents to unite around a seemingly shared interest in demanding corporate accountability. In the broader context of this book, the controversy over this ruling touches upon several major issues: the tension between personal responsibility and policies or social supports to ensure infant safety, the framing of parents as differentially able to negotiate risk, and even the gendered responsibility for infant sleep safety.[126] In this instance, the vocal interests of co-sleeping parents swayed Commissioner Baiocco to vote against a rule whose general spirit (child protection) she broadly supported, and another commissioner to voice "some misgivings." The next chapter, a case study of the public health response to bed-sharing in the City of Milwaukee, will demonstrate that co-sleeping parents are not always met with this level of deference, suggesting that geographic, racial, and economic context matters a great deal in determining "what's best for baby."

3

What's Best for Baby?

Co-Sleeping and the Politics of Inequality

"The average adult weighs roughly twenty times as much as a newborn baby. That's about the difference between your weight and the weight of an SUV." So intones a deep male voice in a radio spot titled "Rollover," first aired in Milwaukee, Wisconsin in June 2010. The ad continues in a direct address to parents, advising them to engage in a brief experiment: Those who believe that it is safe to sleep in a bed with their baby should first ask friends to roll an SUV (an "immovable object") on top of them. Parents who would choose not to try this, the ad continues, are perhaps also smart enough to imagine how a baby feels when being suffocated to death by a sleeping adult. If you love your baby, the announcer concludes, you should know that there is no safer place than in a crib: "it's the best place to prevent a rollover accident—not to mention, a funeral."[1] This chilling advertisement was one piece of a multi-sited public health initiative called the Safe Sleep Campaign, launched by the City of Milwaukee Health Department in 2009.[2]

I will return to this particular promotion shortly, but as this brief introduction suggests, the goal of the Safe Sleep Campaign was to eliminate bed-sharing because of associations between this practice and infant death due to SIDS or accidental suffocation, as mentioned in the Rollover radio piece. Bed-sharing is a common practice in Black families; because bed-sharing is associated with an increased risk of SIDS, some researchers argue that it contributes to racial disparities in infant mortality and thus warrants interventions targeting Black families.[3] The state of Wisconsin has exceptionally high rates of Black infant mortality; from 2013 to 2015, Wisconsin had the highest non-Hispanic Black infant mortality rates in the nation, at 14.28 deaths per 1,000 live births.[4] This high infant mortality rate is primarily driven by five of the state's 72 counties: Milwaukee, Racine, Kenosha, Rock, and Dane counties.[5]

Given high Black infant mortality rates, the heightened likelihood of bed-sharing in Black communities, and the media attention to infant deaths that occurred in an adult bed, it may seem inevitable that a public health campaign was developed with bed-sharing at its center. However, how to conduct such interventions is fraught; prominent SIDS researchers Linda Fu, Rachel Moon, and Fern Hauck acknowledge that "identifying the best ways to implement educational messaging that will be trusted and embraced by Black families is a particular challenge," and without addressing this challenge, success is unlikely.[6] This chapter will unpack the ways that Milwaukee's campaign moved forward without adequately addressing this challenge, opting for the "low-hanging fruit" of eliminating bed-sharing at the expense of a more nuanced approach to community engagement.

The intersections of race, class, and gender impact the experience of parenting in the United States. Public policy, cultural ideologies, and political representations are all components of what Shellee Colen terms stratified reproduction,[7] or a system in which certain groups of people are empowered to reproduce and to parent, while others are disempowered along lines of race, class, nationality, and sexuality.[8] As Barbara Gurr explains in her analysis of reproductive justice within Native American communities, all women experience institutionalized oppression, but particular groups of women (women of color, poor women) bear the burden in specific ways. These experiences do not stem solely from individual choices, as the anti–bed-sharing paradigm would suggest, but rather "they are structurally produced, and they are produced along different axes of identity and social location."[9] Likewise, feminist theorist Laury Oaks follows criminal justice scholars in arguing that certain public policies serve as "crime control theater" (including Safe Haven Laws and Amber Alerts) in which a statistically infrequent but important social problem results in a reactionary public response that gives the appearance of controlling misconduct, if not the effect.[10] The response to SIDS deaths in Milwaukee likewise gives the public appearance of taking a strong stance against behavior posited as harmful to children, without evidence that this is the most important behavioral change to reduce infant mortality, or that the targeted community will benefit from such an approach. It also does so without involvement of the community whose behaviors it aimed to change, which I argue was a key flaw in the campaign's design.

Milwaukee's Safe Sleep Campaign made assumptions about the kind of parenting advice that could be followed by the targeted communities (primarily communities of color), assuming that reducing or eliminating all forms of bed-sharing was the most immediately feasible way to minimize infant death. The strategies employed by the city of Milwaukee are reflective of risk elimination, or the attempt to eradicate what is defined as "risky" behavior (bed-sharing) in its entirety.[11] This approach conflicts with the "risk management" strategies proposed by grassroots activists in the area, who have developed tools in conjunction with the community to teach parents how to co-sleep more safely. Milwaukee's Safe Sleep initiative was flawed in that it held individuals responsible for the problem of infant mortality that is rooted in deep, systemwide inequalities based on race and class. This campaign relied on a neoliberal approach to public health, placing responsibility for preventing bed-sharing deaths on the "private" family unit. It did so without a concomitant effort to address the systemic forces that lead to the kind of massive racial disparities reflected by infant mortality rates in Milwaukee.[12] Such initiatives are part of "the neoliberal trend toward privatization and punitive governance," which "place reproductive responsibility on women, thus privatizing remedies for illness and social inequality."[13] An analysis of the Safe Sleep Campaign is important because the campaign, while well intentioned, is reflective of the broader erosion of women's reproductive and parenting autonomy at the statewide and national levels. The Safe Sleep Campaign is embedded within institutions (of government, medicine, law, and popular media) that assume that mothers, and particularly marginalized mothers, require state intervention to ensure that children are protected from their parents.[14]

The Safe Sleep Campaign utilized striking imagery, foregrounding the ultimate innocent victim (a sleeping newborn), and implying that individual parents are capable of "solving" the seemingly intractable problem of infant mortality. At the same time, the lack of nuance or depth to anti–bed-sharing messages suggests that the targeted parents are not capable of following more complex messages about bed-sharing, like how to do so more safely. Paradoxically, parenting decisions by poor parents and parents of color at times are framed as bad choices, and at others as less choices or decisions than as tradition, instinct, or worse, recklessness and selfishness.[15] This chapter examines how parents of color are scapegoated for problems that are deeply embedded in unequal institutional practices. I consider this campaign from a feminist reproductive justice theoretical lens, because reproductive justice demands that the goals and needs of communities of color are brought from the margins to the center of public health debates.

While Milwaukee's Safe Sleep Campaign included radio and television spots, billboards, bus shelter ads, and outdoor demonstrations, the Rollover public service announcement is a good place to start because it introduces many of the hallmarks of the campaign that invite critique. First, it targeted bed-sharing in part because the health department initially perceived bed-sharing as "low-hanging fruit"—a way to reduce infant death that was much less complex than the systemic "upstream" drivers of infant mortality such as pre-term birth.[16] Second, it reflects the mistaken hypothesis that bed-sharing is a relatively straightforward behavior to change among individual families, without significant consideration of the complex reasons that parents sleep with their children. Finally, with its direct address to the parent, the Rollover ad places responsibility for infant mortality squarely in the lap—or shall we say the beds—of individual families. This radio spot asks new mothers and fathers to view themselves as a potential deadly force in the lives of their fragile newborns, posing a grave threat to a helpless child.[17]

A mother who shares a bed with her child is compared to an SUV, a non-sentient, unfeeling, "immovable object" that could unknowingly crush her child at any time. This comparison is obviously drawn in part for shock value, to frighten parents into complying with the advice given by the health department. Yet it also situates poor parental choice-making as the root cause of bed-sharing deaths, independent from other risk factors. In reality, the vast majority of co-sleeping deaths in Milwaukee do not involve a parental "rollover"; they are attributed to respiratory failure related to the presence of soft objects in the sleep environment (specifically soft mattresses, pillows, blankets, and stuffed animals) often combined with exposure to cigarette smoke.[18] This radio spot misleads parents regarding the potential dangers of co-sleeping, missing an opportunity to educate caregivers on more common risks. Rather than positioning parents as partners in reducing infant mortality (which would be central to a reproductive justice approach), this radio ad situates bed-sharing parents as perpetrators of reckless child endangerment.

Race, Class, and Health Inequality in Milwaukee

While safe sleep is an issue that is applicable to all racial groups, the City of Milwaukee's Safe Sleep Campaign addressed African American parents in particular. The imagery of the campaign reflected the perceived problem, as well as the racial demographics of the city, with three African American babies of the five total infants represented on billboards and ads. At the outset of the Safe Sleep initiative, the Health Department's target was to reduce African American infant mortality to 12 deaths per 1,000 births by 2017.[19] The city specified Black infant mortality because racial disparities in mortality between African American and white infants in Milwaukee are among the worst in the nation.[20] When the Safe Sleep Campaign was launched in 2009, the infant mortality rate in Milwaukee for white babies was 5.4 deaths per 1,000 live births, while the rate for African American babies was 14.1 deaths per 1,000 live births.[21] While infant death rates for Hispanics were also higher than those for white infants, the city did not set specific goals for other minority groups because, according to the Health Commissioner, the city needed to focus on "the toughest neighborhoods where the problem is worst . . . We're not going to leave anyone out, but we have to focus on where the problem is."[22]

In order to understand this logic, it is useful to know more about the demographics of the region. According to the US Census Bureau, around the time that the Safe Sleep Campaign began, African Americans made up 40 percent of the residents of Milwaukee, nearly equal to the number of white residents (44 percent), and significantly higher than the next minority group, Hispanic or Latino (17.3 percent). The relatively high percentage of African Americans in Milwaukee is significant in comparison to the proportion of Black people in the state of Wisconsin as a whole, which is only 6.3 percent.[23] A National Public Radio segment titled "Why Is Milwaukee So Bad for Black People?" described the state as, statistically, "one of the worst places in the country for African Americans to reside."[24] These statistics include the fact that Wisconsin high schools suspend Black students at the highest rate in the nation,[25] and that in recent years, national test scores reveal the largest achievement gap between Black and white students in the country.[26] These are alarming pieces of data given what some researchers and social justice activists have termed the "school-to-prison pipeline."[27] African Americans in Wisconsin are concentrated in Milwaukee and a handful of other cities, and racial disparities are replicated in economics, segregation, incarceration, health care, and education.[28]

Such disparities in Milwaukee are in part reflective of broader national and historical trends. In conjunction with employment discrimination, Milwaukee's segregationist housing practices of the early twentieth century concentrated Black families into certain urban neighborhoods, while white residents moved to the suburbs. Indeed, "by 1990, Black Milwaukeeans overwhelmingly lived in the same inner city neighborhood areas that had been decisively designated for their grandparents and great grandparents 70 years earlier."[29] With the loss of industrial jobs by the end of the 1970s and in the decades that followed, massive unemployment contributed to increasing numbers of Milwaukee residents living in "concentrated poverty tracts" (where 20–40 percent of residents lived below the federal poverty line) or "extreme poverty tracts" (where 40 percent or more live below the line). According to *Milwaukee Journal Sentinel* reporting in the series "A Time to Heal," "by 2014, 145 of the city's 209 census tracts—home to almost three-quarters of the city's population—had at least 20 percent of the population living in poverty, and more than one out of four Milwaukeeans lived in neighborhoods of extreme poverty."[30] As reporter John Schmid argues, Milwaukee now "sets the national extremes of distress," including the highest index of concentrated poverty of the nation's 100 biggest metro areas, and the lowest rates of upward mobility in the 50 largest cities. These outcomes reflect not only economic distress, but also both extreme trauma among the city's most vulnerable residents and remarkable resilience among those who organize to provide aid, resources, and healing.[31]

Economic inequality, segregation, and historical trauma also impact children's health, beginning even before birth. While a great deal of attention is paid to prenatal care (of which access and quality are racially stratified in Milwaukee),[32] prenatal care is not a form of primary prevention and has limited efficacy in reducing premature birth and low birth weight.[33] The majority of infant deaths in Milwaukee are due to complications of prematurity.[34] Premature birth is racialized in Milwaukee; almost two-thirds of African American infant mortality is attributed to complications of prematurity, as compared to one-third of white infant mortality.[35] According to the Centers for Disease Control and Prevention (CDC), risk factors for premature birth include a mother's age, race, and poverty level, with Black women, very young or older women, and poor women at highest risk. Premature birth correlates with low birth weight; Black infants are three times more likely to be born at a low birth weight than are white infants, which is a significant factor in the Black-white infant mortality gap.[36] This gap also ties back to segregation and income level, with the highest concentration of infant death occurring in zip codes with the lowest median income.[37] The four Milwaukee zip codes with the highest infant mortality are contiguous, and are all located on Milwaukee's predominantly African American north side; more than a quarter of all families within these zip codes also live below the poverty line.[38] Stress, long working hours, and environmental conditions—all deeply racialized structural factors—also lead to premature birth (and some birth defects).[39]

Stress itself is both a gendered and racialized factor impacting pregnancy; women who are heavily burdened by stress due to the lived experience of gendered racism may be more likely to experience negative pregnancy outcomes.[40] Living with racism and poverty can increase the levels of stress hormones in the body, which have what is called a "weathering" effect on the health of women.[41] The Wisconsin Pregnancy Risk Assessment Monitoring System (PRAMS) uses a population-based survey to gather data on the experiences of those who have recently given birth. Their 2016–2018 report found that roughly one-quarter of women of color reported experiencing interpersonal racism in the year before their babies were born, and 43 percent of the women living in poverty had the stress of moving to a new address during that time period.[42] In other words, women exposed to persistent and systemic stress have an increased likelihood of premature birth, as well as chronic health conditions like hypertension and diabetes.

Milwaukee's 2017 Fetal Infant Mortality Review (FIMR), which analyzed infant mortality data from 2012 to 2015, concluded that birth outcomes are influenced by the social determinants of health, or "the social and economic factors that shape the environments in which we live, work, play, and age."[43] In her study of racism and premature birth, anthropologist Dána-Ain Davis adds to this the lens of "diagnostic lapses" that contribute to poor birth outcomes. Diagnostic lapses refer to the way in which "professionals make or neglect to make medical decisions, thus exacerbating the vulnerabilities of a racially or ethnically marginalized group."[44] Examples include downplaying or dismissing the symptoms of women of color, or failing to address their concerns about their pregnancies. Diagnostic lapses are significant, Davis argues, because they add complexity to the social determinants of health lens, that can at times deflect from the centrality of racism and the reality that Black women at all socioeconomic levels have disproportionately high rates of pre-term birth.[45]

As this evidence demonstrates, race impacts how inequality and difference are experienced within economic and political systems.[46] While the sobering statistics on racial disparities in infant mortality are well-known, and many are cited on the Milwaukee Health Department's Safe Sleep website, the focus of the Safe Sleep Campaign was on changing the sleep behavior of individual families. This neoliberal approach to public health is not new, but rather a continuation of practices that have prioritized personal responsibility for illness, disease, and death.[47]

Bed-Sharing and Child Safety

What was the impetus for the initiation of Milwaukee's Safe Sleep Campaign? The push to end bed-sharing was not only coming from the city's health department, but also from its administration; Milwaukee Mayor Tom Barrett described the problem as "embarrassing" and "frustrating," with "neighborhoods in the city where the infant mortality rate is higher than it is in some third world countries."[48] The health department reported that between 2006 and 2009, the years preceding the launch of the Safe Sleep initiative, there were 89 infant deaths related to SIDS or accidental suffocation. Of these 89 deaths, 46 (51.7 percent) died while sleeping in an adult bed.[49] The Milwaukee Health Department's Safe Sleep Campaign website states that the high level of bed-sharing deaths over the last decade had prompted the department to initiate their "provocative" prevention campaign.[50]

The question of whether bed-sharing can be done more safely often seems to hinge on whether additional risk factors are present. Approximately 15 unsafe sleep deaths occur in Milwaukee in a given year, and most of those involve additional risk factors.[51] Risk can be introduced by the sleep environment and sleep position. In a safe sleep environment, as defined by the American Academy of Pediatricians, a child sleeps alone, on their back, in a crib, with no blankets, pillows, or toys. Any deviation constitutes unsafe sleep.[52] Keeping in mind that risk factors are often multiple, the most common is bed-sharing *with* blankets, pillows, or other soft items in the sleep area (occurs in an average of 10 out of 15 infant deaths). Additional risk factors, in order of frequency, include exposure to cigarette smoke (9), an infant placed to sleep on their stomach or side (6), alcohol or drug use by the caregiver (3), the presence of bedding or soft objects *without* bed-sharing (2), and overlay, or suffocation by another person (1).[53] Prematurity is the second risk factor in about half of the infant mortality cases in which unsafe sleep is determined to be the primary risk factor, suggesting that prematurity and unsafe sleep are deeply intertwined.[54]

Research on bed-sharing deaths in other parts of the country reinforce the significance of multiple risk factors. In a study of infant deaths in Alaska, researchers found that 13 percent of deaths occurred while bed-sharing, but 99 percent of those had at least one associated risk factor, primarily maternal tobacco use or sleeping with an impaired person. The authors concluded that the most effective way to lower infant mortality is to focus on risk factors for babies in any sleep environment—especially parental substance use and infant sleep position.[55] That being said, while parental drug or alcohol use is likely to garner the most attention because it taps into the discourse of reckless or careless parenting, the Milwaukee Health Department notes that from 2005 to 2008, fewer than 18 percent of caregivers of infants who died in bed-sharing deaths were using drugs or alcohol at the time of the incident. In contrast, 68 percent of those infants were exposed to second-hand smoke.[56] Smoking cessation, however, was not integrated into the Safe Sleep Campaign.

Based on data like this, many proponents of co-sleeping argue that bed-sharing is not an independent risk factor for SIDS/SUID and thus should not be the primary focus of infant mortality campaigns. In other words, they argue, bed-sharing has to co-occur with other "risky" behaviors or conditions—such as smoking, drug and alcohol use, or prematurity—to be significantly unsafe for infants. A 2018 *National Public Radio* article interviewed multiple SIDS researchers to answer the question posed in the article's headline: "Is Sleeping with Your Baby as Dangerous as Doctors Say?" SIDS epidemiologist Peter Blair noted that while certain circumstances (like sleeping with a baby while drinking or using drugs, or sleeping with a baby on a sofa) are always unsafe, influential studies in the early 2000s that linked bed-sharing with SUID risk also had important methodological issues. As discussed in chapter 2, some early studies did not differentiate between sofa-sleeping and bed-sharing, or included cases in which babies were bed-sharing with parents who drank or smoked. Biostatistician Robert Platt analyzed for the AAP the two existing studies that included infants who were bed-sharing without additional risk factors; the limited evidence they provided found that bed-sharing without additional risk factors did not increase SUID rates in babies over 3 months of age. In babies under 3 months, bed-sharing increased risk of SUID about threefold. Pediatrician Ed Mitchell told NPR that the severity of this threefold risk increase depends greatly on the individual baby; "if you take a very, very low risk and multiply by three, the risk will increase, but it will still be a low risk." In contrast, bed-sharing with a premature baby whose mother smokes and drinks could elevate that baby's risk of SUID from moderate to high, Mitchell argues.[57]

Other co-sleeping proponents contend that the United States is in fact a cultural anomaly in its negative attitude toward co-sleeping, in part due to American beliefs about privacy, sex, and marital intimacy. Some tout the benefits of bed-sharing for infants, such as increased arousal (meaning wakefulness), and ease of breastfeeding, both of which are believed to reduce SIDS rates.[58] Yet most proponents of co-sleeping do not deny that sharing a bed can correlate with infant mortality. Rather, they clarify that evidence of co-sleeping is not always causally linked to infant mortality. Despite this, the two are often conflated: When a deceased infant is discovered in an adult bed, the media often attributes the death to co-sleeping, even when the cause of death was not related to the sleep surface.

The potentially tragic consequences of this slippage can be seen in the 2009 story of a six-week-old Milwaukee infant who was found dead in her mother's bed on Christmas morning. The *Milwaukee Journal Sentinel* attributed the child's death to co-sleeping, and presented it as evidence that the message about safe sleep was not getting through to parents,[59] effectively holding the mother responsible for her child's death. In an interview on a Milwaukee-based Fox news program, Dr. Patricia McManus of the Black Health Coalition of Wisconsin (BHCW) stated that the mother was temporarily institutionalized in a psychiatric hospital after her name was made public by the press. Weeks later, medical reports concluded that the child's death was not related to sharing a bed, but the woman's life had already been irrevocably impacted by the public response, in addition to the terrible loss of a child.[60] While demographic information about the race or socioeconomic status of the family was not available, Dr. McManus stated in the same interview that her organization typically works with low-income people and people of color.

The response to parents accused of causing bed-sharing deaths is reminiscent of what feminist theorist Anna Lowenhaupt Tsing has called "monster stories," which "advise women of a new public agenda in which children, like fetuses, must be saved from their own mothers."[61] Tsing studied women in the United States who were charged with jeopardizing the lives of their newborns by giving birth unassisted, and found that the image of the endangered newborn taps into other discourses in the United States like anti-abortion rhetoric and fetal and child protection (and, I would add more recently, the discourse of fetal personhood). In *Reproducing Race: An Ethnography of Pregnancy as a Site of Racialization*, an insightful ethnography of race and pregnancy in a New York City hospital, anthropologist Khiara Bridges likewise argues that low-income pregnant women are frequently situated as "unruly bodies" or "biological dangers within the body politic."[62] Black parents in Milwaukee are similarly framed as a problem population whose embodied parenting practices threaten child safety. In other words, "Black women become wedged between embodying risk and being the targets of intervention."[63] Through the lens of the Safe Sleep Campaign, the "unruly" mother is either ignorant of safe sleep guidelines or is unwilling to comply with them, and thus continues to rely on her own beliefs about parenting rather than acquiescing to medical authority. While parents are certainly not without responsibility for sleep safety, their individual agency must be put within a broader social context. To do otherwise contributes to:

> viewing "parenting" as the cause of, and solution to, social problems. In conditions where ideas about how to effect broader social change are elu-

sive, change is envisioned only where it seems possible to enact it, for example, in the management of the small-scale relations between individuals, especially those between parent and child.[64]

In other words, the turn toward personal responsibility and individualized solutions may result from the seeming intractability of root causes like poverty or institutionalized racism, but these are problems that parenting cannot solve. As an analysis of campaign materials demonstrates, the Safe Sleep Campaign employs the image of the endangered newborn in particular in ways that discursively position careless parents as a menacing threat to children's health.

Tombstones, Knives, and Guerilla Warfare

The City of Milwaukee's Safe Sleep Campaign website includes an archive of the materials and events featured in the initiative, including seven billboards/posters (two layout versions of "Tombstone," two of "Knife," three of "Babies Should Always Sleep in a Crib"), three radio spots, one television spot, a 2010 Safe Sleep Summit, an outdoor mattress installation, a Pack 'n Play Safe Sleep installation at a mall, and the initiation of a yearly Safe Sleep Sabbath[65] during September (Infant Mortality Awareness month) in which faith leaders raise awareness of infant mortality. The website also includes 13 links to newspaper articles about the campaign, radio and television interviews with health department employees, and the Cribs for Kids Facebook page.[66] The marketing agency involved also filmed 75 videos of women in the community talking about safe sleep and other topics involving infant mortality. The intent was to share these videos on social media sites, but funding issues limited their reach. Local youth groups and fire department staff also went into neighborhoods in zip codes with the highest rates of infant mortality and passed out signs that families could put in their windows designating their house a "safe sleep home."[67]

Advertising materials for the campaign were created by Serve Marketing; Serve is a nonprofit, all-volunteer advertising agency that was founded by a Milwaukee marketer. Serve describes its work as "provocative" and "controversial"; it has created campaigns for various organizations about shaken baby syndrome, sexting, statutory rape, child sex abuse, and teen homelessness.[68] The company does not shy away from controversy, noting on its website that the Milwaukee anti–bed-sharing campaign "drew the ire" of an unnamed local health group.[69] Other previous work that Serve has completed for the city of Milwaukee includes billboards featuring bare-chested and shame-faced pregnant boys (including young men of color) with the tagline, "It shouldn't be any less disturbing when it's a girl. Teen pregnancy. Stop ignoring it."[70] The city's positive appraisal of this teen pregnancy campaign influenced its decision to work with Serve on the Safe Sleep Campaign materials. The City of Milwaukee Health Department had data to show that the teen pregnancy campaign was effective, and its provocative imagery had garnered positive feedback. Serve was also attractive to the city because they offered their services pro bono. Working on a voluntary basis for the city allowed Serve to develop projects that they believed would benefit the community, while also experimenting and building their portfolio with materials that potentially pushed the envelope.[71]

After Serve created the marketing materials for the Safe Sleep Campaign, they had to pass through a chain of approval at the Health Department. During this process, concerns were raised by Health Department staff, particularly about the "Knife" billboard ad and the "Rethink Your Position" television spot, which I will discuss below. At least one individual also questioned the campaign's exclusive focus on risk elimination (ending all bed-sharing) rather than risk management (teaching parents how to bed-share in a safer way). But according to those within the Health Department, the desire from leadership to be seen as hard-hitting and provocative was a significant factor in the direction the campaign took. The final link in the chain of approval was the Health Commissioner, and with his consent, the campaign materials were rolled out.[72]

Between 2010 and 2012, the city ran the "Tombstone" and "Knife" PSAs on billboards and transit shelters in locations including addresses in West and South Milwaukee, and nearby Greenfield, and West Allis (part of the metro area).[73] The "Tombstone" ads were the first to be rolled out in 2010. They depict an adult bed with rumpled blankets and two pillows (marking it as an unsafe sleep environment), with the headboard replaced by a tombstone. The tombstone reads: "For too many babies last year, this was their final resting place." Additional language on the image warns, "Think twice before sleeping with your baby. The safest place is in a crib."[74]

While this PSA does direct readers to the City's Safe Sleep website, it fails to inform its audience of any risks specific to this unsafe sleep environment, instead offering the suggestion that all adult beds are equally dangerous. While a viewer who is familiar with safe sleep guidelines may recognize the significance of blankets and pillows as a risk factor, parents who are already co-sleeping with their children in a similar environment may not identify what they could change to make the situation safer. The ad presumes that parents are prepared to make an arguably radical behavior change (to stop co-sleeping altogether) based on very limited, albeit frightening, information. This "sound bite" model of intervention attempts to translate a complicated issue into a few short words, which often results in many unanswered questions. Research demonstrates that individuals are more likely to adopt the advice offered by a public health intervention if they fully understand the rationale behind the message. This PSA does not explain why a crib is safer, or what belongs in a safe sleep environment.[75] The ad places full responsibility for preventing infant death on individual parents. Moreover, by urging parents to "think twice," the messaging insinuates that co-sleeping is not the result of a parenting decision or philosophy, but rather reflects a lack of foresight.

A neoliberal approach such as this distracts from dismantling social structural factors such as barriers to health services, housing discrimination, affordable childcare, and other forms of institutionalized racism. It treats health outcomes as a result of "lifestyle" issues; the effects are then conceptualized as matters of personal choices, with individual solutions.[76] When health outcomes are viewed through "lifestyle explanatory paradigms," beliefs or behaviors that are deemed problematic are attributed to the lifestyle of racial or cultural groups, independent from larger social forces.[77] The Safe Sleep Campaign utilizes a "risk discourse" about bed-sharing that focuses on risk that is internally imposed by lifestyle choices. As Deborah Lupton argues, "risk discourse provides a powerful rationale, cloaked in the 'neutral' language and practice of public health and health promotion, to cast blame upon stigmatized minority groups for their state of health."[78] This focus on individual responsibility for infant mortality blames the victims and personalizes political issues. It ignores social factors like systematic inequality that make it almost impossible for members of some groups to take control of the factors that cause problems such as infant mortality.[79] By privatizing health outcomes, this tactic diverts attention away from state responsibility for social conditions.

The Safe Sleep Campaign is reflective of what historian Rachel Lousie Moran terms an "advisory state project," or government initiative that aims to "encourage citizens to engage in behaviors that cannot be explicitly legislated within the American political context."[80] Advisory state projects, according to Moran, utilize neither physical force nor law, but are rather more subtle in their attempts to direct the behavior of the populace. While Milwaukee's campaign was certainly anything but subtle, it similarly encourages changes in parental behavior without challenging overarching power structures that contribute to the perceived social problem—in this case, infant mortality. Like some of the advisory state projects that Moran investigates, such as children's nutrition and welfare programs, it also does so with an emphasis on the responsibility of mothers for children's health and well-being.

The "Tombstone" PSA also sets up the state and the targeted community as if they are in opposition to one another, rather than potential partners with a shared goal of creating a healthy community. Lupton notes that public health promotion often exhibits a "strange tension" in how targeted communities are conceptualized, "between the vision of the rational, active, responsible citizen and the citizen who needs much encouragement, assistance, and persuasion on the part of state agencies to 'do the right thing.'"[81] The Tombstone PSA takes the latter approach, suggesting that communities who bed-share must be made to comply with public health guidelines, by utilizing guilt, fear, and the imposition of a unitary standard of "good parenting." A reproductive justice approach, in contrast, might seek input about how local parents are bed-sharing (sharing a "family bed" versus falling asleep with a child on the couch, for example), their motivations for bed-sharing, and work to mobilize community support for raising awareness of potential risks. Milwaukee's then Health Commissioner Bevan Baker illustrates the stance taken by the city, describing the controversial billboard PSAs as a set of "guerilla tactics" to combat infant mortality; militarized language such as this could be interpreted as the City of Milwaukee being at war with a certain segment of its residents.[82]

Figure 3.1. City of Milwaukee Health Department "Tombstone" ad, January 2010. Source: Milwaukee Health Department Safe Sleep Campaign website. https://city.milwaukee.gov/health/Safe-Sleep-Campaign.

A similar discourse is produced in another component of the Safe Sleep Campaign, an installation effort in which 36 mattresses and two couches were placed along the meridian of Sherman Boulevard and Capitol Drive, in an intersection that is located in a low-income area of northwestern Milwaukee. The mattresses contained orange outlines of babies, with provocative phrases like "Imagine how many babies would still be alive if they'd slept in a crib?" and "Babies who sleep here don't always wake up."[83] The outline of the babies is reminiscent of the outline of a corpse at a crime scene, an image familiar to the public from crime drama and movies, where it is usually employed to signify that a murder has been com-

Figure 3.2. City of Milwaukee Health Department Outdoor Mattress Campaign, July 2010. Source: Milwaukee Health Department Safe Sleep Campaign website. https://city. milwaukee.gov/health/Safe-Sleep-Campaign.

mitted. To viewers of these images today, the orange outlines might bring up more recent associations with the bodies of actual Black men and boys lying in the streets, victims of police violence, and the social justice movements that have arisen in response, such as Black Lives Matter.

In addition to the shape, the *color* orange also symbolizes caution, danger, and crime. The way that these images link the tragic death of an infant with crime, and even murder, situates the parents or caregivers as perpetrators of the crime, rather than potential partners in reducing risk. Moving mattresses and couches—pieces of indoor furniture—outdoors and into the streets is also jarring and attention-grabbing, suggesting public surveillance of what typically remains within the allegedly private sphere. In other words, this juxtaposition of intimate home furnishings with the street, which is in many ways an emblem of public space, suggests the permeability of the supposedly private sphere in the name of child safety. Milwaukee Alderman Willie Wade told the press that the installation was meant to be "in their faces" [they, presumably being parents], adding, "we don't want them to have the excuse that they didn't know."[84] Yet again, the combination of this language and the imagery of the campaign positions parents and city officials in opposition to one another, even if individuals like Baker and Wade (both members of Milwaukee's Black community) did not intend for this takeaway.

Perhaps even more shocking are the "Knife" ads, released in 2011. These two advertisements depict a white and African American baby, respectively, dressed only in a diaper and lying in an unsafe sleep environment— they are each in what appear to be adult beds, surrounded by loose bedding, and in unsafe sleep positions (one on his stomach, the other on his side). Most conspicuously, of course, both babies are lying next to what can only be described as a butcher knife or a meat cleaver. The main text of each ad reads, "Your baby sleeping with you can be just as dangerous."[85] The wording—"your baby sleeping with you"—posits bed-sharing as the primary safety risk, yet the visual represents multiple risk factors for suffocation and SIDS beyond a shared bed (both sleep position and the presence of loose, soft bedding). Creating a false equivalency between

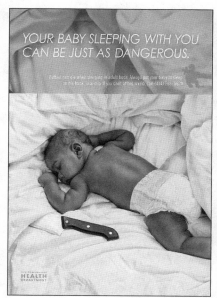

Figure 3.3a-b. City of Milwaukee Health Department "Knife" ad, November 2011. Source: Milwaukee Health Department Safe Sleep Campaign website. https://city. milwaukee.gov/health/Safe-Sleep-Campaign

the alleged dangers of bed-sharing and the undeniable dangers of a knife-adjacent newborn rhetorically criminalizes a very common practice, thus construing any "guilty" viewers as bad parents.

And yet, where exactly are the parents in this advertisement? This explicit imagery—a helpless infant sleeping face down next to a deadly weapon—is glaringly missing a key actor in the bed-sharing blame game, that being the supposedly irresponsible parent who is sharing the bed with her child, and putting the child's life at risk. The absence of the parent makes the image more frightening, and takes parenting (as a verb, a thing that we *do*) literally out of the picture. The children in these ads are abandoned to their grim fates, not sleeping in a bed with parents who have consciously chosen to put them there. In addition, the knife stands in for and symbolizes the physical embodiment of the parent—perhaps even more explicitly than in the "Rollover" radio spot, this PSA positions the parent as deadly to their child.

This advertisement draws upon cultural messages of the vulnerable child to create an emotional impact on viewers. In *Vulnerability Politics: The Uses and Abuses of Precarity in Political Debates*, Katie Oliviero argues that sensationalistic representations of iconic figures (such as children or fetuses) as vulnerable or threatened can be used strategically to create political traction.[86] In this anti–co-sleeping message, the child is both inherently vulnerable because of their age and undoubtedly threatened by the presence of a weapon.

This vulnerability is highlighted in other components of the campaign, such as the radio spot titled "Helpless." This PSA begins, "Newborn babies are among the most helpless creatures in the world," then goes on to list the things a newborn baby cannot do "even if their lives depended on it," including repositioning bedding that may be blocking their airway. After asking the listener to imagine themselves in the position of the helpless infant, the voiceover instructs parents that if they should still choose to sleep with their baby, now they know "what she's up against."[87] This statement shifts the locus of vulnerability from that which is inherent to all newborn "creatures," to vulnerability that is created by the (now fully informed) but careless parent.

For the Safe Sleep Campaign to work, individuals must recognize co-sleeping as a social problem. Mothers experience more pressure to address a social problem like this than do fathers, because women are held responsible and accountable for managing the vulnerability of children.[88] Feminist theorist Laury Oaks noted a similar discourse in campaigns aimed at reducing tobacco use by pregnant women in the 1990s. While Oaks was analyzing representations of the fetus, rather than the child, she found a parallel emphasis on vulnerability, arguing that "antismoking messages often draw on the widespread emotional appeal of the public fetus, depicting fetuses as vulnerable individuals who demand maternal protection and care."[89] Oaks likewise argues that framing maternal smoking as a social problem, and as a form of maternal-fetal conflict, creates space for the surveillance of and regulation over women's conduct during pregnancy.[90] Co-sleeping must also be conceptualized as a social problem (thus its linkage to infant mortality) in order to merit a public health solution. Mother blame is a powerful tool that undergirds public health campaigns that aim to change women's behavior; negative outcomes, ranging from prematurity or low birth weight, to SUID, are construed as evidence that mothers did not subsume their own desires (for cigarettes, for an extra hour of sleep, for cuddling with their baby) to the health of the child. Public health campaigns are one of many intersecting discourses that disproportionately place the onus on women to self-discipline in order to minimize risk.[91]

Significantly, feminist analyses of public health campaigns ranging from preconception health, exposure to environmental toxins during pregnancy, and tobacco use, find that such campaigns are racialized in their approach to maternal audiences. White mothers are consistently framed as more educable, responsible, and willing to change to protect their fetuses or infants.[92] While the Safe Sleep Campaign utilizes images of both light-skinned and dark-skinned infants, three of the five babies in the poster/billboard PSAs can be read as African American. The three radio spots are all voiced by the same man, arguably a sound-alike of the Black American actor Morgan Freeman. The representations of Black infants and authoritative Black male voice imply that Black children are particularly vulnerable to the irresponsible, careless, or selfish decision making of Black parents. This could, of course, be explained by the high rates of Black infant mortality in Milwaukee that the campaign aimed to eradicate. However, in analyzing preconception public health campaigns, Miranda Waggoner notes that "when public health messages try to reflect demographics and at-risk groups, they in effect produce powerful symbols that reproduce stereotypes and ignore the systematic inequalities that inform the demographic realities regarding health disparities in the United States."[93] In other words, while choosing Black infants and Black authority figures to represent the problem may be "pragmatic," these figures cannot be separated from socially sedimented and racist stereotypes about parenting and risky behavior. This representation could arguably have a different connotation if it were created by, or in collaboration with, the communities it is representing—examples of this type of effort will be addressed later in this chapter.

An additional component of the campaign materials created by Serve, and what the agency itself describes as the most effective,[94] was the "Rethink Your Position" television spot. The PSA opens with what is meant to look like footage of a woman's bedroom from a black and white camcorder, including the viewfinder, the time (10:04pm), and the abbreviation REC (for recording) next to a red dot to indicate that the camera is on. The next few seconds reveal a time lapse of the remainder of the night, in which the woman tosses and turns across the bed, dragging blankets and pillows into various positions as she sleeps. The scene then cuts to the same woman placing an infant into the bed with her, with the question, "Still think sleeping with your baby is a good idea? The safest place for your baby is in a crib," followed by the phone number to call for a free Pack 'n Play.

Many assumptions are embedded within this 32-second spot, including that sharing a bed with a baby does not change how a mother sleeps. Dr. James McKenna, an anthropologist known for his commitment to safe co-sleeping, conducted studies on breastfeeding mothers and babies while they slept in a laboratory in the 1990s. Based on his findings, he argues that mothers and babies respond to one another's physiological cues during sleep, and that rather than flailing about, breastfeeding mothers position their bodies in specific ways to protect and respond to their infants.[95]

Most troublingly, however, is that this PSA promotes the fallacy that babies who co-sleep are likely to die from overlay. Viewers are meant to mentally re-create the time lapse scene of the woman thrashing and rolling about the bed with a vulnerable infant beside her (or underneath her). However, as previously mentioned, of the roughly 15 annual co-sleeping deaths in the city of Milwaukee, between 0 and 1 are attributed to parental overlay. The misconception that parents are rolling over onto their babies is significant because it increases the stigma surrounding co-sleeping without pointing parents in the direction of more evidence-based risks to infants such as soft bedding and exposure to second-hand smoke. Like the "Knife" print ad and "Rollover" radio PSA, it situates the embodied parent as a vector of risk.

This television spot is unique in the campaign in that, unlike the aforementioned examples, it explicitly includes a mother figure rather than relying on an object (a knife, or a car) to stand in for the parent. This may provide compelling advertising material, but overlay is more likely to occur when an infant is sleeping with a sibling or adult other than their mother, when the adult does not realize that a baby is in the bed, when co-sleeping occurs on a couch or chair, or (still infrequently) when the adult has been using drugs or alcohol. Misleading information about the dangers of bed-sharing can have serious consequences; a 2010 study of almost 5,000 mothers in the US found that more than 55 percent of mothers fed their children on couches or chairs at night, and 40 percent of those mothers reported falling asleep with their infants during feeding. Given that co-sleeping on a couch or chair presents a far greater risk of accidental suffocation than does co-sleeping on a bed (almost eight times higher), the misrepresentations of the dangers of bed-sharing may unwittingly put children in riskier sleep environments.[96] While this PSA may have been successful in increasing the number of parents who contacted the Health Department for a free crib (a program that I will discuss further), it also spread misinformation about the primary causes of co-sleeping deaths.

It is important to remember that roughly 80 percent of infant mortality in Milwaukee is due to a combination of prematurity and birth defects,[97] both issues that are linked to poverty, racism, and inadequate health care. The mother-blame inherent in these public service announcements distracts from institutional responsibility. While Milwaukee's campaign is purportedly gender-neutral in its targeting of parents, it is mothers that our society ultimately holds responsible for the well-being of children, and particularly of infants.[98] As the feminist scholar Laura Briggs argues, in the last several decades, parenting (and, I would specify, mothering), has increasingly been framed as something "easy to get wrong," as reflected in the emergence of new fears about vaccination, childhood disability, harm, and death. Where problems like childhood disease, accidents, even SIDS, were once construed as senseless tragedies, sympathy is increasingly replaced by blame, casting mothers as criminals and children as victims.[99]

Safety is also frequently marketed as a commodity that can be purchased by vigilant parents. As will be discussed in chapter 5, parents receive the message that their newborns are fragile and endangered through advertising for products like wearable baby monitors. These devices purport to alert parents if their newborn has stopped breathing during the night, use hospital-grade pulse oximeters to measure baby's blood oxygen level at home, and offer remote monitoring of baby's vitals via smartphone apps. Whether these tools offer any measurable increase in safety, or merely the sense of risk management, is debatable. However, even this sense of security is stratified by class, with low-income parents often priced out of access to high-tech monitoring systems, or even brand new (and thus smoke-free) cribs and bedding.

Barriers to Safe Sleep Success

Milwaukee's campaign does attempt to address the issue of cost as it pertains to infant sleep surfaces. The small print on the "Knife" ad reads, "Babies can die when sleeping in adult beds. Always put your baby to sleep on his back, in a crib" followed by a number to call for a Pack 'n Play (a portable bassinet). This ad does provide a potential solution to bed-sharing for parents who cannot afford a crib for their child, and offers parents a way to keep their infants in the same room without sharing a bed. While the goals of this direct service initiative are laudable, further research is necessary to determine whether the requirements to receive a crib create barriers for marginalized communities, and what might be the limitations of the Cribs for Kids program.

For one, in order to receive a crib, parents must contact the organization Cribs for Kids, for which Milwaukee became a site in 2009.[100] Cribs for Kids is no stranger to controversy; the same program was behind a provocative billboard advertising campaign in low-income neighborhoods in Pittsburgh. The Pittsburgh ads showed a hearse carrying a miniature coffin with the words "Your baby belongs in a crib, not a casket."[101] The executive director of the program explained that in order to get the message across, "We thought maybe we have to hit them right between the eyes," again relying on metaphors of a violent and combative relationship between parents and those promoting safe sleep. Cribs for Kids distributes a portable crib, a fitted crib sheet, pacifiers, a safe sleep board book, a sleep sack (wearable blanket), and educational materials to parents.[102] In order for Milwaukee parents to receive these benefits, the family must attend a one-hour appointment at a Milwaukee Health Department clinic location at which a public health educator provides them with safe sleep materials and education, and they have to agree to a follow-up phone call to answer questions and reinforce the material.[103]

As this suggests, families must expose themselves to potential state intervention in order to receive this benefit. Requiring individuals to come into contact with potential agents of the state as a prerequisite for assistance creates barriers for communities that are already over-surveilled and over-policed.[104] The feminist legal theorist Dorothy Roberts notes that children of color are routinely removed from their homes for reasons including inadequate housing, which may make parents hesitant to acknowledge that they lack basic provisions for childcare, or to come into additional contact with mandatory reporters.[105]

The question of whether free cribs are effective in reducing SIDS and accidental suffocation deaths is complicated. Research suggests that many parents bed-share regardless of the availability of other sleep surfaces, like cribs.[106] For example, one study found that a crib or bassinet was in the home in at least 47.8 percent of cases in which a baby died in an unsafe sleep environment. The authors examined the reasons why parents chose alternative sleep surfaces. In addition to "situational" reasons (like baby was crying or being fed) and parental/infant preferences, parents also reported misconceptions about infant sleep safety. Some believed that babies were less safe in a crib because they lacked adult supervision and were likely to succumb to "crib death." The authors of this study argue that crib donation programs are "important, but limited in their reach."[107] While these authors recommend comprehensive and detailed safe sleep education for parents, other studies have found that even parents who consider themselves to be aware of risks are still co-sleeping. A Canadian study published in 2008 analyzed questionnaires submitted by 293 "highly educated" mothers concerning their sleep practices; more than 70 percent of parents reported bed-sharing on a regular or occasional basis, with 88 percent stating that they knew there were some risks associated with the practice. These results were similar to a US study, which found 76 percent bed-sharing rates, and a British study that reported a 65 percent rate of bed-sharing.[108] As critics of Milwaukee's Safe Sleep Campaign have noted, deaths attributed to bed-sharing in Milwaukee have continued to occur in rooms that contained an unused Pack 'n Play or crib.[109] As part of a risk reduction strategy, the fact that the Pack 'n Plays were not used by all parents, or used every time, does not mean that the outreach has failed, but that is not a panacea for bed-sharing.

Finally, some research studies have suggested that while bed-sharing is common across lines of race and ethnicity, some communities of color bed-share more consistently than do white parents, and for reasons that are not tied to socioeconomic status. A large population-based study of mothers in Oregon found that over 40 percent of Black and Hispanic mothers reported that they "always" co-slept with their infants. Rates of co-sleeping did not change significantly with income level among Black and Hispanic mothers as it did with some other ethnic groups (including white mothers). The authors concluded that programs that give away free cribs might lack efficacy if most women are bed-sharing for reasons other than a lack of space.[110] To reiterate, this does not mean that programs that distribute Pack 'n Plays are inherently flawed; from a reproductive justice perspective, access to fundamental childcare resources like a clean, smoke-free Pack 'n Play supports the ability of parents to care for their children. According to the Milwaukee Health Department, the number of cribs requested in that city increased from 671 in 2009 to 2,043 in 2011, which likely indicates that the campaign was successful in raising awareness of the availability of free cribs.[111] I outline the limitations to reiterate that the link between infant mortality and co-sleeping is complex, and that programs that aim to change individual behavior should be one component of risk-reduction efforts that address the broader social determinants of health.

As previously mentioned, co-sleeping may have different resonance among communities of color, and thus community health outreach regarding safe sleep requires significant cultural competency. However, "culture" has also been used in the bed-sharing debates as a thinly veiled means to critique the parenting of communities of color. The parenting practices and traditions of people of color and ethnic minorities in the United States have frequently been viewed with skepticism, as "Other" to the standard or norm of white parenting.[112] Another of the radio spots in the Safe Sleep Campaign explicitly identifies "tradition" (often a synonym for cultural difference or backwardness) as a misguided and dangerous justification for bed-sharing, declaring that "if you think sharing a bed with your baby is simply a nice family tradition, a way to feel a special bond with your newborn, well, we've got some news for you. The safest place for a baby is always in a crib."[113]

Scholars of public health parallel how the "lifestyle" and behavior of marginalized groups are used to explain problems like infant mortality with the resurgence of biological determinism in the form of the geneticization of disease. Both downplay the social construction of race and reinforce the role of personal responsibility for health.[114] According to Bridges, even when culture is understood as learned rather than biological, it can still be perceived to have a powerful effect on outcomes. She argues that

> the modern concept of culture shares that foundation of radical, unchangeable, nonnegotiable, and deterministic alterity. When we understand that culture can be used to signify fundamental, insurmountable difference (i.e. radical Otherness), then cultural stereotypes and assumptions about the way people from/within certain cultures "just are" may produce the same effects produced by racial discrimination.[115]

Culture has been used to explain health disparities ranging from cardiovascular disease to HIV/AIDS, and in doing so can reify racial difference and obscure the effects of racism and structural inequality.[116]

An example can be found in a local Fox News investigative report on bed-sharing deaths in Milwaukee in January 2015, which was tellingly headlined "Culture vs. Calamity." The title invokes the racialized narrative of a "culture of poverty" among communities of color, while also marking cultural "difference" from the middle-class white norm as the cause of the "calamity" of infant death. The segment, which questions whether co-sleeping deaths should be criminalized, begins with a recorded 911 call in which parents inform a dispatcher that their 12-day-old baby is no longer breathing after his intoxicated father fell asleep with him on the couch (pixelated images from the segment suggest a man of color). The segment follows with a voiceover announcing that, "eight years after Milwaukee health officials first declared co-sleeping a crisis babies are still dying while sleeping with adults."[117] The images shown during this voiceover include several still photographs of adult beds (presumably those in which co-sleeping deaths occurred), followed by a picture of a Black baby doll, and then images of malt liquor cans and bottles. While the language in the segment is race-neutral, the imagery is not. The Black baby doll and "guilty" person of color racialize co-sleeping deaths, while the inclusion of malt beverage cans and liquor bottles pathologizes the families in which they occur.

Representations such as these contribute to what is known as a "deficit model" in assessing parenting practices, in which differences observed (or imagined) between the parenting practices of minorities and those considered the standard (white, middle-class, Americans) are interpreted as shortcomings rather than "adaptive strategies," or even improved re-imaginings of normative family structure and practice.[118] This perspective was institutionalized in a 1965 government study called the Moynihan Report, which tied the economic and social problems of contemporary Black families to what it termed a pathological, matriarchal family structure.[119] More recent legislative efforts include Wisconsin's attempt to drug-test some recipients of its food assistance program, FoodShare. The plan was put into place under the previous administration of Governor Scott Walker, and is opposed by the current governor, Tony Evers, who is attempting to prevent its implementation.[120] The paternalism behind such legislation is similar to the risk elimination stance toward bed-sharing. The risk elimination position assumes that some parents cannot understand or be trusted with nuanced messages about safety, and therefore must be confronted with blanket prohibitions on practices that have the potential for harm.

Medicine and public policy may actually be working together to reinforce the message that parents require surveillance in gendered (and racialized ways). As Barbara Gurr argues in *Reproductive Justice*, mainstream health care discourses, including an evidence-based medicine approach, may fail to capture what she calls the "social aspects of reproductive health care." These include the "broader political, economic, and social forces" that shape the experience of and interactions with institutions of medicine.[121] Guidelines for reproductive behaviors like alcohol use during pregnancy, cesarean deliveries versus vaginal births, and caffeine consumption while nursing are part of an environment in which lower risk is valued more highly than parents' own knowledge about their bodies and their babies. As Gurr argues, an over-reliance or uncritical acceptance of empirical measures can discredit alternative ways of knowing about health, and "these processes have always been not only sexed and gendered but also raced and classed, and thus cannot be extricated from social and political drives toward homogenization and assimilation, masked as efficiency."[122]

Oaks found similar messages by health educators concerning smoking during pregnancy. She argued that health education "mobilizes a moral discourse in which pregnant women ought to follow strict antismoking recommendations even if experience indicates that it is unnecessary. From an antismoking perspective, all women who smoke are irrational risk takers."[123] Anti–bed-sharing messaging often positions parents who co-sleep as taking unnecessary chances, and delegitimizes their own assessments of the risks and benefits of the practice. Alternative ways of knowing that are not backed by scientific research or data are dismissed, which may disproportionately affect women and people of color whose epistemologies are marginalized in science and medicine.[124]

B'More for Healthy Babies

An interesting contrast to Milwaukee's Safe Sleep Campaign is one in a city with similar demographics and racial disparities in infant mortality, and with a safe sleep initiative that began around the same time period. Baltimore in the mid-2000s was experiencing a devastatingly high infant mortality rate of 13.5 percent, with Black infants five times more likely to die than white infants.[125] The Baltimore City Health Department partnered with CareFirst BlueCross BlueShield to begin strategic planning in 2008, and with the Family League of Baltimore produced a report on the city's infant mortality crisis in 2009. After securing funding from CareFirst BlueCross and the state of Maryland, B'More for Healthy Babies was launched in 2009. While it is spearheaded by the

Baltimore City Health Department, the initiative also involves partnership with over 150 public and private entities.[126]

As in Milwaukee, the Baltimore City Health Department identified bed-sharing as a leading, and theoretically modifiable, risk factor contributing to infant deaths. The city reported that 85 percent of deaths occurred on a sleep surface other than a crib, and 78 percent were attributed to bed-sharing.[127] Addressing safe sleep was thus central to the first phase of the B'More for Healthy Babies initiative, which began in 2010 and encompassed healthy and safe parenting. The initiative then rolled out healthy pregnancy programs in 2011 that would enroll women in prenatal care, increase home visits, and encourage smoking cessation, followed by Healthy Baltimore in 2012 that would "focus on the importance of good health on a person's ability to live life to the fullest and have healthy babies."[128] The health department emphasizes community and system collaboration and outreach, including hospitals, schools, social work, nonprofit groups, and individual families.[129]

Like Milwaukee's campaign, B'More for Healthy Babies utilizes bus shelter and billboard ads, and radio spots. Communications materials for the campaign were developed by Johns Hopkins Center for Communication Programs, which also evaluates the initiative's effectiveness. The campaign utilizes the widespread ABCD safe sleep messaging (Babies should sleep **Alone**, **Back**, **Crib**, and **Don't** smoke), as well as the tagline "SLEEP SAFE: Alone. Back. Crib. No Exceptions." Notably, the website and materials also include the *why* behind each of these tenets. For example, the assertion that babies should sleep on their back is paired in campaign materials with a justification that babies are less likely to choke while sleeping in the supine position. As Moon, Hauck, and Colson argue, individuals are more likely to follow public health guidelines if the rational is also clear to them;[130] this may be particularly significant concerning safe sleep advice because what lay people believe to be safe is often well intentioned but flawed. For example, some parents put their babies to sleep on their stomachs specifically because they believe (incorrectly) that babies are *less* likely to choke if they spit up or vomit in this position.[131]

Like in Milwaukee's campaign, B'More for Healthy Babies does not shy away from the message that unsafe sleep can result in infant death. It does represent this outcome quite differently, through a Safe Sleep

Campaign video that is screened at hospitals, WIC sites, jury duty lo-cations, detention centers, Department of Social Services offices, and social media.[132] The video features three Baltimore parents who lost their children to SUID or accidental suffocation. In the video, two Black mothers and one white mother share their stories of how their infants died while sleeping in an adult bed. Other Baltimore parents explain the ABCD message, while the video demonstrates a safe sleep environment by showing a Black infant sleeping in an otherwise empty crib, wearing a sleep sack, and using a pacifier. The mothers, including one who is a Baltimore physician, also share research about how sleeping in the prone position or with a parent increases the risk of infant death and statistics on the frequency of bed-sharing deaths.

One of the mothers in the video, Dearea Matthews, told reporters that she initially rejected the health department's request to participate in the campaign, but eventually complied because she believes that she would have listened to safe sleep recommendations if they were coming from a real mother rather than a handout or fact sheet.[133] The emotion-laden video also emphasizes, in the women's own words, how much they loved and continue to love the babies that they lost. The video reinforces maternal responsibility for infant safety by selecting only mothers to participate, by screening the videos in locations like birth centers and WIC offices, and ending with the message "every baby counts on you." Yet by including these heartfelt expressions of maternal love and dedica-tion, the video tempers the potential for stigmatizing or demonizing the mothers who have lost their children.

Why does this approach matter? Consider the different ways that in-fant mortality can be represented—one is numerically, through aggre-gated data. The infant mortality rates of different racial groups have been cited frequently throughout this book, and were used by both Milwau-kee and Baltimore to determine which populations should be targeted for public health campaigns. As feminist sociologists Monica Casper and Lisa Jean Moore argue, the problem of infant mortality is frequently represented quantitatively, with a focus on what infant mortality rates represent (like a nation's health status), or what they explain (like racial disparities in healthcare access). While these quantitative data are im-portant, Casper and Moore argue that they are often utilized in policy work at the expense of a focus on the actual babies whose lives are lost, or the real parents who grieve these deaths. When this happens, aggre-gated data "drive rationalized policy devoid of empathy and care."[134] When the problem of infant mortality is discussed purely through sta-tistics, "aggregate problems seek aggregate solutions," which are likely to focus on individual behavior.[135] The Safe Sleep videos created by B'More for Healthy Babies centralize the names, pictures, and stories of babies who died in their sleep, from the perspectives of their mothers. Casper and Moore argue that representing infant mortality in ways like this of-fers a "different register" for understanding the problem of infant mor-tality, and perhaps one more conducive to empathy, to locating pathways to empower parents, or even collective action.

Unfortunately, the video does not address how risk may differ for infants based on variables like age, prematurity, or prenatal exposure to smoke, or how parents increase or decrease risk through behaviors such as drug and alcohol use, smoking, or creating a safer sleep environment when they do co-sleep. Overall, however, the video offers information and education for parents beyond the shock- or fear-inducing tactics of Milwaukee's campaign materials. Moreover, to a lesser, but arguably still significant extent, B'More for Healthy Babies does incorporate fathers as "safe sleep ambassadors." In one video, Black fathers interact with their children at home and at work, while explaining the significant role that men play in enabling safe sleep, including talking to other men and educating older siblings about sleep safety.[136] By integrating fathers into the safe sleep audience, the initiative normalizes paternal involvement in safe sleep and recognizes men as part of a communal effort to promote infant health.

Baltimore's initiative has resulted in significant declines in infant mor-tality and in racial disparities. By 2017, the overall infant mortality had dropped 35 percent, including a 64 percent decrease in the Black-white infant mortality gap.[137] The City of Baltimore was also recognized as the semifinalist for the Harvard Kennedy School's Innovations in American Government award, which "highlights exemplary models of government innovation and advances efforts to address the nation's most pressing public health concerns."[138] Meanwhile, in Milwaukee, deaths attributed to bed-sharing have continued while the Safe Sleep Campaign wound down (while the city does not offer a clear "end date" for the campaign on its Safe Sleep website, the last posted events and materials date from

July 2012). In 2017, 25 deaths were attributed to an unsafe sleep environment, up from roughly 13 deaths in 2016.[139] According to the 2017 Fetal Infant Mortality Review (FIMR) Report, 15.9 percent of infant deaths from 2012 to 2015 were attributed to the combined categories of SIDS, SUID, and accidental suffocation.[140] Milwaukee mayor Tom Barrett acknowledged to local news media that, "The message is clearly not getting through, and we need to do a better job of making sure this message is heard."[141]

What might explain the relative success of Baltimore's campaign as compared to Milwaukee's? While my data collection and analysis of B'More for Healthy Babies were far more limited than that of the Safe Sleep Campaign, Baltimore's approach emphasized community collaboration and outreach that addressed multiple and intersecting factors impacting the health of the whole family. One partner, the Annie E. Casey Foundation, points to the combination of public and private funding sources that allow for creative approaches and a depth of resources that would not otherwise be available. The Foundation also emphasizes the importance of family engagement efforts like home visits for new mothers that are provided by trusted community partners. Finally, the Annie E. Casey Foundation's analysis of B'More for Healthy Babies concludes that "adopting an explicit focus on racial equity is critical. Addressing racial disparities in health, or in any other sector, requires a deep understanding of underlying systemic and historical forces."[142] B'More for Healthy Babies addresses the role of racism in Black infant mortality, which lessens the stigmatization of Black parents as poor decision makers. By including Baltimore families in the campaign, whether as safe sleep ambassadors or to share their own stories of loss, B'More for Healthy Babies situates parents as responsible and caring partners in reducing infant mortality rather than as vectors of risk.

This is not to say that the City of Milwaukee Health Department, or the advertising agency responsible for Milwaukee's Safe Sleep Campaign, had any kind of racist intentions in promoting their message. Their goal was to reduce infant mortality, particularly among communities that have alarmingly high rates of infant death, and that is admirable. However, the health department is operating within a larger system of racial oppression, and regardless of their intentions, the *effects* of this campaign are unjust in that it targets individual families rather than tackling the social determinants of health that are stratified by race and class. The disjuncture between the goals of this public health campaign and its reception are not unique to Milwaukee, as demonstrated by Miranda Waggoner's analysis of the CDC's campaign to promote "preconception health" (including urging all women of reproductive age to refrain from drinking alcohol). Waggoner finds that public health officials were taken aback when what they conceptualized as a reproductive justice initiative to expand healthcare access was instead viewed as retrogressive and essentialist by academics and the public. According to Waggoner, "thinking about reproductive risk is not one-dimensional. Policy initiatives can use reductionist and gendered frameworks while also attempting to advance reproductive justice."[143] The goal of the Milwaukee Health Department was to reduce racial disparities in infant mortality, which is a crucial step in addressing health inequities in that city. Unfortunately, they did so initially by beginning with the "low-hanging fruit" of bed-sharing deaths, and their intentions did not take into consideration the lived realities of the city's residents.

Prior to the city's launch of the Safe Sleep Campaign, the Black Health Coalition of Wisconsin's Milwaukee Healthy Beginnings Project began its own initiative aimed at promoting safe sleep in Milwaukee called Babies Sleeping Safe. According to Dr. McManus, the BHCW began with focus groups including Hmong, African American, and Latino participants. In these focus groups, BHCW staff asked community members questions about their views on infant sleep safety, and what their current sleeping practices were. They used this information to create a brochure titled "Babies Sleeping Safe: Co-Sleeping with Your Baby." The brochure acknowledged that families often co-sleep with their babies for reasons including personal preference, ease of breastfeeding, bonding, and to respond promptly to a crying infant. The next page listed seven steps toward safe co-sleeping, including unsafe places for a baby to sleep (like a couch or chair), what to do if you're taking medication that could impact responsiveness, the dangers of soft bedding and pillows, and the advice that parents should never sleep with their baby if either partner has been using drugs or drinking alcohol. Additional tips include that parents should not smoke near their babies, or allow their infants to overheat while sleeping. The brochure includes the phone number, website, and email address for the BHCW.[144]

Based on the information that the BHCW had gathered from the community, they created a brochure that started from the reality that parents were co-sleeping with their infants, and took an approach meant to reduce the risk of SIDS or accidental suffocation, rather than attempting to eliminate the practice of co-sleeping. This is demonstrated even through the title of the brochure, which pairs the phrase "babies sleeping safe" with "co-sleeping with your baby"; this title authorizes the possibility that co-sleeping can be done more safely, which did not exist within the framework of the Safe Sleep Campaign. According to McManus, the "Babies Sleeping Safe" campaign was built on the belief that caregivers are open to thinking about parenting in new ways, and to learning and changing behaviors. However, she emphasizes that for this kind of public health education to be successful, the source must be trusted and well-known in the community. The Black Health Coalition of Wisconsin's initiatives, according to McManus, are built around the needs of the community, from scheduling meetings that take place after school hours, to providing small transportation stipends that allow parents to attend, as well as childcare and food during events. As McManus says, "To try to get better outcomes, they've [members of the community] got to be included. You can't just do this for people."[145]

The City's Safe Sleep Campaign failed to do what the BHCW centralized, which was working in partnership with the targeted communities to understand the problem and its potential solutions. Focus groups were not conducted by the Milwaukee Health Department or Serve Marketing to ascertain infant sleep practices within the Black community, or to gather feedback on the campaign materials themselves. According to a representative from Serve, Mayor Barrett may have shown the images to Black mothers and grandmothers who worked in City Hall and were residents of the "inner city."[146] The decision not to use focus groups either in the early phases to determine how residents co-sleep and why (as the BHCW did) or even to assess the efficacy of the advertising campaign after it was created seems to have been a serious omission. Not only do we know in retrospect that the campaign was considered offensive and ineffective by many, but according to McManus, many residents that she spoke with were baffled by the messaging of the campaign. She reports that the BHCW had a previously scheduled community meeting on the day that the controversial "Knife" ad was released. Many of those who attended, McManus recalls, did not make the connection that the butcher knife in the bed next to the baby was meant to stand in for the parent, or represent the danger that the parent posed while co-sleeping. McManus concluded that Serve was not entirely to blame that the ad did not resonate with parents, but in her words, "in the city, there's a cultural divide and an economic divide, and Lord, if you're both 'cultural' and poor, you know, you really felt that you just don't seem to know anything."[147] In other words, the lived experience and knowledge of the targeted community was not incorporated into the design of the campaign, resulting in an end product that, at best, did not resonate.

A positive effect of the backlash against the Safe Sleep Campaign has been an increased focus on premature birth and other social determinants of health. As Geoffrey Swain, former medical director for Milwaukee's Health Department, noted in an interview with Milwaukee Public Radio in 2013, deaths associated with premature birth had been vastly overlooked up to that point:

> Most of them are dying in the hospital [of complications of prematurity] . . . You never hear about them. Media never hears about them . . . So what the public is hearing, is they're hearing all about these unsafe sleep deaths, they're not hearing about four times as many babies that are dying of prematurity. So we get this skewed perception about what causes babies to die.[148]

In the wake of the local and national critiques of the Safe Sleep Campaign, the Health Department pivoted toward drivers of prematurity, and racial disparities in premature birth. It emphasized how the lived experiences of systemic racism in Milwaukee contribute to chronic stress, which has a greater impact on health at the population level than does individual behavior. This response by public health staff within the Health Department also influenced Mayor Barrett, who is said to have increasingly spoken publicly about structural factors that impact infant mortality like employment and neighborhood safety, rather than exclusively or primarily emphasizing individual choices and personal responsibility.[149]

Not everyone viewed the campaign's wind-down in the same way; Patricia McManus argued that the city of Milwaukee was not responsive enough to critiques by the Black community, and only pulled back once a negative national and international spotlight was focused on the city. As this suggests, the public health staff and elected officials who had influence over Milwaukee's campaign responded to community critique for a variety of reasons, including political pressure as well as self-reflexivity about flaws in the approach and an ongoing motivation to improve racial disparities in infant mortality. The funding of public health initiatives is also a factor, given that the Health Department relied on a pro bono marketing campaign and was unable to finance focus groups prior to the campaign's rollout, or a follow-up evaluation of the campaign's effectiveness within the targeted community. Without appropriate funding for focus groups up front, formative and summative campaign evaluation, and broader community engagement, the Health Department will be limited in applying what it learned to future campaigns.[150]

Conclusion

From a reproductive justice perspective, this disparity in treatment is not an anomaly, but rather is part of a continuum of reproductive health inequalities that have historical and contemporary resonance in communities of color. For example, individuals that I interviewed in Milwaukee about safe sleep also independently raised the issue of lead poisoning in that city. In the fall of 2017, a former Health Department employee contacted Mayor Barrett and Milwaukee's aldermen to report that Milwaukee families whose children had elevated levels of lead were not receiving appropriate notification, follow-up, or services. Further investigation revealed that thousands of families had not received a letter about how to reduce the lead in their children's blood, and that more than 90 percent of cases were closed before lead levels had declined sufficiently to meet state guidelines. Lead-exposed children in Milwaukee are disproportionately poor and African American, due in part to residential segregation that results in Black families experiencing greater environmental exposure. Health Commissioner Bevan Baker resigned amid this controversy, and was replaced by Black Health Coalition of Wisconsin founder Patricia McManus, who served as interim commissioner until a permanent replacement was appointed in September 2018.[151]

There is disagreement between community health groups like the BHCW and the City of Milwaukee Health Department about the most significant sources of lead in the community and the best course of action to reduce lead levels. While both groups agree that all forms of lead exposure are unsafe, they prioritize different responses. Many Black families live in homes that contain deteriorating lead-based paint, the mitigation of which is the focus of the Health Department's efforts, but the BHCW has also demanded the removal of lead service lines (also known as "laterals") which are lead-containing pipes that bring water into many homes. The relationship between the Health Department and the Black community was already strained by the Safe Sleep Campaign, and has been increasingly adversarial as a result of the controversy surrounding childhood lead exposure.

This adversarial relationship is a significant barrier to addressing the divergent perspectives on whether lead paint or lead in water poses the most significant hazard to Black families today. To Patricia McManus, the city's focus on the removal of lead paint instead of on lead in the water is another example of the Health Department choosing the easy target at the expense of an entrenched, complicated, and expensive one (like tearing up the streets to remove lead water pipes). In McManus's words, the city is again "trying to put a political lens on a public health issue." The reverse is true for a Health Department official, who offered the following assessment of the relationship between the current lead controversy and the Safe Sleep Campaign:

> Our main discussion around . . . infant mortality in the city needs to be about the experience of racism and discrimination, it needs to be about joblessness, it needs to be about criminal justice reform, it needs to be about housing, and evictions, and violence in neighborhoods, and all that stuff. That's the main thing. That's like the deteriorating paint. And safe sleep is like the water. Is it unimportant? No, it's not unimportant. Should we ignore it? No, we should not ignore it. But where should we put most of our effort?[152]

These two individuals expressed very similar critiques of the Safe Sleep Campaign, and likeminded perspectives on the social determinants of racial disparities in health. However, their analyses of the most significant drivers of lead exposure differ. Like the issue of infant sleep safety, the question of how to limit lead exposure involves a balance between individual behavioral change and broader, systemic change. But as these two perspectives suggest, even stakeholders with the same goals may disagree on which issue is the primary driver of negative health outcomes. This could present an opportunity for engagement, debate, and shared knowledge production between these constituencies. However, the adversarial relationship that has grown between the Black community and representatives of the state based on flawed initiatives like the Safe Sleep Campaign and the scandal surrounding the reporting of children's lead levels makes productive collaboration extremely challenging.

This legacy of Milwaukee's Safe Sleep Campaign and how it continues to affect ongoing relationships between marginalized communities and the city of Milwaukee is significant. It demonstrates the importance of centralizing reproductive justice in the research, design, and implementation of public health outreach. Centralizing reproductive justice would start by asking parents, and especially mothers, how and why they co-sleep. It would take their reasons seriously, and ask parents what their baseline needs are to ensure sleep safety. It would consider how parents' decision-making is influenced by environmental factors like a smoke-free, pest-free home, and neighborhood safety. It would not ignore the 15 percent of infant deaths that are attributed to unsafe sleep, but would also balance the response to this issue with the primary drivers of the other 85 percent of infant mortality that cannot be fixed with a slogan, an ad, or any appeal to personal responsibility. As the next chapter will demonstrate, the stakes of this debate are high—controversies about safe sleep are about more than individual choice and behavior—they reflect deeply embedded beliefs about race, class, and parenting. The death of a child is already an unimaginable loss to a parent; when the state decides that a parent's actions are to blame, the tragedy becomes that much greater.

4

"Everybody Loses"

Parents as Perpetrators

In 2015, the Wisconsin Senate Committee on Health and Human Services heard testimony on a first-of-its-kind bill to legislate the circumstances in which parents can co-sleep, or share a bed with, their children. Specifically, the bill proposed to make it a felony to injure or kill an infant by co-sleeping while under the influence of drugs or alcohol. The bill's author, Republican State Representative Samantha Kerkman, followed this up with a second piece of proposed legislation that would require police to take blood samples from any caregiver involved in a "suspicious infant death."[1] Those impaired by drugs, or with a blood alcohol level of .08 or above, would be considered intoxicated, holding adults in Wisconsin to the same standards for sleeping under the influence as for driving.[2] The bill heard by the Committee in 2015 also included the requirement that a physician, nurse-midwife, or other trained healthcare provider supply pregnant women with printed and audiovisual materials about safe sleep and the dangers of co-sleeping while intoxicated at a prenatal visit, or before she leaves the hospital. At that time, parents would be given a form stating that they have been advised of these risks, and that they would share this information with any other caregivers. Parents would not be asked or required to sign the form, but their medical records would indicate whether they received the information.[3]

Kerkman was likely motivated to draft the bill (which would eventually fail to pass the Senate) by reports of 33 infant deaths in Wisconsin that were attributed to accidental suffocation in an unsafe sleep environment in the four years prior. Killing one's child is, of course, already illegal in the state of Wisconsin; public health organizations that opposed the bill emphasized the argument that existing laws criminalizing abuse or endangerment are sufficient, and that further legislation is not necessary.[4] If parents could be prosecuted under existing law—and had been all across the country, as evidence in this chapter will demonstrate—then why craft new legislation that specifies the illegality of co-sleeping while intoxicated? One answer is that the proposed legislation reflected an anxiety that some parents pose a unique risk to their infants, whether through ignorance or carelessness, and that the state must step in to protect these children.

Tellingly, this legislation was built on a deeply flawed understanding of the primary drivers of sleep-related infant death—that parents "choose" to drink to excess and then suffocate their infants—suggesting that the primary impact of the law would be to symbolically criminalize "bad parents." Kerkman's bill was opposed by representatives of public health agencies including the Milwaukee Health Department, the Wisconsin Public Health Association, and the Wisconsin Association of Local Health Departments and Boards, who raised a variety of concerns. Geoffrey Swain voiced the opposition of the City of Milwaukee Health Department in an op-ed to the *Milwaukee Journal Sentinel* the first time Kerkman's bill was introduced in 2013. Swain outlined the conditions that often contribute to sleep-related infant deaths before noting:

> The key terminology here is "risk factors." The risk factors mentioned above are not the same as "causes" of death. Just because an infant is found dead while sleeping next to an adult (risk factor) does not mean the adult rolled over onto the baby and caused the death. Likewise, just because a parent admits to having a drink does not mean that alcohol use actually led to the infant's death.

Swain described the assumption that most infant deaths are caused by drunk or incompetent parents as "wildly inaccurate" and says that the Health Department hopes that the Wisconsin Legislature will "consider the true picture" when reviewing legislation.[5] Kerkman herself had reinforced the misconception that intoxication and rollovers are a significant part of the problem, stating, "When you do drink your body becomes more desensitized, you might not realize that you have rolled over."[6] While it is widely agreed upon by those that study infant sleep safety that bed-sharing is not safe when parents are under the influence of drugs or alcohol, the majority of co-sleeping deaths do not involve drug and alcohol use, and rollovers are the cause of between 0 and 1 of the roughly 15 annual "unsafe sleep" deaths in Milwaukee.[7]

When Kerkman's bill was re-introduced in 2015, Milwaukee Health Department representative and Director of Family and Community Health Jessica Gathirimu testified to the Department's continued opposition in front of the Committee on Health and Human Services. Gathirimu reiterated the Health Department's support of comprehensive safe sleep education, but argued again that the misconception that most co-sleeping deaths result from drunken rollovers is "full of misunderstanding." Gathirimu could speak to this with confidence, having "compile[d] the stories of each and every infant death in Milwaukee" for five years as part of the Fetal Infant Mortality Review team. Gathirimu's testimony reiterated the evidence marshalled by Swain in his 2013 op-ed, and reinforced the message of the Health Department that most Milwaukee parents are trying their best to keep their children safe and healthy, and that education rather than criminalization is the best approach to minimize sleep-related infant death.[8]

At the time of this writing, Wisconsin is seemingly unique in considering legislation addressing bed-sharing deaths, but it is not alone in viewing co-sleeping as a social problem that requires a criminal justice response to control the individual drivers of safe sleep death. This is reflected in Kerkman's statement to the media that people should "make better choices." The framework of choice not only implies a level playing field upon which all choices are equally available, but also implicates the existence of "good" and "bad" choice-makers. The individualized, choice-oriented framework has also trickled down to permeate the rhetoric of the general public. A Wisconsin mother interviewed by a local NBC news affiliated contrasted "good" co-sleeping families like her own with those who might require the threat of a felony: "If they're unable to make good choices on when they drink and how much they drink, they're probably are not [sic] going to make the safe choices about whether their kids should be in bed with them or not."[9] Bad choice-makers do not prioritize the safety of their children, this discourse suggests, and perhaps can only be made to do so by the threat of criminal sanctions.

This chapter analyzes the prosecutions of parents and caregivers for the deaths of children that occurred while co-sleeping between the years

2011 and 2018. I begin with 2011, because it was in this year that the American Academy of Pediatrics (AAP) expanded its guidelines for infant sleep safety from focusing solely on the prevention of Sudden Infant Death Syndrome (SIDS) to reducing the risk of other forms of sleep-related infant death, including an unsafe sleep environment. A safe sleep environment is defined by the AAP as one in which an infant sleeps alone, on their back, in a crib, without loose bedding or toys. As discussed in chapter 2, the AAP revised its guidelines in 2011 after the post-1990s decline in SIDS deaths began to plateau and other sleep-related deaths (such as accidental suffocation) began to rise. The AAP argues that because the modifiable and non-modifiable risk factors for SIDS and other sleep-related infant deaths are similar, safe sleep recommendations should encompass all categories; essentially, the AAP expanded its focus from SIDS prevention to include all sleep-related infant deaths. In the 2011 updated guidelines, the AAP endorsed room-sharing—in which an infant sleeps in a crib or bassinet in the same room as a parent—as a way to reduce the risk of SIDS. However, the policy also stated that the AAP "does not recommend any specific bed-sharing situations as safe."[10] The AAP guidelines are cited extensively in both news media coverage and scholarly analyses of SIDS and co-sleeping as an authoritative and powerful institution shaping the messages that parents receive about infant sleep. As such, AAP guidelines may also influence the law enforcement and prosecutorial response to parents who are held responsible for sleep-related infant deaths.

One reason that the AAP continues to update its guidelines regarding sudden unexpected infant death is because infant mortality rates in the United States, while at an all-time low, continue to remain significantly higher than those of other comparable countries around the world.[11] Sudden Unexpected Infant Death is a component of the overall infant mortality statistics. The Centers for Disease Control and Prevention reports that roughly 3,600 infants in the United States die of Sudden Unexpected Infant Death each year. The term Sudden Unexpected Infant Death (SUID) was created by the National Center for Health Statistics in the early 2000s. It is useful to think of SUID as an umbrella category for the death of children under the age of one, and to remember that it contains three silos: sudden infant death syndrome, accidental suffocation, and deaths with unknown causes.[12] As of 2017, of the 3,600 annual infant deaths that fall into the umbrella category of SUID, 38 percent are categorized within the SIDS silo, 36 percent fall within the unknown causes silo (potentially because a death scene investigation or autopsy was not completed), and 26 percent are categorized in the accidental suffocation/strangulation in bed silo.[13]

That being said, the early 1990s did see an overall drop in the SUID rate, which was largely credited to the AAP's 1992 recommendation that parents start putting babies to sleep in the supine position,[14] and the dissemination of that message through the Back to Sleep campaign, launched in 1994. As discussed in chapter 1, the Back to Sleep Campaign was endorsed by national health organizations including the National Institute of Child Health and Human Development, the AAP Task Force, and SIDS advocacy organizations. The campaign is credited with a remarkable shift in parenting practice and infant sleep norms in the United States, with the majority of infants now put to sleep on their backs.[15]

This story—that sudden infant death rates decreased because babies were put to sleep on their backs—is a primary narrative about SIDS, at least among the public. Less popular attention has been paid to research demonstrating changes in intrinsic and extrinsic SIDS risks.[16] Intrinsic risks include male sex at birth, prenatal exposure to tobacco, low birth weight, and prematurity. Extrinsic risk factors are those that exist in the infant's environment, like soft objects, overheating, prone sleep position, and bed-sharing, as well as postnatal exposure to tobacco smoke.[17] Some of these risk factors have shifted since the early '90s, such as lower overall levels of maternal tobacco use, higher levels of breastfeeding initiation, and breakthroughs in the treatment of premature infants. Also complicating the Back to Sleep success narrative is that the sharp drop in SIDS rates essentially leveled off after 2001,[18] and reductions in infant mortality were not shared equally across racial groups. Native Americans, African Americans, and Alaska Natives continued to experience SIDS more frequently than did white families.[19]

Recent research demonstrates another factor that contributes to the contemporary emphasis on accidental suffocation and a safe sleep environment, one that I argue is deeply significant for understanding the prosecution of parents for co-sleeping deaths. As I will discuss further, the last several decades have witnessed a shift in how unexpected infant deaths are classified. Until recently, many deaths that are currently being categorized as accidental suffocation would have been labeled as SIDS.[20] If we return to the concept of SUID as a broad category containing three silos, we can visualize the infant mortality numbers beginning to shift *from one silo to another*, rather than reflecting an actual overall decrease in SUID deaths. As deaths within the SIDS silo dropped in the early to mid-1990s, deaths within the accidental suffocation in bed silo and the unknown causes silo rose in the late 1990s, even while infant deaths remained relatively constant. According to SIDS researchers, including the AAP's SIDS Task Force, a diagnostic shift occurred: Some deaths that were once attributed to SIDS are now being categorized as one of the other two SUID silos—accidental suffocation or unknown causes.[21] What led to this shift, and how has it impacted public health and even the criminal prosecution of parents?

The Diagnostic Shift

The crux of a SIDS diagnosis is that no other diagnosis is possible— SIDS is, at its core, unexplainable. Historically, theories about the cause of unexpected infant death have gained and lost favor among medical researchers, including that affected babies have an oversized thymus gland, that their deaths are caused by "accidental mechanical suffoca- tion," or by breathing difficulties (apnea).[22] The first formal definition of SIDS was determined by medical professionals, including pediatricians and pathologists, at the Second International Conference on Causes of Sudden Death in Infants in 1969. SIDS was defined then as "the sudden death of any infant or young child, which is unexpected by history, and in which a thorough postmortem examination fails to demonstrate an adequate cause for death."[23] Although SIDS was still a poorly understood syndrome, by the end of the 1960s it had emerged as an official diagno- sis and the terminology spread outward into the lexicon of professional medicine. By 1970, SIDS was accepted as an official diagnosis on death certificates, and in 1979 the World Health Organization assigned SIDS its own medical code in the International Classification of Diseases.[24]

Parents of infants who died unexpected deaths in their sleep were grateful for the medical classification of SIDS because the diagnosis, although frustratingly vague, assured them that they were not alone in their loss, and were not to blame.[25] The definition of SIDS was revised again in 1991, when the US National Institute of Child Health and Human Development Group published the requirements that the death must occur in a child under the age of one, and "remains unexplained after a thorough case investigation, including performance of a complete autopsy, examination of the death scene, and review of the clinical history."[26] This revision was significant because it required a death scene investigation, which could reveal mitigating factors that would exclude a SIDS diagnosis, such as the sleep position of the infant or the presence of soft bedding and pillows.

While the underlying cause of SIDS is still debated by researchers, the most influential theory is that SIDS involves multiple, interacting factors, exemplified by the Triple Risk Model. This model contends that SIDS is explained by the interaction of three factors: infant vulnerability, a critical stage of development, and an environmental trigger or stressor. According to this theory, an environmental stressor like soft bedding while co-sleeping could be quite dangerous for an infant with vulnerabilities such as premature birth or a brain stem dysfunction, whereas a physiologically "normal" infant may have more protective responses (like turning their head to clear their airway).[27] There are no biomarkers that set SIDS and accidental suffocation apart, even in autopsy, and because the deaths occur during sleep, they are typically unwitnessed.[28] SIDS is, in essence, "a diagnosis of exclusion."[29]

The diagnostic shift in the United States is identified as occurring between 1999 and 2001, motivated by multiple factors, including differing diagnostic preferences among pathologists, variations in policies for determining cause of death, and more thorough death scene investigations.[30] The increasingly stringent guidelines for investigating SIDS can involve parents using baby dolls to reenact the scene of their child's death in their own homes, witness interviews, and scene photos. This evidence can reveal risk factors associated with unexplained infant death such as maternal tobacco use, prone sleep position, soft bedding, and bed-sharing. When a death scene investigation, for example, reveals that a baby was found on a couch instead of a crib, or on their stomach instead of their back, these factors potentially pollute the "no known cause of death" purity required for a diagnosis of SIDS.[31] With this additional information, the death certifier may attribute the cause of death as undetermined or accidental suffocation rather than SIDS.[32]

How do these investigations occur? Most US jurisdictions require that the unexpected death of an infant is referred to the coroner or medical examiner, and that the death is investigated by the coroner/medical examiner or law enforcement.[33] These professionals are advised to use the CDC's Sudden Unexplained Infant Death Investigation reporting form and guidelines,[34] which were released in 1996 and revised in 2006. The guidelines are meant to assist in standardizing and documenting the collection of data to determine cause of death classification and improve research on SIDS risk factors.[35] The adoption of these guidelines also may have contributed to shifting diagnoses. A recent study of cause of death determinations found that the number of coroners' offices and medical examiners that reported that they would *not* use the term SIDS on a death certificate rose from 5 percent in 2004 to 50 percent in 2014.[36] Moreover, less than half of the US population is served by a medical examiner, as opposed to a coroner. Coroners are laypeople who are either elected or appointed to the role and "rely on available medical personnel to assist in investigations and perform autopsies," which can affect the quality of the death certification process.[37] If a death scene investigation or a detailed postmortem examination is not completed, a pathologist may feel insufficiently informed to classify a death as SIDS, and instead label it undetermined.[38]

This diagnostic shift, or the pattern of classifying deaths as accidental suffocation or undetermined that at one time would have been coded as SIDS, leads some researchers to conclude that the decline in SIDS rates has been in part due to the changing categorization of infant mortality, rather than a true decrease in SUID deaths.[39] As Jhodie Duncan and Robert Byard conclude in *Sudden Infant and Early Childhood Death: The Past, The Present, and The Future*, "the term SIDS has become increasingly controversial . . . this has resulted in a decrease in the application of the term as a diagnosis, with many professionals classifying cases into other categories and employing terms such as 'undetermined,' 'unknown,' 'unascertained,' or 'ill-defined,' despite the fact that cases fulfil the criteria for SIDS."[40] This diagnostic shift is apparent not only in the United States, but also in countries including England, Wales, and Australia, where SIDS rates declined during the 1990s and deaths attributed to other factors rose.[41]

As a result of the diagnostic shift, infant mortality numbers seem to reflect a decrease in rates of SIDS (for which no one is to blame), with some of those deaths now attributed to other causes including accidental suffocation (for which caregivers may be held responsible and prosecuted). This allows for selectively prosecuting "bad" [read: drug-using, young, unmarried, unemployed] parents for deaths that might otherwise be considered tragic accidents. Whether the diagnostic shift is warranted or valid in eventually clarifying SUID deaths is outside of the scope of this project. However, the potential unintended consequences may include an erosion of the validity of the SIDS diagnosis, which has also been undermined by the lingering belief held by many in the news media, politics, and even in some areas of public health, that most unexplained infant deaths are preventable.[42] This position is not only implied, it is often quite explicit, as in the title of a 2012 article in the Illinois *Daily Herald*, "Most Sudden Infant Deaths Are Preventable, Studies Show," or in the comment by a Milwaukee radio host that babies are dying because "pigs of mothers" are too lazy to put their infants in a crib. A portion of infant deaths that were once considered nonpreventable may now be read as abuse, or even murder, particularly when accused parents occupy already marginalized identities.

The data analyzed for this chapter are based on 29 instances of caregivers who were prosecuted for their role in the death of a child who died while sharing a sleep surface with that adult.[43] As I have argued thus far, the diagnostic shift in determining the cause of unexpected infant death has led to a greater number of deaths that are classified as undetermined or accidental suffocation rather than SIDS.[44] All of the children in this data set died in what the American Academy of Pediatrics would define as an unsafe sleep environment, meaning that the babies were not sleeping alone or in a crib.[45] The cause of death for most infants was listed as some variation of asphyxia, overlay, or accidental suffocation. Medical examiners and coroners labeled some of the deaths "undetermined," but often noted a history of co-sleeping, or that the death was "likely suffocation." Only one was described as SIDS, and one as unexpected death in infancy, with a history of co-sleeping. The frequency with which infant deaths in this data set were categorized as asphyxia or undetermined reinforces the reality of the diagnostic shift, in which deaths that involve risk factors such as co-sleeping are unlikely to be categorized as SIDS. By examining the commonalities between cases in which parents are prosecuted for co-sleeping deaths, this research reveals some potential unexpected consequences of the diagnostic shift in terms of the precarity it may create for the parents and caregivers of deceased infants.

The charges leveled against caregivers when a co-sleeping death occurs vary widely. For the data gathered in this study, charges ranged from misdemeanors (from misdemeanor endangering the welfare of a child to misdemeanor involuntary manslaughter) to felonies (including intentional child abuse resulting in death, aggravated manslaughter, and negligent homicide). Despite efforts in Wisconsin, no states have specifically criminalized co-sleeping. Given all of this, it is difficult to track prosecutions stemming from co-sleeping deaths because the charges are varied, they are not tied to a specific activity that has been criminalized, and there is no comprehensive data source at the state or national level that records prosecutions for co-sleeping deaths. As a result, news coverage of co-sleeping deaths is the most comprehensive source of such cases. To create a data set, I searched the databases LexisNexis and US Newsstream for media coverage of co-sleeping deaths from 2011 to 2018. After identifying names of caregivers, I again searched these two databases for additional news coverage, as well as alternative internet search databases in order to determine further characteristics of cases. I also used public records, primarily publicly available court documents. I was able to obtain court documents that included the charge and the disposition for 28 of the 29 cases.

Using the media coverage and court documents available for each case, I coded for demographic data (name, age, race) and case details (address, year, cause of death, location of death, substance use at time of death, charge, sentence). I used these case details to determine the region in which each death occurred (Midwest, West, South, or Northeast) and the median household income based on census tract. Because of the nature of this data collection, the amount of information available for each case was inconsistent, and thus some cases have more data missing than others. For example, one case may have resulted in the publication of ten discoverable news articles, while another case was written about only once. In addition to coding for demographic data and case details, I recorded written notes on the available documents for each case. These notes were then analyzed for recurring themes, which emerged from the characteristics of the cases themselves. Through this method, three major themes emerged: first, the role of parental substance use; second, the significance attributed to safe sleep counseling; and third, the loss of more than one child to unexpected infant death. While these themes were developed using data from all of the cases, I then selected two to three cases for each theme that were either representative of many others or unique in what they revealed about the prosecution of co-sleeping death. I briefly introduce the selected cases before contextualizing each theme. Finally, I selected pseudonyms for the cases that are discussed in detail in the chapter. While all of these cases involve public records, it is my hope that the use of pseudonyms may spare some of the families involved from the additional distress or trauma resulting from a public discussion of a personal tragedy.

One limitation of this research is that the data set of 29 cases is undoubtedly a major undercount of parents charged in these circumstances. That is because there are surely many cases that are not covered by the news media, or news media coverage that is not archived in the two primary databases that I selected. This is due in part to other limitations such as the lack of laws specifically criminalizing co-sleeping, and the inexistence of a comprehensive database that compiles these charges. Despite this limitation, the data set gathered does offer a greater window into the criminal prosecution of bed-sharing deaths than is available in the existing literature.

Demographics

Of the 29 cases selected, in 28 a parent was charged with the death of an infant, and in one case a non-parent caregiver was charged (the adult son of a daycare provider). I was able determine the age of parents and caregivers at the time of arrest in all of the cases; the 25 female caregivers in this study ranged in age from 17 to 42, with an average age of 28 years old and a median age of 27. The ten male caregivers in the study ranged in age from 22 to 50, with an average age of 30 and a median age of 28. Geographically, the most cases were clustered in states in the Midwest

(13), followed by the Northeast (8), the South (7), and the West (2). The state with the most cases was Pennsylvania (which constituted seven of the eight cases in the Northeast region); as I will discuss further, Pennsylvania also stands out for its proactive legislation and activism aimed at reducing SIDS and accidental suffocation deaths.

The race or ethnicity of caregivers could be determined for 18 of the caregivers; race was only coded when it could be verified in court or prison documents. Of these 18 caregivers, 12 were white, four were Black, one was Asian/Pacific Islander, and one was Native American. Interestingly, racial identifiers were not used in any of the news media coverage of the cases; news media often included mug shots or other photographs of the accused, perhaps in part to stand in for racial identification. The limited demographic data make it difficult to draw conclusions about how race impacts prosecutions for co-sleeping deaths. However, research on related areas such as Jeanne Flavin and Lynn Paltrow's groundbreaking study of arrests and forced intervention on pregnant women demonstrates that along with low-income women, women of color are disproportionately impacted. As Flavin and Paltrow argue, these findings are "consistent with well-documented racially disproportionate application of criminal laws to African-American communities in general and to pregnant African American women in particular."[46] Moreover, research demonstrates that in multiple states and in federal courts, African American defendants were less likely to have charges dismissed and more likely to receive plea deals that included prison or jail time.[47] Given this, further research is necessary to assess how race impacts whether parents are arrested, charged, and prosecuted for co-sleeping deaths.

The majority of parents charged for co-sleeping deaths in this study were of low socioeconomic status. The median household income for caregivers was determined for 27 of the 29 cases based on the census block of each home address.[48] The median household income in the United States for 2018 was $70,573. Median household incomes in this data set ranged from $20,294 to $117,188, with an overall median household income of $46,304. On average, the median household income for caregivers in this study was roughly $19,000 lower than the median household income for the state in which they resided. In other words, most of the caregivers in this study were likely poorer than average.

While it may seem unexpected on the surface that socioeconomic class emerges more strongly than race as a factor that ties the cases together in this data set (keeping in mind that race could not be identified for all cases), legal scholar Michele Goodwin argues that class often matters as much as race in the related area of fetal protection laws; while Black women are often the "canaries in the coalmine," poor white women are also targeted by interventions into reproductive autonomy and childrearing.[49]

These findings align with those of Paltrow and Flavin in their study of 400 arrests and forced interventions among pregnant women and mothers. Paltrow and Flavin found that socioeconomic disadvantage was the overwhelming commonality between the cases that they gathered, with over 71 percent of women in their study qualifying for indigent defense.[50] Legal scholar Jennifer Collins had similar findings in a study of caregivers who were prosecuted when their children died of heat stroke after accidentally being left in the car. Collins found that "blue-collar" parents were four times as likely to be prosecuted as wealthier parents.[51] Poverty not only impacts the defense that parents are able to afford should they go to trial; in my data set, it also potentially influences whether infant deaths were viewed as accidental or as the result of child abuse and neglect.

For example, both the courts and media returned repeatedly to markers of class status when assessing the guilt of parents whom I will call Amy and Ryan. The twenty-five and twenty-eight-year-old parents were charged with felony child neglect resulting in death after their one-year-old and three-month-old children died on the same night while sleeping in bed with both parents. Amy admitted to using alcohol before sleeping with the children, and Ryan had used both alcohol and marijuana. Both parents were sentenced to 3–15 years in state penitentiaries. Media coverage of the case noted that the family lived in a mobile home, they frequently slept all together in the living room, and that the children's beds were unmade and covered in clothing. As in this case, common problems that define poverty such as a lack of food, clean clothing, or appropriate childcare are often definitionally categorized as child mistreatment.[52] Linda Fentiman uses the "reasonable person heuristic" to explain how prosecutors, jurors, or judges may assess women accused of crimes against their children; assuming that a "reasonable person" would have foreseen the potential risks of co-sleeping and avoided them allows others to maintain faith in a just world. Because mothers are typically the last to interact with a child before their death, blaming the mother attaches meaning to a senseless tragedy,[53] especially one like suffocation that seems to require a "doer" behind the deed.

In Amy's sentencing and commitment order, the Circuit Court Judge listed "matters taken into consideration" including appearance, education, and gendered expectations of behavior, all of which are inflected by socially constructed beliefs about class. For example, the judge described Amy as a "poor, dysfunctional woman" with no more than an eighth-grade education and a "vocational history in housekeeping." The judge used Amy's body as a "matter taken into consideration," noting without additional comment her multiple tattoos, as well as nipple and tongue piercings. Finally, the judge asserted that "the average person knows how to maintain a clean house and how to protect his/her children." The judge connects cleanliness with parenting when using this "reasonable person/parent" standard, but this allegedly neutral heuristic is inflected by gendered stereotypes that result in disproportionate mother blame.[54] As the judge's comments make clear, Amy not only violated laws and social norms by harming her children, she also violated gender norms by failing to maintain a clean home and marking her body with tattoos and sexualized body piercings. When the judge in Amy's case says that the "average person" knows how to maintain a household *and* protect their children, he not only ties the two together, but also blames bad mothering for the harm to the child.

It is not uncommon for housekeeping to stand in as a measurement of appropriate femininity and good motherhood among women accused of violent crimes. Legal scholar Emma Cunliffe finds a similar discourse in the infamous case of Waneta Hoyt, a mother who murdered five of her children over the course of several years in the 1960s and '70s. This case was significant because the deaths of multiple Hoyt children were initially held up as evidence of the apnea theory of Sudden Infant Death Syndrome, until Hoyt later confessed to smothering the children to stop them from crying. In *Murder, Medicine, and Motherhood*, Cunliffe notes that media coverage of Hoyt's trial focused extensively on the fact that she had not finished high school, and that the family lived in a trailer park. In essence, media coverage of Hoyt, Amy, and other women in my data set imply that the gender transgression inherent to being a poor mother, and especially a poor mother who lacks the time, resources, or energy to maintain her home, is relevant to the death of a child. Poverty and uncleanliness are gender transgressions that signify "bad motherhood," and "bad mothers" harm their children.

Cunliffe contextualizes this mother-blame within the circumstances of unexpected infant death. The treatment of Hoyt, Cunliffe argues, is consistent with a general trend toward criminalization of parents for child abuse and infanticide in the late twentieth century that was "tied specifically to a mistrust of mothers in the context of unexplained infant death."[55] Not only are mothers more likely to be the primary caregivers of children, and thus more likely to have the opportunity to kill a child or discover the child's body, but blaming the mother also fills in a frustrating gap in scientific knowledge about the actual causes of unexpected infant death.[56] The diagnostic shift likewise offers an alternative to the "unknowns" of a SIDS diagnosis by shifting many infant deaths into the accidental suffocation or strangulation category.

As previously mentioned, cases in this data set all involved infant deaths that occurred while sharing a sleep surface with an adult, as opposed to unexplained deaths or suffocation that happen while a baby is sleeping in a crib. Of the 31 babies who died,[57] I could ascertain the location of death in 30 of the infants.[58] Of these, 22 babies were found sharing a bed or mattress on the floor with an adult,[59] five were on a couch or couch cushions on the floor, two were on the floor, and one was in a reclining chair.[60] The charges against parents in these cases varied widely, ranging from misdemeanors to felonies. In some states in the United States, more than 95 percent of all criminal convictions are made through guilty pleas;[61] this holds true for the sample here, in which most parents resolved their cases through a plea of guilty or no contest. Of the 29 cases, I was able to determine the resolution of 28 cases; one was not yet disposed at the time of this writing. To the best of my knowledge, 22 caregivers were convicted of at least one felony, and 12 were convicted of lesser misdemeanor charges. Every individual whose case was disposed was convicted of at least one offense.

Themes

Three characteristics were most salient among the cases in this data set: first, that parents or caregivers were using drugs or alcohol while co-sleeping; second, that the accused had lost more than one infant to SUID; and third, that parents or caregivers had been previously counseled not to co-sleep by social services or medical authorities. While not every case shares all of these characteristics, many of these strands overlap in individual stories. The following sections will discuss each theme in more detail and highlight two or three cases that fit within each theme.

Parental Substance Use

JANET

Janet, a 32-year-old white woman living in the Midwest was arrested following the death of her 28-day-old infant. Janet was not sleeping with her child at the time of the baby's death; she had put the infant into the bed with her husband before leaving the room to take a bath. When she returned, the baby was nonresponsive. Morphine and Subutex (a medication used to treat opioid addiction) were found in the home. Janet was initially charged with felony endangering the welfare of a child in a ritual or ceremony; she eventually pled guilty to misdemeanor endangering the welfare of a child. She received a two-year suspended imposition of sentence, and two years of unsupervised probation. A suspended imposition of sentence means that no sentence is imposed as long as she follows the parameters of her probation; should she fail to do so, a judge can impose any sentence up to the maximum for the crime of which she was convicted. Media reports do not indicate that her husband was charged in connection with the death.

LEAH

Leah, a Native American woman living in the Midwest, was 26 years old when her three-month-old died while sleeping with her on a mattress on the floor. Leah was intoxicated at the time of the infant's death; according to the baby's father, Leah's alcohol use had contributed to the surrendered custody of her older daughter. Prosecutors in the case reported to news media that the decision to charge Leah with felony second-degree reckless homicide and felony child abuse was influenced by her history of alcohol use and past interactions with Social Services. Leah pled no contest to the charges against her and was sentenced to one year in jail and 14 years of probation, including the conditions that she commit to absolute sobriety and comply with random drug and alcohol testing.

JENNA AND ADAM

Jenna and Adam, 30 and 24 years old respectively, were living in the Midwest when they were each charged with felony and misdemeanor counts of child endangerment. Both parents were under the influence of alcohol and marijuana when their four-month-old died while sharing a bed with them. The couple had a history of investigations by Social Services regarding the four children who lived in the home. Both pled guilty to misdemeanor child endangerment, and both received 180 days in jail, with 90 days stayed, and two years of probation.

The most pervasive commonality between the 29 cases that I gathered was the parental use of drugs or alcohol. Of the 29 cases, in 23 at least one of the caregivers either admitted to or tested positive for using alcohol or illegal drugs before co-sleeping with the child. In three of the remaining six cases, news reports noted that drugs were found in the home, or that the accused had a history of drug or alcohol abuse.[62] The severity of the substance abuse varied within the data set, and is also difficult to quantify due to the nature of these cases. Because SUID typically occurs at night, when families are asleep, law enforcement may be testing parents for substance use many hours after the death of the infant. Some parents were clearly impaired by "hard" drugs such as heroin while sleeping with their children, while others are reported as having a history of drug or alcohol abuse.

Given these limitations, this research could not identify the exact narcotics used in each instance, but opioid use was evident in multiple cases. These include synthetic opioids such as hydrocodone and oxycodone (often known by its brand name, Oxycontin) as well as heroin and morphine. The time period in which these cases occurred also coincides with an opioid epidemic in the United States. The CDC divides the opioid epidemic into three waves; the first beginning in the 1990s as prescriptions of opioids increased, the second wave initiated in 2010 and marked by heroin overdoses, and the third wave starting in 2013 and notable for overdoses of synthetic opioids. Currently, an average of 130 people in the United States die per day due to opioid overdose.[63] For years, pharmaceutical companies pushed physicians to prescribe more opioids to more patients, and research indicates that 80 percent of those who abuse opioids had a prescription for these medications before their abuse began.[64]

The opioid crisis is reflective of how deadly the neoliberal rhetoric of individual choice and personal responsibility can be. The response to the crisis is slowed by lawmakers who hesitate to approve funding for treatment and first response measures due to stigma and stereotypes about addiction, while the pharmaceutical companies that manufacture synthetic opioids continue to profit. Stigma surrounding opioid and other illegal drug use is particularly strong for pregnant women and mothers; using these substances garners greater social censure, regardless of harm, than alcohol or tobacco.[65] More than eight times as many women are incarcerated in the United States currently than in the 1980s, largely through drug-related offenses, and nearly half of women in prison are Black.[66] Moreover, the majority of incarcerated women are mothers, and often single parents who are responsible for their households. Despite calls for corporate accountability, it is individuals who are largely held accountable for the real or perceived consequences of substance abuse, as this data set demonstrates.

In some cases, the implications of substance abuse are quite clear; for example, one father seemingly nodded off while using heroin, and failed to check on the infant next to him on the couch even after a friend warned him that the baby appeared to have died. In other cases, however, the link between substance use and infant death is more tenuous; for example, when a caregiver reported moderate alcohol or marijuana use that may or may not have led to impairment. Bed-sharing with an impaired person is a recognized risk factor for SUID, but at the same time does not establish a causal link to infant death. That being said, more than 80 percent of cases in this data set involved allegations of drug or alcohol use; claims of parental substance use may take on a heightened significance in the criminal justice system regardless of their severity. Mothers in particular are held to a pernicious societal double standard regarding alcohol use, in which excessive drinking is culturally equated with maternal failure.[67] As violence against women expert Jody Raphael argues, "women in our society are burdened with the responsibility of transmitting moral values and attitudes thought to immunize against drug abuse. When they become addicts themselves, the crime is thus considered more serious."[68] Indeed, Raphael argues that mothers who use drugs are viewed as not only failing at their maternal role, but rejecting their female role as well.

Janet's case speaks to this issue. Unlike every other parent or caregiver in this data set, Janet was arrested for child endangerment even though she was not the adult sleeping in the bed with the deceased baby. This is not to suggest that the father of the baby should have been charged, but rather that Janet's case is unusual in this data set in that she was not physically present in the area where the child died. News coverage of Janet's arrest does not note if she tested positive for drugs, but she is described as "admitting" that spoons in the home contained opioids. As Jeanne Flavin argues in *Our Bodies, Our Crimes*, women and girls are divided by institutions like the criminal justice system into binary frameworks of bad/good, offenders/mothers. "Not coincidentally," she argues, such systems "reinforce these distinctions by effectively barring women who use drugs, commit crimes, or are battered from ever being considered 'good' or deserving of societal benefits and protections."[69] Feminist theorist Natalie Fixmer-Oraiz adds that our cultural understanding of "bad" mothers is dependent upon the intensive mothering that we expect from "good" mothers. If good mothers are imagined to be selfless and exclusively child-centered, then "those who dare to parent while poor and undocumented or ill or addicted" are worthy of criminalization.[70] Janet's arrest likewise reinforces the gendered asymmetry in parental responsibility for the welfare of children; in the social welfare and criminal justice system, mothers are held culpable for outcomes whether they were actively or passively implicated.[71] Motherhood is framed as a totalizing identity, wherein mothers have the capacity to predict and prevent risks that they may not even fully understand, let alone control.[72] Janet was ultimately held accountable for her failure to foresee her child's death.

The criminal justice crackdown on parents who use drugs and alcohol in this data set is similar to how women are treated for substance abuse during pregnancy. While a criminal justice response to substance abuse or to unsafe sleep deaths is not inevitable, it is also not without precedent. One aspect of the erosion of women's reproductive rights and autonomy in the United States has been the criminalization of women's conduct during pregnancy, from drug and alcohol use to miscarriage and stillbirth. The 1980s witnessed a national panic over "crack babies" and the underclass of primarily Black youth that would allegedly emerge from this crisis. Politicians and news media fanned the flames, despite evidence that the effects of prenatal drug exposure were inseparable from factors linked to poverty such as homelessness, tobacco use, and domestic violence.[73] While further research has debunked the racist claims and fearmongering, author of *Medical Apartheid* Harriet Washington argues that "the imaginary crack baby epidemic remains real in the minds of most Americans, providing yet another exemplar of African American 'bad mothering'" and driving prosecutions of Black pregnant substance abusers.[74]

Concern shifted to methamphetamine use in the 1990s, and opioid addiction in the 2000s. The American Civil Liberties Union (ACLU) first documented the prosecution of pregnant women for drug use in 1990; within two years there were 160 prosecutions in 22 states. Among those cases, about 75 percent of those prosecuted were women of color.[75] This criminalization of mothers has been aided by the growing acceptance of fetal personhood, or the ideology that the rights of citizenship are bestowed at conception, and thus embryos and fetuses are "persons" who must be protected from the women who carry them. In 1998, for example, the Supreme Court of South Carolina decided that "a viable fetus is a person" and thus "a woman who uses illegal drugs while she is pregnant can be charged with neglect, manslaughter, even murder."[76] Currently, 23 states classify substance abuse during pregnancy as child abuse, and 25 states require healthcare professionals to report suspected prenatal substance use to law enforcement.[77]

Flavin and Paltrow found that the majority of cases in which pregnant women experienced unwanted interventions or arrests involved allegations of drug use. Yet, as the authors argue, the risks posed by the drug most commonly alleged to have been abused (cocaine) are difficult to disentangle from other issues like exposure to maternal tobacco use and other factors in the external environment. A similar conflation occurs with co-sleeping deaths, in which substance use is cast as the singular or primary cause of the fatal outcome. As previously discussed, unexpected infant deaths are often categorized as undetermined, or accidental suffocation (as opposed to SIDS), when risk factors like co-sleeping or parental substance use are also present. However, prematurity and maternal tobacco use are two of the most significant risk factors for SIDS,[78] which can exist independently, or co-occur with bed-sharing and parental substance use. Yet the cultural significance attributed to drug and alcohol use, especially by mothers, eclipses these other risk factors. As Fentiman argues, all actors in the criminal justice system, including police officers, medical examiners, judges, and juries, are impacted by the social construction of risk, and tend to have a preference for monocausal explanations that identify individual actors as having the capacity to foresee and prevent catastrophic outcomes.[79]

How does the criminalization of pregnant women for drug use relate to the prosecution of parents for co-sleeping deaths? For one, the former relies upon the presumption of maternal-fetal conflict, or the idea that pregnant women and their fetuses are separable entities with divergent interests. While the latter involves children, rather than fetuses, I would argue that fetal personhood and maternal-fetal conflict exist on a continuum that does not end with birth. Indeed, women have been charged with crimes like delivery of a controlled substance after their babies were born because narcotics allegedly passed from the mother's body through the umbilical cord to the newborn child. Additionally, the *New York Times* Editorial Board argues that laws initially designed to protect women who are victimized (like feticide laws) then embolden prosecutors to turn these laws against women themselves. They give the example of the highly publicized murder of pregnant Laci Peterson in 2002, which inspired Texas legislators to pass the Prenatal Protection Act in 2003. Prosecutors used the Act, which defined a fetus as an "individual" before birth, to charge pregnant drug users with providing a controlled substance to a child. At least 50 women were arrested in one Texas county that year based on this interpretation. Even after a defendant successfully appealed her conviction based on the argument that pregnant women could not be charged under the Texas law, others in Texas continue to be arrested under similar circumstances.[80]

Parents who are charged with felonies for co-sleeping deaths are frequently described by prosecutors, judges, and others as irresponsible,
bad parents, and vectors of risk to their infants. In some of these cases, it
is clear that parental substance abuse contributed to an unsafe environment for children. However, it also seems that the socioeconomic status,
age, race, and education of many of the parents inclined authorities to
perceive them as risky, dangerous, or bad caregivers from the outset.
And hindsight bias (based on the knowledge that a child died under the
supervision of these adults) implicitly confirms these perceptions.

As this suggests, the link between drug and alcohol use is closely tied
to the social construction of "good" versus "bad" parenting, particularly
for mothers. The contemporary "moral construction of poverty" continues to posit poor mothers as deviant, irresponsible, and immoral,
and upholds the myth that poor women are more likely to harm their
children than are their wealthier counterparts.[81] Sociologist Jennifer
Reich contends that "gender further defines failed parenting, with a
special form of contempt reserved for mothers, particularly those who
are unmarried" such that "women receive the bulk of state scrutiny."[82]
Race also intersects with gender and class in ways that create additional
precarity for mothers of color. Leah, for example, is a Native American
mother who had a history of interactions with child welfare services,
including relinquishing a child for adoption, allegedly because of her
problems with alcoholism. Native American families, of course, have
a long history of trauma with regard to government intervention into
childrearing. Leading up to and throughout the twentieth century, the
US government routinely removed Native American children from their
homes and the custody of their parents based on the belief that Native
mothers were inherently ignorant, incapable, and even a danger to their
own children.[83]

The extent to which a family interacts with social services is also
closely related to their social class. As Virginia Eubanks argues in *Automating Inequality: How High-Tech Tools Profile, Police, and Punish the
Poor*, poor families have more frequent interactions with mandatory reporters like social workers, therapists, and law enforcement officers who
may be likely to view their parenting practices with heightened skepticism. Higher income families have greater access to private resources

when they find themselves in need of assistance, including legal support, which buffers them from the systems and databases that increase surveillance and monitoring. Once parents are enmeshed within these systems, they experience what Eubanks calls "poverty profiling," or interventions based not necessarily on individual behaviors, but on their class status. As Eubanks argues, "parenting while poor means parenting in public."[84] Leah, Jenna, and Adam all had prior interactions with social services for their children, and thus were all "parenting in public."

The implications of poverty extend beyond interactions with social services; the authorities such as law enforcement and medical practitioners who investigate unexplained infant deaths are primed to view disadvantaged families as inherently unhealthy, and to interpret signs of poverty (like inadequate housing or crowded living arrangements) as indicative of a dangerous and uncaring environment for children.[85] These class biases then frequently intersect with race, given the intertwining of race and socioeconomic status in the United States. In other words, unacknowledged biases about what types of mothers, living in what kind of neighborhoods, are likely to drink excessively or use drugs, could influence whether or not an infant death is assumed to be suspicious. These implicit biases could also impact the decision about whether or not to test a grieving parent for drug or alcohol use. Although no data exist at this time to prove this specific hypothesis, research on the drug testing of pregnant women can provide some support. A 1989 study found that medical professionals were ten times more likely to report pregnant patients for drug use if they were African American than if they were white.[86] A more recent study from 2007, of 8,487 women, found that Black women and their babies were 1.5 times more likely to be tested for illicit substances than were non-Black women and infants, even though Black women were not more likely to test positive. Other factors that were associated with being drug tested included unemployment, low educational status, being unmarried, and having public or absent health insurance.[87]

Finally, it seems reasonable to assume that law enforcement and prosecutors may share similar preconceived beliefs as do medical professionals. Prosecutors have enormous power to determine charges in the American criminal justice system, a system of mass incarceration in which the number of imprisoned people has quadrupled since the 1980s.[88] In Leah's case, for example, prosecutors decided to bring charges because of her history of alcohol abuse and interactions with social services. Women's criminal histories of course also impact how they will be perceived, given that justice-involved women and girls are "often looked upon as 'doubly deviant,' violating both gender and legal norms."[89] It is not uncommon for prosecutors to load up on charges in order to avoid time-consuming and costly trials by pressuring the accused to accept a plea agreement. Women accept plea deals for a variety of reasons; in Michele Goodwin's study of fetal protection laws, prosecutors told Goodwin that many women accept plea deals out of fear, including the fear that their alleged crimes against fetuses or infants will be "inflammatory" to a jury and result in a longer sentence.[90] These fears may have been stoked by the fact that few women could afford a private attorney; prosecutors told Goodwin that they "noticed a difference" in the quality of representation for those who did obtain private legal counsel. The well-grounded fear that juries are primed to respond punitively to women accused of harming their children, combined with low-quality representation and extensive charges, are likely to encourage women to accept plea deals.

In my data set, some parents were charged with felonies before pleading to misdemeanors. For example, Jenna eventually pled guilty to misdemeanor endangering the health and welfare of a child, but was originally charged with felony child endangerment and two misdemeanors. She served 90 days in jail; in the state in which she resided, a conviction for felony child endangerment results in a prison sentence of no less than two years, and no more than ten.[91] Twenty of the parents in this data set were convicted of felonies. As felons, they may lose access to public housing, experience voter disenfranchisement, be ineligible for student loans, and in some cases, be denied access to benefits like the Supplemental Nutrition Assistance Program (SNAP) or Temporary Assistance to Needy Families (TANF).[92] Many of these individuals are also the parents of surviving children; these consequences of a felony conviction that disproportionately impact the poor—limiting access to affordable food, housing, and education—will create significant hardship for families already reeling in the wake of an infant's death and in some cases a period of incarceration.

For many women, problems with drugs and alcohol began before they became mothers. Pregnant women face barriers when seeking drug or alcohol treatment, including insufficient medical insurance, scarcity of treatment centers, lack of childcare during treatment, stigma, fear of detection, and loss of child custody. As a result of these barriers, drug-using pregnant women are likely to avoid medical care.[93] Their concerns are justified, given that 17 states have laws that categorize substance abuse during pregnancy as a form of child abuse, and in three states it is grounds for civil commitment.[94] Any laws or policies that dissuade women from seeking prenatal care can have negative effects for both women and children. Native American women like Leah already receive lower levels of prenatal care than do white women; limited prenatal care combined with elevated levels of alcohol and tobacco use during pregnancy contribute to high rates of infant mortality for Native women.[95] As a policy matter, children's health would be better served by investing less time and resources on the criminalization of substance abuse and of poverty, and shifting these resources to mental health services and the drivers of substance abuse disorders (like trauma, poverty, chronic stress, and adverse childhood events).

Jenna and Adam's case reveals many of the ways in which poverty and substance abuse intersect in the prosecution of parents for infant death. Jenna used alcohol and marijuana during her pregnancy and had multiple investigations by Child and Family Services involving her four children. When visited by social service agents prior to the infant's death, the home was deemed as meeting "minimum standards of care" but was without heat, and all of the family slept downstairs. Jenna and Adam admitted to using alcohol and marijuana before sleeping with their four-month-old child, and both had alcohol in their systems (Adam's blood alcohol level significantly higher than Jenna's) when tested. The infant's death was attributed to unexpected death in infancy with a history of co-sleeping, but prosecutors argued that the baby was smothered by one of the intoxicated parents. The judge clearly agreed that substance abuse had caused the death, telling Jenna that she had "failed as a mother," and Adam that he was "just failing period," concluding that "the baby's dead because the two of you were stoned and dead drunk."[96]

Jenna and Adam's lawyers pushed back against the narrative presented by the courts. They argued that the government was overstepping its bounds by intruding into family life, and was trying to tell individuals how to parent. The attorneys may have been responding in part to statements made to the media by the county coroner, who blamed the infant's death on his assumption that either Jenna or Adam drunkenly rolled over on and suffocated the baby. The coroner also told the media that he was personally "against" co-sleeping. These statements resulted in a response to the relatively small midwestern newspaper by none other than anthropologist James McKenna, perhaps the best-known proponent of co-sleeping in the United States. McKenna's letter to the newspaper argued that the coroner's comments were generalizations that were meant to stigmatize parents for co-sleeping. McKenna noted that while the coroner may have a personal opinion about co-sleeping, it did not align with that of millions of Americans who routinely co-sleep safely.

McKenna pointed out that while the AAP condemns co-sleeping, the practice is accepted by the World Health Organization and UNICEF in part because co-sleeping facilitates breastfeeding. McKenna's letter to the newspaper is interesting not only because he was responding to a specific case in which infant death was attributed to co-sleeping, but also because his letter attempted to put co-sleeping back into its broader context. McKenna's account stands in contrast to the way that co-sleeping is routinely described by law enforcement and the courts, where it is attributed to laziness and selfishness, and cast as an obvious risk to children. For example, police and prosecutors in the cases studied here described co-sleeping as a "willful disregard of a known, unjustified, and extremely high risk"; "irresponsible," and evidence that mothers are "unwilling to make sacrifices." These statements reflect a neoliberal discourse in which individuals are personally responsible for managing risk, and women in particular are culpable for children's health. The statements also assume that individuals experience risk in similar ways, however Jenna and Adam's living situation make clear that this is not the case. As Deborah Lupton argues, "Risk discourse tends to assume universal experience and ignores social differentiations, such as ethnicity and social class. Yet there is a class difference in the manner that people are exposed to risk: wealth may buy safety from risk while poverty attracts risk."[97] There is also a gender difference in responsibility for managing risk. In *Using Women: Gender, Drug*

Policy, and Social Justice, Nancy Campbell contends that mothers who violate gender norms by using drugs are marked as "spectacular failures" requiring intensive government intervention.[98] "Good mothers" are expected to be constantly vigilant, foreseeing and preempting the risks of everyday life.[99] Mothers whose children die while co-sleeping are framed as having chosen risky behavior over the safety of their children. McKenna provides a counterpoint to readers, many of whom are likely to have shared a bed with their own infants, in which co-sleeping is not necessarily pathological. However, Jenna and Adam's case, like many others, suggests that co-sleeping is a suspect practice when parental substance use and poverty intersect.

Previously Counseled

ELIZABETH

Elizabeth was 25 years old, living in the South, when her 18-day-old son died in her bed after she fell asleep while feeding him a bottle. The medical examiner attributed her son's death to "possible overlay" and co-sleeping. Elizabeth had also lost her first child, a 13-day-old daughter, in similar circumstances. The medical examiner described this death as an accident due to "probable overlay" and co-sleeping. Elizabeth was charged with felony aggravated manslaughter of a child; like most parents in this study, she attempted to plead to a lower charge. In an unusual turn, the judge rejected her initial plea, which would have resulted in a six-month jail sentence and 15 years of probation. He later accepted a no contest plea to neglect of a child with great bodily harm, and sentenced her to four years in prison and six years on probation.

AMBER

Amber, a 28-year-old white woman living in the Northeast, was initially charged with the suffocation death of a child after her two-month-old son died of asphyxiation while sleeping alone on a couch. Although this death did not involve co-sleeping, Amber served 85 days in jail after pleading guilty to contributing to conditions that caused a child to be in need of assistance. Five years later, another son died at age two months while sleeping in bed with Amber and her three-year-old daughter. Amber pled no contest to felony counts of involuntary manslaughter, criminal homicide, and child endangerment, and received a sentence of 11–22 years of incarceration, and two years of probation.

In at least 15 of the cases in this data set, news media reported that the accused parents had been counseled against co-sleeping prior to the death of their child. For the purposes of this project, "previously counseled" refers to any documentation that a parent received safe sleep education before the death of their child. As this section will discuss further, safe sleep education/counseling was often either provided by hospital staff after the birth of a baby, by a pediatrician after parents "admitted" to co-sleeping, or mandated by social services when a child was injured or died. Having received some form of safe sleep education was consistently presented as evidence of higher-order negligence on the part of the parent. In Elizabeth's case, the death of her first child prompted this additional counseling by medical professionals and other authorities. Media reports make clear that the counseling Elizabeth had received served as evidence that she had committed a crime; as the county sheriff told news media, Elizabeth was given a "pass" in the death of her first child, but continuing to co-sleep after multiple warnings meant that she was wantonly risking the life of her second child.

This statement was consistent with that made by law enforcement or court officials in many other cases: Previous counseling was a mitigating factor in the sentencing order for one defendant and was mentioned in an arrest affidavit for another. Parents in two separate cases were noted to have violated the contracts they signed with social services in which they agreed not to co-sleep; in another case, a district attorney said that co-sleeping after being counseled equated to "an extreme indifference to the value of human life." Other examples of the response to parental disregard for safe sleep education abound (and some will be discussed below), but as these suggest, parents who were educated about safe sleep are seemingly less sympathetic to the courts and more culpable for the death of their children.

As advice against co-sleeping has gained public health traction, some hospital maternity wards are moving toward a model in which all new parents are educated about safe sleep before they can be discharged with their infant. In 2010, Pennsylvania passed the Sudden Infant Death Syndrome Education and Prevention Program Act, which required that hospitals and birth centers provide parents with educational materials about safe sleep prior to discharge, and that parents sign a statement acknowledging receipt of these materials, one copy of which remains on file at the medical center. The act notes that hospitals and birth centers will not be criminally or civilly liable if a parent does not follow the advice offered in these educational materials but makes no similar guarantee for the criminal or civil liability of parents. Other states that have legislated safe sleep education in hospitals include California, Florida, Illinois, Michigan, Nebraska, and Texas; these laws primarily require providers to distribute materials such as pamphlets or videos that explain the risk of SIDS, and how to reduce these risks.[100]

The Pittsburgh-based organization Cribs for Kids, which depicts itself as instrumental in passing Pennsylvania's law, describes this legislation as the cornerstone of its Hospital Certification Initiative. The initiative offers hospitals three certification levels (Certified Safe Sleep Hospital, Certified Safe Sleep Leader, and Certified Safe Sleep Champion) based on their compliance with and leadership on providing safe sleep policies, staff training, parental education, and supplies such as cribs.[101] The Cribs for Kids certification program criteria also note that provision of safe sleep materials must be documented in a patient's chart. An interactive map of Safe Sleep Certified hospitals on the organization's website shows dozens of locations around the country.

City health departments are also promoting safe sleep education in hospitals. As discussed in chapter 3, Baltimore, Maryland's "B'More for Healthy Babies" Campaign, for example, is considered a model for success in reducing infant mortality rates. The campaign, described as "an integrated model of policy, service, community, and individual behavior change," has included standardized safe sleep education at all Baltimore birthing hospitals since 2010.[102] Individual hospitals have also instituted such measures; a community teaching hospital in Boston, for example, launched an initiative to increase safe sleep education that provided safe sleep training to nursery staff, ensured "bed checks" in hospital nurseries, and required parents to watch a video about safe sleep and sign a statement of commitment to the "ABC" (babies sleep Alone, on their Back, in a Crib) model. Documentation that parents have signed the statement of commitment then becomes part of the patient's electronic hospital record.[103]

The impetus behind educating parents about safe sleep is surely a worthy one; hospitals, health departments, and organizations like Cribs for Kids want to reduce the likelihood that infants will be placed in what the AAP defines as unsafe sleep environments. Yet multiple cases within this data set demonstrate an unintended consequence of mandatory safe sleep education. The documentation that parents have been advised on safe sleep practices then follows the family as part of their medical history or case file, and can be weaponized as evidence of informed negligence should a child die. And yet advice is exactly what this is; bed-sharing is not against the law in any state in the country, and is indeed touted as the best way to promote breastfeeding and bonding by popular parenting philosophies like attachment parenting.[104]

In other words, mandatory education about co-sleeping becomes a form of reproductive duress. I define reproductive duress as occurring when individuals or institutions in positions of power apply pressure or enact constraints that limit the agency of those making reproductive or parenting decisions. Parents who want to leave the hospital with their baby have little alternative but to accept the safe sleep materials, but doing so signals that should they decide not to follow these guidelines, they have made an informed choice to risk the life of their child. That this documentation could be used against a parent is not just theoretical; the district attorney prosecuting one mother in this sample said that his decision to proceed with criminal charges was *based on* the fact that she had received counseling about co-sleeping while in the hospital. Because of this, he claimed, he would have indicted her for criminally negligent homicide and second-degree manslaughter even if she had not been using drugs.

Amber was also counseled about safe sleep before being discharged from the hospital, by social services, and by her pediatrician six days prior to the death of her second child. Amber's lengthy prison sentence is remarkable given that she was not under the influence of drugs or alcohol at the time of the child's death. It was undoubtedly impacted by the repeated documentation that she received safe sleep education, as well as the fact that she had previously lost a child to SUID. News coverage of Amber's trial also highlighted her other deviations from ideal motherhood, including having had seven children (five surviving) with multiple fathers by the age of 30. The judge who sentenced Amber was particularly disturbed by her refusal to defer to safe sleep guidelines, stating, "It has taken two dead babies . . . for you to finally, I hope, accept that you don't always know better." The district attorney stated that Amber "lacked common sense," contending that "there are other alternatives to sleeping on top of a child." While the judge criticized Amber for valuing her own judgment over that of experts, the DA suggested that she does not care enough to consider alternatives to co-sleeping. The DA also framed the child's death as a specifically gendered failure, contending that "the child relied on her as a protector, and [Amber] betrayed the ultimate bond between a mother and a child."

Amber's mother offered an alternative perspective in an interview with news media. She argued that the death of Amber's first child was unrelated to the sleep surface (essentially contending that the child died of SIDS rather than positional asphyxia or accidental suffocation), and that the fear of SIDS was what motivated Amber to co-sleep. This framing repositions what the courts interpreted as arrogance, noncompliance, and carelessness as instead maternal nurturance and concern. Amber's mother also noted that people disregard safe sleep guidelines every day without being criminally charged. Her statements normalize a choice that law enforcement described as "an extreme indifference to the value of human life." They also imply that some parents may be more vulnerable to criminal prosecution than are others.

In addition to maternity wards and pediatrician's offices, parents may receive mandated safe sleep education through interactions with social service agents such as Child Protective Services. Counseling in this form will disproportionately target low-income parents who interact with the state in order to receive public resources such as subsidized childcare, publicly funded health care, or nutritional assistance. Because poor families do not have the economic flexibility to rely on private services rather than public ones, "poor people's lives may be subject to greater public scrutiny than their middle- and upper-class counterparts."[105] Like parents who are required to receive safe sleep education before leaving the hospital, parents who are counseled not to co-sleep by agents of the state have limited agency to refuse such directives, which are then documented and can be used against them.

The potential for safe sleep education to be used against parents was also evident in the proposed Wisconsin bill that would have criminalized co-sleeping while intoxicated. In its companion bill, healthcare workers and nonprofit organizations were required to counsel pregnant women or new parents on the dangers of co-sleeping. As part of this counseling, parents would be provided with printed and audiovisual materials about co-sleeping while intoxicated, and would be given a form stating that they had been advised of the dangers and would share that information with any other caregivers. The bill stated that no signature line would be included on the form, which alleviates some concerns that this information could be used against parents at a later date. However, the person who provided the materials would be instructed to note in the individual's medical records that they had been counseled, creating documentation that could potentially be used in a criminal investigation.[106] Given this, the proposed bill in Wisconsin had the potential to further the weaponization of safe sleep education, despite the fact that this requirement was seemingly included in order to gain buy-in from skeptical public health constituencies in the state.

In *Fixing Families*, sociologist Jennifer Reich notes that mothers who are enmeshed in the child welfare system are expected to perform deference to case workers and to be empowered to make good choices in order to be reunited with their children. However, the level and parameters of acceptable "empowerment" are limited; if women become *too* self-directed or self-confident, they may make choices that do not align with the goals of the state. This concept speaks to the punitive (even if unintended) effects of mandatory safe sleep education. Parents are expected to defer to the expertise of organizations like the AAP that determine safe sleep guidelines, and to be empowered by the education they receive from hospitals, pediatricians, and case workers to make good choices for their children. But if mothers trust too much in their own expertise and are unfortunate enough to experience the death of a child, then their decision to act against the education they received is framed as exponentially more irresponsible. As Reich argues, "being empowered and deferring to the state are incompatible."[107] This is clear in the cases of mothers who argued that they co-slept, despite being counseled against it, when their children were sick, because they feared losing another child to SUID, or because they were nursing. Although these reasons are identical to the reasons that thousands of other parents co-sleep without incident every night, with the hindsight provided by the child's death, the conclusion drawn by the courts is that these parents had every reason to know better.

I identify this statistically infrequent but vicious cycle of mandatory safe sleep education, infant death, and prosecution of parents as a form of reproductive duress. It is one that aligns directly with the contemporary neoliberalization of health, and the expectation of self-governance, which requires individuals to manage their own likelihood of encountering risk through personal responsibility and self-actualization. As Debra Cossman argues, "the very logic of health care policy is increasingly premised on this individualized model, and those who fail to self-regulate are at risk of being constituted as blameworthy, failed citizens."[108] In our current "age of responsibility," parents who were previously counseled about the dangers of co-sleeping and then do so anyway are held exponentially more responsible for any negative outcome that might occur, regardless of the relatively low risk of death and pervasiveness of the practice. The neoliberal ethos of accountability and personal responsibility are "now a way to coerce people to engage in the right, responsible behavior—with the threat of punishment never too far out of sight."[109]

In Elizabeth's case, the punishment meted out by the judge also included the provision that she should have no contact with minors, and that any children born to her during her incarceration or probation would be surrendered to the state. The judge clarified that "no contact with minors includes your own children." The provision that a mother cannot have contact with minors, including her own future children, is more common in cases in which mothers have had their parental rights terminated. The Adoption and Safe Families Act of 1997 allowed courts to terminate an individual's parental rights based on that parent having previously lost custody of a different child, such that "a parent's past actions are conclusively determinative of future conduct."[110] Unsurprisingly, judges are more likely to restrict the reproductive decision making of women than of men.

According to reproductive justice scholar Rachel Roth, courts have restricted women's reproductive autonomy for three primary reasons: child abuse and neglect, criminal activity not involving children, and drug use, with the majority of cases falling under the category of child abuse.[111] Elizabeth had not previously had her parental rights terminated, but seems to have been treated similarly because of the death of her children. Including this provision as part of the plea agreement severely constrains Elizabeth's future reproductive autonomy, given the length of her sentence and probation. This provision is also reminiscent of controversial judicial decisions that require the use of birth control as a condition of probation. Norplant, the first long-acting reversible contraceptive, gained notoriety in the early 1990s when a California judge gave a defendant the choice of seven years in prison or one year in jail followed by the implantation of Norplant.[112] Elizabeth's plea agreement utilizes reproductive coercion through the threat of terminated parental rights, rather than potential jail time.

The criminal justice response to parents whose children die after they were counseled against co-sleeping is troubling. This model produces an uneasy precedent for other public health issues; in this political moment we can surely imagine a future in which women who are educated about the risks of potentially procreative sex are then prevented from accessing Plan B or access to abortion should they "choose" to become pregnant (and of course this is very close to reality for the thousands of women whose de facto access to contraceptives has been slowly eroded in the last several decades). In the interest of public health, parents should be able to welcome education about infant safety without the threat that this education will be used against them should the worst outcome occur. And for some parents in this data set, the worst outcome occurred more than once.

Multiple Deaths

TYLER AND SHARON

Tyler, age 28, and Sharon, age 27, are an African American couple living in the Western United States. In 2014, the couple's first son died while sleeping in bed with his parents. His death was listed as undetermined, but the medical examiner noted that it occurred in what the AAP defines as an unsafe sleep environment. When their second child also died in an unsafe sleep environment two years later, the medical examiner stated in an interview that he could not determine the cause of this death either, but that both were "likely" caused by accidental suffocation. The second death led law enforcement to revisit the death of their first child. Sharon, pregnant with her third child, was convicted of misdemeanor child abuse and reckless endangerment in the death of her second child and was sentenced to 18 months of probation. Tyler pled guilty to misdemeanor child abuse in that case and was sentenced to 270 days in jail.

CARRIE

Carrie was 33 years old and living in the Southern United States when she was charged with felony involuntary manslaughter. Within 18 months, Carrie had lost two children to SUID, with both deaths occurring while co-sleeping. Police and family members suspected that her history of alcohol abuse played a role in the death of both infants. She received a suspended sentence of 10–21 months and five years of probation, including the provision that she does not have custody of children under the age of five.

Like Carrie, Tyler, and Sharon, Elizabeth (whose case was summarized in the previous section) was also one of eight families in this data set (over 25 percent) who were reported to have lost more than one infant to SUID. This history was cited in the news coverage and court documents as evidence that the parent had committed a crime. For example, the affidavit used in Elizabeth's arrest noted that she was being charged with a felony because her son "was killed in the same manner as her first child . . . due to her own culpable negligence and without lawful justification." Evidence that Elizabeth had been previously counseled during her first and second pregnancies (by Department of Health staff, case workers, hospital staff, and a primary care doctor) was listed seven times as probable cause evidence in her arrest affidavit.[113] The county sheriff was likewise quoted as saying, "She was irresponsible and as a result, she's got two dead babies. It's time for her to go to prison. It's time for her to pay the price," and "This lady doesn't get it. Because of this lady's recklessness, because of her disregard of all the instructions and rules, her second child died and that's why criminal charges are brought against her today." Poor mothers in particular are expected to practice austerity and self-discipline in every realm of their lives if they want to raise their own children;[114] mothers who have lost multiple children are portrayed as unwilling to sacrifice their own comfort or desires to protect their babies. Like Amber, who was sentenced to 11–22 years in prison after her second baby died of SUID, Elizabeth received one of the lengthier sentences in this data set, at four years.

Tyler and Sharon were another couple who were charged with the death of two infants after their second child died in a manner similar to their first. The senior deputy district attorney in charge of the case focused explicitly on personal responsibility and individual behavior as the cause of the children's death, stating, "Parenting is one of the most important responsibilities you'll ever have. It requires you to make sacrifices, requires you change your behavior, and requires you to put someone other than yourself first. Sadly, [Sharon] was unwilling to do these things, and as a result she put her son's life at risk." Sharon was described as a smoker and heavy drinker who had consumed alcohol during her pregnancy and been arrested for driving under the influence.

The arrest affidavit also implicated Sharon's gender failure by returning repeatedly to the unkempt state of the house. Several paragraphs were spent describing the home as "filthy," and scattered with trash, dirty diapers, empty liquor bottles, and cigarette butts. As discussed earlier, a well-kept and clean home is considered a measuring stick of maternal dedication in American culture and is also cast as a matter of a woman's personal work ethic, moral standing, and unselfish demeanor. This, of course, erases the differential access to resources that allows wealthier mothers the option to outsource this responsibility (often to lower-income women and women of color) and to afford to rent or buy homes that are not neglected or environmentally hazardous due to lead paint, rodents, or insects. Notably, this attention to home cleanliness has long haunted SUID parents. In *Rest Uneasy*, Brittany Cowgill notes that in the 1960s, when SIDS researchers began visiting bereaved parents after the death of an infant, they were often assessing the home environment for cleanliness and hygiene, and the mother for her perceived level of "appropriate" grief. She argues that in the 1960s and '70s, "lower-class and minority families were distinctly disadvantaged and mistreated in the aftermath of SIDS," and in the rare instance that a family was criminally charged for the death, they were either poor, people of color, or both.[115]

Like in other cases, Sharon and Tyler's affect was also presented as evidence of criminality. The arrest affidavit contends that Sharon was not upset as paramedics attempted CPR on the child, but rather was "mad," and that at the hospital neither Sharon nor Tyler were "panicked or crying." Because care for a child's well-being is considered foundational, even "natural" for parents (particularly for mothers), for the police report to describe the couple as uncaring is particularly damning. Black women are also stereotyped as angry in American culture, which is often a way to silence them and delegitimize their feelings and lived experiences.[116] A few sentences later, however, the report notes that both parents threatened suicide upon learning that the child had died, and were hospitalized on a mental health hold. The report does not attempt to reconcile these two emotional poles, or acknowledge the wide range of responses to shock and trauma that might be expressed by parents. In this case, as in Elizabeth's, the death of a second child serves as evidence of parental negligence, and failure to put the needs of the child first. In sociologist Jennifer Reich's study of parents in the child welfare system, she found that Child Protective Services wholeheartedly embraced the dominant construction of mothers as naturally self-sacrificial, nonviolent, and nurturing. Women implicated in the CPS system were thus inherently "bad mothers."[117] Sharon is similarly always-already a bad mother as described in this police report—her home is unkempt, her affect is wrong, and *her child is dead*. Sharon's guilt requires no further investigation based on cultural standards of what it means to be a mother.

In Elizabeth's, Carrie's, Tyler's, and Sharon's cases, of course, they have lost not one child but two. While one can understand intuitively why two deaths may appear more suspicious and concerning than one, some research suggests an increased susceptibility to SIDS among siblings of SIDS victims. While this link is still debated among SIDS researchers, some findings indicate that the likelihood of SIDS death is up to four times higher among SIDS siblings than the general population,[118] and others indicate an increased incidence among siblings of two to ten times.[119] The AAP's Task Force on Sudden Infant Death Syndrome cites an "87 percent probability that a second SIDS death within a family would be of natural cause," and thus "the task force supports the position that the vast majority of either initial or second sudden unexpected infant deaths within a family seem to be natural rather than attributable to abuse, neglect, or homicide."[120] Moreover, the Triple Risk Model would suggest that these SIDS siblings may have had a genetic predisposition to SIDS that interacted with a critical stage of development (the infants' age), and an environmental stressor such as overheating or the presence of bedding and pillows. Because SIDS and accidental suffocation are physiologically indistinguishable from one another, medical examiners often must rely on other information, like evidence of substance abuse or sleep location, to reach a cause of death. Even when substance abuse and SIDS/accidental suffocation are correlated, it does not mean that parental substance abuse causes these deaths. That being said, medical examiners are not coming to conclusions outside of socially constructed beliefs about motherhood; if only "bad" mothers drink or use drugs, then the evidence of this behavior points to maternal culpability. Legal scholar Emma Cunliffe argues that "bad moms" play an important role in SIDS discourse; medical research has failed to conclusively determine the cause of these deaths, and mother-blame fills that explanatory space.[121]

Carrie was quite clearly identified as a "bad" mother in the press. She was reported as having four arrests for drunk driving, and her ex-husband and other family members explicitly blamed the death of her two sons on her alcohol abuse. Carrie told hospital staff that she must have rolled over on her first son, a four-month-old who suffocated while sleeping with her. The medical examiner initially categorized this death as accidental suffocation, but state officials later changed the cause to "undetermined." Carrie's second son, an eight-month-old, also died while co-sleeping with her, this time on the couch; she reported that she awoke to him lying face up in her arms (as opposed to clear positional asphyxia, such as face down, or trapped between her body and the cushions). His death was ruled to be accidental suffocation with co-sleeping as a contributing factor. The county attorney prosecuting the case explicitly stated that charges were brought because of the multiple deaths, saying, "She's had two infants die and so that automatically makes this case different from folks who have an isolated incident of a child's death."

Interestingly, Carrie's case was taken up by a state newspaper as an example of the failure of medical examiners in the state to appropriately investigate infant deaths. The newspaper was not necessarily arguing that Carrie was not responsible for the deaths, but rather that, as her ex-husband said, "If there had been any serious investigation after [Child One] died, I feel like [Child Two's] death wouldn't have happened." An investigation by the newspaper revealed that state medical examiners rarely conduct death scene investigations, which are a requirement for a death to be categorized as SIDS, and sometimes are not the ones to conduct an autopsy. They found that medical examiners had visited the scene of only 2 percent of infant deaths in the year prior to the publication of the article, relying on law enforcement to perform tasks such as death scene reenactments and interviews with parents. Nearly a dozen national experts interviewed for the story noted that police officers are not medically trained and do not have the experience with infant death cases that a trained medical examiner would bring to a death scene investigation. The medical examiner in charge of investigating the deaths of Carrie's sons also did not conduct a death scene investigation or speak to the parents after either death, although a deputy coroner did visit the home after the second child died. The newspaper also notes that Carrie was not charged with her son's death until their reporters began investigating. While Carrie's case raises the issue of how infant deaths are investigated, it also reiterates the question of why parents would cooperate with death scene investigations—which are critical for researching and potentially preventing further unexpected infant deaths—if participating puts them at risk for prosecution. The article ends with a quote from Carrie's lawyer, who would not allow her to speak with the press, but concludes that "no matter what happens, everybody loses."

Conclusion

If we return briefly to the contemporary medical understanding of SIDS, researchers believe that SIDS is likely to occur when an infant with an intrinsic vulnerability is exposed to an environmental stressor at a critical stage of development.[122] Many of the environmental and intrinsic factors that make an infant vulnerable are also characteristics that overlap with poverty, including pre- and postnatal exposure to cigarette smoke, premature birth, and low birth weight. These factors are often outside of the control of individual parents who may lack access to affordable nutrition, comprehensive prenatal care, and smoking cessation aids, or who also experience the daily stress of racism and poverty that contribute to negative birth outcomes. Despite these structural factors, the correlation between SIDS and poverty has long been attributed to bad parenting, and particularly bad mothering by poor women. Historically, "crib death" was attributed to the immorality and vice of poor mothers, if not outright neglect or infanticide.[123] As theories about SIDS were developed, researched, and sometimes abandoned throughout the mid-twentieth century in the United States, "SIDS correlations with certain groups of people (such as lower-class Americans) and certain behaviors (such as smoking) contributed to colloquial assumptions that SIDS was associated with 'lower home standards . . . and . . . a lower standard of infant care."[124]

Today, the lingering association of unexpected infant death with parental culpability remains, and poor parents and parents of color continue to be those families deemed likely to harm their children. Because there is no biomarker or autopsy finding that distinguishes SIDS from accidental suffocation, differentiating the two relies on the investigation and interpretation of individuals. These investigations are not always standardized, and categorization of infant death varies widely.[125] Even when these individuals are equipped with the expertise and opportunity to fully investigate an infant death, they still do so within a culture that stigmatizes the parenting practices of the poor. Moreover, because substance abuse and being a "good mother" do not align in American culture, evidence of drinking or drug use is assumed to have contributed to the death of an infant even when no definitive causation exists. And all of this is happening amidst a diagnostic shift from SIDS to accidental suffocation that has created a pathway for the prosecution of parents whose characteristics or behaviors mark them as socially deviant.

The prosecution of parents for co-sleeping deaths reinforces the multiple layers of law, policy, and discourse that distrust and even criminalize parenting by poor women. They shore up the "moral construction of poverty"[126] and rely on gendered constructions of good mothers. And more broadly, they contribute to a neoliberal paradigm of health that overemphasizes personal responsibility at the expense of structural causes of poverty, substance abuse, and infant mortality. Despite the failure of bills that would streamline these prosecutions, as intended in Wisconsin, it is clear from this data set that existing legislation can and is being used to prosecute co-sleeping deaths, and that safe sleep education is being weaponized as evidence of parental failure. Fetal protection efforts by states provide a chilling example of how old laws have been reinterpreted, expanded, and applied in ways that criminalize pregnant women, and new laws utilized in unintended ways—the effects are potentially harmful not only to women but also to fetuses and children if they dissuade women from seeking out medical care or substance abuse treatment.[127] If safe sleep education is used as evidence to prosecute parents for unsafe sleep deaths, parents may attempt to avoid such counseling and hospitals and public health educators may hesitate to provide it in ways that can be tracked or documented. In the short term, we must advocate for parental access to safe sleep education that is community-led, culturally competent, and completely divested from the criminal justice system or any form of surveillance and tracking. On a broader scale, we must support collective action to interrupt the criminalization of poor women's reproduction, which is definitively tied to racial justice. If we fail to do so, this data set demonstrates that the parenting practices of poor people are already and will continue to be criminalized, and with results in which "everybody loses."

5

Advertising Infant Safety

Gender, Risk, and the Good Parent

In an episode of the British science fiction television show *Black Mirror*, a single mother experiences a scare when her young daughter wanders away from a playground and is briefly lost. After this close call, the mother opts to have a cutting-edge technology called Arkangel implanted directly into her daughter's brain. The device streams biometric data, location tracking, even a livestream of everything in the child's field of vision, to a tablet that her mother can monitor 24 hours a day. While the implant cannot directly protect her daughter from harm, the mother experiences relief and a renewed sense of security due to the steady stream of data and seamless surveillance that the device provides. Given the mistrust of technology that animates this dystopian series, it is not surprising that the experiment does not end well, to say the least.[1] The premise of the *Black Mirror* series is to demonstrate the potentials of technology that lay just in the future; technologies that do not exist yet, but are not hard to imagine using in a few years' time. Kurt Workman, the chief executive of the baby care company Owlet, also imagines a future in which parents have greater access to their children's biometric data. Owlet sells "peace of mind" to new parents through a wearable baby monitor—a "smart sock"—that transmits an infant's biometric data such as heartrate and pulse from the device to the parent's cell phone via Bluetooth technology. Workman anticipates that "the wearable future will include every single baby coming home from the hospital with a health monitor."[2] Workman's prediction may be feasible—as of 2020, Owlet reported that it had tracked more than 600,000 babies using their smart socks, priced at $299 each.[3]

As this convergence of dystopian science fiction with contemporary technology suggests, today's parents are expected to be fearful and anxious about the safety of their children. At the same time, they are inundated with information about how to mitigate perceived risk. Safety is increasingly tied to proffering up one's intimate data for measurement, cataloguing, and health assessment. Parents are advised that using technology to log a baby's hours of sleep, breathing patterns, temperature, or heart rate will give them advance notice of illness or abnormality. Despite the reality that infant mortality is greatly stratified by race in the United States,[4] infant safety products are marketed as if every baby is equally vulnerable. Moreover, the use of biometrics in everyday life is increasingly normalized as a security tool; many mobile device users unlock their phones via a fingerprint or facial recognition scan, and the Transportation Security Administration (TSA) plans to roll out facial recognition software at airports across the country.[5] Feminist theorist Shoshana Magnet defines biometrics as "the science of using biological information for the purposes of identification or verification."[6] Digital biometrics acquire biological information through the use of technology, and then store the data for further analysis by individuals, corporations, or the state. Biometric surveillance is frequently used to sort populations, and to maintain boundaries or borders; it relies on the disaggregation of the body into pieces of data.[7] As Magnet notes (and thoroughly critiques), the public has received messages from scientists and the technology industry that biometrics are essential to our safety, and that they protect us from twenty-first-century threats like crime and terrorism.[8]

In the arena of health and wellness, biometric devices supposedly protect us from more intimate and internal threats that may be lurking even when our children sleep.[9] The Juvenile Products Association reports that the infant safety industry, which includes tech products like infant wearables as well as blankets, sound machines, and cribs, is valued at more than $325 million a year.[10] The infant safety industry has grown alongside campaigns like Back to Sleep, which have demonstrated that despite the well-documented difficulty of changing individual behavior, a certain proportion of caregivers will make sleep-related changes if convinced that doing so will reduce risk. The labor of responding to shifting safe sleep guidelines is undeniably gendered; research on the gendered division of childcare suggests that mothers are likely to be responsible for selecting devices like baby monitors, and of "monitoring" the monitor when it is in use.[11] Parents receive messages that the world their families inhabit is increasingly insecure, and the burden of addressing each new risk is disproportionately undertaken by mothers.[12] Mothers receive messages from advertisers and the media that they will be empowered through consumerism; they may engage in what sociologist Norah MacKendrick terms "precautionary consumption," aware that it is their own responsibility to find the best products to optimize their children's health.[13] As the baby safety technology industry reinforces the message that sleep is risky, "good" mothers are pressured to become experts in mitigating this risk, primarily through their role as consumers.

Previous chapters have outlined the emergence and shifting nature of safe sleep guidelines, the attendant public health campaigns meant to encourage public compliance, and the potential criminal consequences for certain groups of parents when they fail to do so. A neoliberal, consumerist health agenda isolates the individual family unit from the broader social determinants of health, such that the prevention of negative outcomes is framed as a matter of positive lifestyle choices. Moreover, private companies profit from market-based solutions to social problems, whereas structural and systemic fixes come at an economic and political cost. The market has long recognized the value in products that tap into parental anxiety, and thus safe sleep messaging that focuses on how parents can change their behaviors (like influencing the sleep environment) rather than structural and systemic change (like the stress of racism, or environmental hazards) aligns neatly with consumer-based, privatized solutions to which access is stratified by class.

This chapter builds on that argument, using Owlet, a wearable infant monitor, as a case study. I analyze Owlet's marketing materials, including videos, product descriptions, frequently asked questions, and disclaimers, as well as the images of parents, babies, and safety devices on the website. Through a feminist science studies–informed analysis of infant wearables, and the marketing of Owlet in particular, I argue that the contemporary moral imperative of health intersects with both the biomedicalization of infant sleep and the gendered expectations of intensive motherhood. In other words, infant sleep is increasingly framed as necessitating medical and technological intervention, and mothers are responsible for making sure they get it. These trends explain in part why products like Owlet gain traction, and also why parents are stigmatized and potentially criminalized when their children do *not* sleep safely. Companies that sell infant sleep safety benefit from neoliberalism in ways that extend beyond the relentless focus on personal responsibility for health. They are also operating within a regulatory environment in which such products can be sold without FDA approval, and tech companies can utilize consumers' data with few limitations. It is important to note that while I focus on Owlet in this chapter, it is not this specific product that I locate as the "problem"; the Owlet Smart Sock could be pulled from the market at any time (as many other wearable devices have been). However, the economic, political, and cultural attitudes and values about parenting and personal responsibility that it signals would remain intact, and continue to inform practice, policy, and law.

The Evolution of Monitoring Sleep

Since their inception, baby monitors have been reflective of the anxieties of the time period in which they are created. The first ever baby monitor, called the "Radio Nurse," was released by the Zenith Radio Corporation in 1937. The Radio Nurse was intended to reduce risk and lessen parental anxiety; after the Lindbergh baby was infamously kidnapped from the family's home in 1932, Zenith's president requested that his team of engineers create a listening device for nurseries.[14] The Radio Nurse was not successful with the public, with flaws that in some ways would foreshadow the privacy and surveillance concerns about contemporary high-tech monitors. The device utilized the same radio frequency as garage door openers and car radios, such that the drivers of passing automobiles could potentially listen in to the baby's nursery. Given that the monitor was invented to prevent kidnapping, parents were concerned that they might be transmitting the location of their sleeping infant.[15]

As the Radio Nurse demonstrates, infant safety products have long been tied to socially constructed beliefs about threats to the well-being of children, often focusing on the exceptional rather than the mundane. As historian Peter Stearns outlines in *Anxious Parents: A History of Modern Childrearing in America*, the highly publicized murder or kidnapping of children (like the Leopold and Loeb murder of a Chicago boy in 1920, or the Lindbergh kidnapping) heightened parental anxieties despite their infrequency. By the 1970s, the child or teen runaway captured national attention, aided by the introduction of the iconic milk carton campaign, meant to bring home missing children by having their images appear on kitchen tables across the country.[16] The 1980s marked a shift from "child provision," or government programs that supported women and children, to "child protection," which encouraged the private sector and nonprofits to fill the gap by offering individualized solutions for child safety.[17] As this suggests, while some of these issues reflected cultural panics out of proportion to the actual threat posed to children, the attention they received also reflected cultural priorities about which children were worthy of care and concern. The more mundane threats posed to poor children and children of color by poverty and institutional racism such as unequal access to education and mass incarceration were less likely to be sensationalized in sympathetic ways. Instead, parents during the Reagan era were warned by media, law enforcement, and the government about kidnapping and child exploitation, reinforcing the notion that "the world was not secure for children."[18]

The private sector responded by producing child safety products, including an early wearable device produced in 1985 called the Kiddie Alert, which allowed parents to attach a transmitter to their child—if the child wandered further away than the pre-set range of 25–200 feet, an alarm would sound.[19] It presumably took some time for the popularity of such monitors to take off, given that even in 1987, devices like the Gerry Baby Safetronics Deluxe Baby Monitor ($50) were described as "electronic luxuries" by the *New York Times*. By 1999, however, the same newspaper described audio baby monitors as "ubiquitous," while predicting that in the future, television would take over this task and offer a "picture-in-a-picture" of the sleeping baby on the living room TV screen.[20] In the 2000s, baby monitors did indeed evolve from audio-only to include video (albeit primarily on a device-specific handheld screen). This innovation was met with skepticism by, again, the *New York Times*, which described the $200 Graco I-monitor Digital Color Video Baby Monitor as "Truman Show-esque," referring to a 1998 film in which Truman Burbank, played by Jim Carrey, finds out that he has been under constant surveillance since birth as the unwitting star of a reality television show.[21]

Despite such concerns that monitors may be too invasive, research suggests that parents utilize them for a variety of reassurance-related purposes. Sociologist Margaret Nelson, who interviewed nearly 100 parents of varying socioeconomic status, found that while contemporary parents may spend time agonizing over *which* baby monitor to buy, the vast majority never consider foregoing a device altogether.[22] Nelson also analyzed reviews of baby monitors on a product review website and found that parents report utilizing monitors because they view babies as either in need of care, or requiring adjustment and control. Babies are posited as inherently at risk—Nelson specifically cites the risk that babies will stop breathing—and thus require constant surveillance. Monitors serve as harm reduction, which "involves a range of behaviors from managing factors that predispose illness to preventing illness from transforming into more serious problems."[23] Parents can gain a sense of agency and control over their feelings of vulnerability if they believe that a monitor can preempt illness or death. These findings demonstrate how an ethos of risk management has permeated parents' consumer choices, as has the assurance that parents can mitigate risk by taking personal responsibility for managing safety.

Monitors are utilized as risk management devices by parents who may believe that these devices can reduce the risk of unexpected infant death. Nelson analyzed online reviews of baby monitors; she found that parental anxiety was a leading motivator for their purchase. As one parent wrote, she and her husband "were nervous wrecks because of the SIDS risk."[24] An audio- or video-based monitoring system does not actually have the potential to prevent SIDS, but because new parents are socially conditioned to be "nervous wrecks," and encouraged to alleviate anxiety through consumerism, this quote makes sense. It is reflective of the uneven history of medically monitoring vulnerable infants, the perceived fragility of infant life, and the powerful symbolism of baby monitors as a risk reduction tool for anxious parents.

Monitors of a different type have been used in relation to SIDS as recently as the 1980s, which may explain the public perception that a baby monitor can reduce the risk of SIDS death. Brittany Cowgill's *Rest Uneasy*, a detailed history of Sudden Infant Death Syndrome in the twentieth century, outlines how a now-discredited theory of SIDS led to widespread use of home breathing monitors in the 1970s and '80s. These monitors, which attached to the infant through wires that detected vital signs, were first prescribed in the early 1970s. During this time period, the theory that SIDS was caused by irregular breathing, or apnea, had taken hold among US SIDS researchers. As a result, thousands of families with high-risk infants purchased cardiorespiratory monitors that could supposedly alert parents if their infant stopped breathing. Monitors were prescribed for children who had been diagnosed with "near miss" SIDS deaths, irregular breathing, or were the siblings of babies who had died of SIDS.[25]

Critics of the home monitors argued that they were ineffectual at preventing infant death, produced false alarms, were expensive, and were stressful for parents. The physician who popularized these devices acknowledged that they were not always effective for SIDS prevention; in language reminiscent of that used by Owlet today, he said that he recommended them "based less on a conviction that home monitoring would prevent SIDS than as a way of reducing the anxiety of parents."[26] Using the monitor tied parents to their home whenever their infant was asleep, often kept them awake throughout the night by triggering dozens of alarms per day, and caused marital and financial stress. Despite these significant deterrents, parents reported that the alarms decreased their anxiety and gave them a sense of control; "for them, the possibility that a monitor could save their child far outweighed whatever problems the device may have introduced . . . they perceived that every time they responded to an alarm, they were saving their child's life."[27] As Cowgill's research demonstrates, the efficacy of a monitor in reducing risk may not directly correlate to the perceived value for parents.

The use of home cardiorespiratory monitors gradually declined (although never entirely dissipated) as evidence of their efficacy failed to materialize, and the American Academy of Pediatrics issued a statement in 2003 that such monitors should not be used exclusively for the prevention of SIDS.[28] While the apnea theory of SIDS lost support, parents continued to worry about whether their newborns were breathing, and thus continued to utilize commercial baby monitors and other child surveillance systems. The twenty-first century has been marked by a boom in the baby technology industry, due in part to the increased processing power of which small devices are capable.[29] Contemporary baby monitors include features like two-way audio, HD video that can be streamed on multiple devices, a log of how long the baby slept, video tracking of the baby's breathing patterns, data on the humidity and temperature in the baby's room, and syncing with devices like the Amazon Echo to remotely control night lights and lullabies.[30]

The Market for and Marketing of Wearable Infant Monitors

While monitors have become increasingly sophisticated, it's worth a reminder that they are designed to be used with healthy babies. Unlike the apnea monitors of previous decades, today's commercial monitors are not selected because a baby has specific risk factors. Rather, they exemplify an anticipatory notion of risk, and a belief in the power of pre-detection. According to sociologist Dorothy Nelkin, anticipatory risk requires healthy individuals to foresee future dangers and act upon them in advance, often through a reliance on medical experts (or, in this case, pseudo-medical devices). Doing so "depoliticizes" risk, situating risk reduction as an individual mandate as opposed to a public health or community concern.[31]

Notably, the market for baby tech also aligns with what is accepted among adult consumers, such as the popularity of wearable technologies as a fitness accessory.[32] The impetus behind these devices, that health is a fluid and ever-changing project of the self, requiring proactive self-discipline, is normalized by contemporary "wellness" culture. Wellness evokes lifestyle trends like raw juice cafes, oxygen bars (where individuals can pay to inhale "pure" O_2), or Westernized adaptations of yoga and meditation. While the core concepts of wellness culture date back to what was known as "life reform" in nineteenth-century Europe, the modern concept of wellness is linked to the 1950s. It was then that Dr. Halbert L. Dunn differentiated wellness from health, arguing that while health is the "absence of illness," wellness refers to an "active, ongoing pursuit."[33]

In addition to the "lifestyle" marketing of trends in diet, fitness, and mental health, the concept of wellness has also been adopted by corporations that encourage or even require employees to participate in workplace wellness programs to reduce stress, lose weight (and potentially save money on insurance costs).[34] In other words, while wellness is in many ways an individual project, it has also been institutionalized in ways that benefit corporate hegemony. Other institutions, such as schools, are also introducing biometric self-tracking to children, where they might wear a heart rate monitor in gym class that informs the teacher on whether the class is meeting targets.[35] Wearables encourage data collection at the micro level (the number of steps taken, ounces of water consumed, hours of sleep per night), and "promise greater control over health, safety, and emotional well-being through intimate data gathering."[36] As biometric tracking and data collection become increasingly normalized as a responsible way to maintain wellness, it is little surprise that parents would adopt similar technology for their infants.

The market for wearable infant monitors has seen multiple new entrants in recent years. Brands include Mimo, which monitors sleeping position, body temperature, and breathing rate through a turtle-shaped sensor attached to a baby's clothing ($200); Monbaby, which tracks respiratory motion and sleep position via a button attached to clothing ($170),[37] and the Snuza Hero ($110), which monitors a baby's breathing through a device that clips to the infant's diaper. Other devices, like Sproutling, which measured heart rate, skin temperature, motion, and sleep position via a leg band ($300), or Baby Vida, which used pulse oximetry to detect oxygen saturation levels ($150), have been removed from the market after disappointing sales or quality concerns. Baby Vida was created by Mollie and Jeff Evans after their twins contracted a respiratory illness that required the parents to check frequently on the infants' breathing.[38] As will be discussed below, their company went out of business after a widely disseminated study in the *Journal of the American Medical Association* revealed that the device was almost entirely ineffective. Efficacy aside, the price tags associated with these monitors arguably stratify access to them, marking them as high-status goods likely to end up on the baby registries of upper-income parents. As such, they reinforce the uneven playing field on which women compete to be considered "good mothers" even if all mothers are expected to live up to the same socially constructed standards.

This chapter will focus on Owlet because it is the leader in the wearable monitor industry and offers the best-selling line of Owlet Smart Socks. Owlet was founded in 2013 by four male graduates of Brigham Young University, and launched its first "smart sock" device in 2015. The smart sock is now on its third generation, which can be bundled with an Owlet "cam" (a video monitor that streams to a parent's smartphone), or each device can be purchased a la carte. The third-generation Smart

Sock uses a pulse oximetry device strapped to the infant's foot (what they call the "sock") to track the baby's heart rate, oxygen levels, and sleep duration. The pulse oximetry device in the Owlet Smart Sock is similar to the monitor that might be attached to one's finger at a doctor's office to check the oxygen saturation level of blood. Low oxygen saturation is known as hypoxemia, which can result from breathing trouble. Pulse oximetry data from the Smart Sock then transmit via Bluetooth to a base station, which parents can livestream through Owlet's app on their smartphone. Parents receive an alert from the app if the sock's reading leaves what Owlet terms "the safe zone." The Owlet app provides "historical information" mined from the Smart Sock to the parent. This app collates weeks, months, or years of an infant's biometric data, allowing parents to take a "proactive" approach to their infant's health, to "analyze sleep trends and analytics." Parents are encouraged to review the data in order to make choices about when to put their baby to bed, or how long to let them nap. When parents are not using the app (like while they sleep), they are alerted to any potential problems via the Owlet base station. This device glows green if the smart sock does not detect abnormalities, or triggers an alarm with sounds and lights if, as its website says, "something appears to be wrong." When the camera and Smart Sock 3 are purchased together, parents can combine the pulse oximetry data with high-definition video, two-way audio, and a room temperature sensor.

If today's parent is urged to amass, track, and record data about their infant in order to maintain perfect vigilance, then Owlet's success may lie in its promise to offer valuable, and otherwise unknowable, insights into a child's health. The main page of the Owlet website includes an image of the smart sock, the base, and a smartphone with the app open, next to the phrase "knowing is best." This phrase conjures up, but subtly alters, the saying "father knows best," suggesting that the knowledge produced by technological monitoring is superior to the "instincts" of a parent, or even the sensory "data" that parents have historically relied on—their eyes, their ears, the touch of their hands. It also implies the antithesis, that without this technology, a parent lacks knowledge about their baby, and thus may be unable to provide the best care. As Magnet argues, "unlike the unruly material body, biometric bodies offer up a text," or "a thing, a more easily governable entity."[39] Owlet transforms the biological processes of each infant into data, and encourages parents to read and interpret the data in order to understand and respond to their baby. Digital data are perceived to be more trustworthy because they are supposedly neutral, accurate, and objective; even a non-medical device can exude scientific or medical authority.[40] While many new parents express frustration when they do not know what their infant wants—are they hungry? Uncomfortable? Sick?—Owlet transforms the messiness and unknowability of infant care into the clean lines and clarity of a line graph.

According to a study conducted by researchers affiliated with Owlet, 75 percent of parents reported that they use the monitor for "peace of mind."[41] What constitutes "peace of mind" is somewhat nebulous, however. Given that the device measures oxygen saturation levels, one might assume that Owlet provides parents with peace of mind that their child is healthy and breathing. As previously mentioned, the shadow of SIDS hangs over infant sleep, and many new parents obsessively check their child's breathing out of fear of this little-understood disease. However, Owlet does not directly claim that the "peace of mind" that it provides is that which comes from knowing one's baby is safe from SIDS. This is intentional, given that Owlet is marketed as a consumer device—one not regulated by the FDA—rather than a medical one.

Medical versus Lifestyle Devices

Owlet carefully walks the line between marketing its product as exclusively a lifestyle/general wellness device or a safety product, potentially broadening its prospective audience by appealing to parents who want both. As a lifestyle device, Owlet promises parents more and higher quality sleep, based on the cultural script that all new parents are perpetually sleep-deprived.[42] As a safety device, Owlet spokespeople acknowledge that their products cannot prevent SIDS. The Owlet user agreement, which consumers accept when they are "purchasing, installing, downloading, or otherwise accessing" their products, states that the products are not medical devices:

> They do not and are not intended to diagnose, cure, treat, alleviate or prevent any disease or health condition, or investigate, replace, or modify

anatomy or any physiological process. They are consumer products intended to promote general well-being. Never use our Products to replace
good parenting, common sense, or appropriate medical care.[43]

This statement seeks to indemnify Owlet from any responsibility for
injuries or deaths that occur while the product is being used, while
also implying that such harm would result from parental failure (to be
"good" parents, to use common sense, or to seek out medical treatment)
should it occur. On the other hand, Owlet researchers argue in a peer-
reviewed journal that "this type of monitoring can provide parents and
physicians valuable information about infant health, potentially alert
when an infant is in crisis and enabling timely interventions."[44] The
carefully negotiated wording speaks to the slippery way in which terms
like health and wellness are used in contemporary American culture,
and how weighted they are with moral implications.

Consider two messages: First, that the best way to ensure an infant's
health is to monitor their vital signs while they sleep. Alternatively, that
only negligent parents let their newborns sleep with no medical monitoring, and risk missing the warning signs of a serious health emergency.
In *Against Health*, Jonathan Metzl and Anna Kirkland define heath as "a
concept, a norm, and a set of bodily practices whose ideological work is
often rendered invisible by the assumption that it is a monolithic, universal good."[45] They argue that when behaviors are framed as "health"
issues, a "wider set of assumptions" can be made about an individual's
actions and choices.[46] Essentially, Metzl and Kirkland argue, utilizing a framework of "health" allows the latter message to be embedded
within the former, such that health-related decisions are intimately tied
to morality, character, and worth. Peter Conrad likewise links health to
morality, and contrasts medicalization with health promotion. Unlike
medicalization, which constructs a biomedical solution for what was
once a social problem, health promotion "proposes behavioral or lifestyle changes for previously biomedically defined events."[47] The focus
on behavioral or lifestyle change aligns with the rhetoric that individuals
are capable of shaping health outcomes. Rather than waiting passively
to detect illness in a child, parents have a moral imperative to track and
collect data, and technoscientifically monitor their infant's health *prior*
to illness.

Wearable monitors are also advertised as offering parents "peace of mind," suggesting that if parents adopt the practice of using a Smart Sock, for example, they may at minimum reduce their own anxiety and potentially mitigate their child's risk of serious illness. Owlet emphasizes its supposed stress reduction benefits on social media platforms, like Instagram, where influencer moms and mommy bloggers share sponsored posts echoing how Owlet provides them with peace of mind, reduces their anxiety levels, and allows them to sleep without worry.[48] Tama Leaver likewise finds that Owlet utilizes endorsements from microcelebrities on the Owlet blog who write sponsored testimonials about their own use of the product. The content produced by these microcelebrities, Leaver finds, is all organized in formulaic ways with similar photographs, messaging, and repetition of phrases like "peace of mind."[49] Emotional and mental health is central to contemporary claims about wellness, which promise that the pursuit of health will reduce anxiety and increase agency and self-efficacy.[50] Whether or not technology like wearable monitors actually improves infant health becomes secondary to the sense of wellness that they ostensibly provide.

The way in which technological innovation and biological data collection differentiate wearable monitors from traditional monitors also marks this as a form of biomedicalization. Practices of biomedicalization centralize the potentials of technoscience to transform health and bodies, both through treatment and enhancement or optimization.[51] Wearable monitors reflect the biomedicalization of infant sleep safety by emphasizing the optimization of health and the anticipation of risk through technoscience. As Clarke and colleagues argue, health and illness are "becoming individual moral responsibilities to be fulfilled through improved access to knowledge, self-surveillance, prevention, risk assessment, the treatment of risk, and the consumption of appropriate self-help and biomedical goods and services."[52] As this definition suggests, it is not just disease but *health* that can be biomedicalized, as we see in the consumer biomedical monitoring of healthy infants. Clarke et al. argue that while health is seemingly more biomedicalized as individuals increasingly screen, surveil, test, and track their health at home, it may be perceived as less medicalized *because* it happens at the home rather than the clinic, and is administered by oneself, rather than by a physician.[53] This may feel like the perfect middle ground for anxious twenty-first-century parents who have integrated technology into their homes and bodies for decades. Wearable monitors offer a biomedical safety net that is seemingly appropriate for all infants, without medical supervision.

Of course, Owlet cannot make specific claims about its ability to prevent illness because it has not been approved as a medical device by the Food and Drug Administration. However, to ascertain that the device is a consumer rather than a medical product, consumers will have to do some virtual digging. The "Frequently Asked Questions" page on Owlet's website includes the query, "Does Owlet guarantee the safety of my baby?" paired with the answer, "No . . . the Smart Sock is not a FDA-approved medical device and is not intended to diagnose, cure, treat, alleviate or prevent any disease or health condition or investigate, replace or modify any physiological process. You are responsible for the health and wellbeing of your baby and following safe sleep, health, and care guidelines." The disclaimer page also notes that the device's "notification thresholds" are "not as stringent as a medical monitor," despite another FAQ about pulse oximetry that compares the Owlet device to a pulse oximeter at a doctor's office. These statements seemingly counter other claims made on the website that the Smart Sock can assure parents that their baby is okay, in part by pivoting to each parent's personal responsibility. Because Owlet is marketed as a consumer device, the company does not have to support the claim that they can reliably alert parents if a baby's heart rate or oxygen level has changed, that they allow parents to "see" a baby's breathing patterns in real time, or can assure parents that a baby is "sleeping soundly."[54] It is not hard to imagine that parents who do not read the fine print, carefully peruse the website, or look up corporate disclaimers may perceive the device as a piece of medical equipment. In contrast, the executive director of the ECRI Institute, which protects consumers from unsafe medical technology, describes Owlet as "more like a toy in the way it's being regulated."[55]

Pediatrician Christopher Bonafide and colleagues note, however, that the FDA may have the authority to regulate infant wearables if they choose to do so, given that "apps that transform a mobile platform into a regulated medical device" are within their oversight, including apnea and breathing monitors, and oximeters.[56] Given this, Bonafide et al. argue, products like Owlet could be classified as a FDA class II medical device which "requires that the makers demonstrate 'substantial equivalence' to a legally marketed device."[57] For now, the Owlet disclaimer notes that the Smart Sock "assists" rather than "replaces" the parent, followed by a list of ways that the monitor should not be used, like on infants who have been prescribed an apnea monitor or pulse oximetry device by a physician, or as an "excuse" for unsafe sleep habits. The Smart Sock, the makers argue, is intended for healthy babies, to produce insights into wellness rather than prevention of disease. This statement, of course, belies the circular logic of their marketing strategy, in which healthy babies are always at risk of becoming sick babies, and thus require constant monitoring.

Research on the reliability of the wearable monitors reveals mixed results. A study published in the *Journal of the American Medical Association* compared the efficacy of Owlet and Baby Vida (which, as previously mentioned, has since been pulled from the market) to that of an FDA-approved pulse oximetry device. The study tested Owlet and Baby Vida on 30 infants that were hospitalized for non-life-threatening conditions by using an FDA-approved device on one foot, and switching between the two consumer devices on the other foot. They found that Owlet detected hypoxemia (low levels of oxygen in the blood), but did so inconsistently, while Baby Vida failed entirely to detect the condition, and gave incorrect low pulse rates.[58] Bonafide, a co-author of the study, concluded that "there is no evidence that they'll help kids, and there's some evidence of potential harm," including that parents will fail to use evidence-based SIDS prevention measures, and incur expensive and unnecessary trips to the hospital based on false or misleading alarms.[59] Critics point out that the makers of wearable monitors benefit for the gray area in which they operate. Medical device evaluator David Jamison argues that "we're letting companies make a lot of money by making an end-run around the FDA. It [a wearable infant monitor] looks and smells like a medical device, but we're not going to call it that."[60] The ability of corporations to avoid regulation is a key component of neoliberal economic policies;[61] as discussed in chapter 2, the makers of infant safety devices benefit from a system that presumes that the industry will set appropriate safety standards and guidelines.[62]

The American Academy of Pediatrics also objects to the use of wearable infant monitors. Their 2016 safe sleep guidelines continue to warn against the use of any home cardiorespiratory monitor and state that such monitors have not proven to detect SIDS risk even when utilized in hospitals by trained staff. The statement concludes that "there are no data that other commercial devices that are designed to monitor infant vital signs reduce the risk of SIDS."[63] When asked directly about these devices by the media, Dr. Rachel Moon, the chair of the AAP's task force on SIDS, has replied that there is no evidence that the devices work. She also raises concerns that parents will not follow evidence-based recommendations to prevent SIDS. Moon states, "we're worried people will become complacent. If they have a monitor they might feel they can put their baby on its belly to sleep, or sleep with their baby."[64] Some media outlets report limited evidence that parents may do just what Moon fears. When contacted by the *Washington Post*, the founder of a popular safe sleep group on Facebook acknowledged that he has seen a "significant" proportion of parents admit that they engage in what the AAP considers unsafe sleep practices because they are also using a wearable monitor.[65] These reports are, of course, anecdotal, and also return to the AAP's broader underlying assumption that parents can only be trusted with one message about infant sleep safety, and that is ABC (Alone, Back, Crib). If wearable devices are perceived to undermine the existing safe sleep guidelines, it is unlikely that the AAP would endorse their use.

Despite these limitations, Owlet's website prominently features parental testimonials to "sell" the life-saving capabilities of the device. Parents are uniquely situated to promote the product, because their authority is personal and experiential rather than medical or scientific. As the public's trust in the impartiality of medical authorities has declined in recent decades, the appeal of patients (or in this case, parents) as marketers for medical products has grown.[66] Parents can offer testimonials as to what they *believe* the product was responsible for—even saving their child's life—and have no clear incentive other than gratitude for the health of their infant. Owlet's parent testimonials are situated next to adorable photos of (primarily white) babies who have benefitted from the device; one father reports that he took his baby to the hospital after receiving an alert of a high heart rate, leading to a diagnosis of Wolff-Parkinson-White Syndrome. This father is also identified as an Emergency Medical Technician (EMT), lending medical authority to his experience.

The message these testimonials generate is that infant sleep is inherently risky, and that parents have a personal responsibility to mitigate that risk by monitoring their child. Laura Mamo, Amber Nelson, and Aleia Clark argue that corporations produce risk in order to justify the need for their product; they demonstrate this through an analysis of Gardasil, the vaccine that protects against human papillomavirus (HPV). The makers of Gardasil construct girlhood and girls' bodies as at risk, and the HPV vaccine as a common-sense and empowering form of risk reduction. Once the vaccine is on the market, parents have a "moral responsibility" to access it for their children, or they are failing to protect the health of their daughters' bodies.[67] Wearable monitors contribute to a similar neoliberal imperative; if monitoring and surveillance can allegedly alert parents to a life-threatening risk, then the device is more akin to a car seat (a moral—and legal—requirement) than a traditional baby monitor. Owlet frames the Smart Sock as a commonsense safety product through the language and imagery used on its website.

For example, the website's homepage features a laughing mother playing with an Owlet-wearing baby girl, next to the phrase "Know Your Baby is OK: Track your infant's heart rate and oxygen levels while they sleep." A logical interpretation of that tagline would be that (a) infant sleep is risky, (b) Owlet *can* accurately and consistently track heart rate and oxygen levels, and (c) knowing an infant's heart rate and oxygen levels will also allow you to know that the infant is "ok" (read: not at risk for infant death). Watching the app conflates the baby with the data; if the data are at a normal baseline, then the baby is "ok." This elision is a core component of biometric self-tracking and surveillance, in which "the distinction between the body as 'thing' and the digital representation of that 'thing' is leveled out."[68] For example, in one parental testimonial a mother writes, "each time I wake up at night I glance over at the base station and I'm reassured by the green light that all is well." According to this logic, checking on the green light is equivalent to checking on the baby; the totality of the baby's needs are ensured by the absence of risk, which is promised by the presence of the green light.

Wearables also posit monitoring as equally necessary for all infants, because all parents require the "peace of mind" that the products purport to ensure. According to Miranda Wagonner, the practice of anticipating risk is increasingly common in contemporary medicine, "with the distinct feature of treating otherwise healthy populations as if they are already potentially diseased."[69] Healthy infants, in this case, are anticipated to be always at risk of illness or death, and thus this risk must be dealt with before it emerges. If, as I have argued, "peace of mind" equates to health and safety during sleep, then the infant safety industry would have consumers believe that all infants require monitoring because illness or death can strike at any time. However, this message elides the very unequal risk of infant mortality in the United States. According to the Centers for Disease Control and Prevention, rates of infant mortality for African American babies are 11.4 out of 1,000 live births, followed by American Indians/Alaskan Natives at 9.4, Native Hawaiian/Pacific Islander at 7.4, Hispanic infants at 5.0, non-Hispanic white infants at 4.9, and Asian infants having the lowest levels of infant mortality in the United States at 3.6 deaths per 1,000 live births.[70] All infants in the United States are not equally likely to experience life-threatening illness or unexplained crises while they sleep; in fact, Black and Native American children are twice as likely as white infants to succumb to SIDS.[71]

The market for infant wearables suggests that the ability to mitigate the risk of infant mortality is in the hands of individual parents, accessible through the purchase of appropriate safety products. Yet, as chapter 3 discussed in greater detail, racial disparities are far more reflective of intersecting, structural causes of infant mortality such as racism and poverty than they are of individual behaviors. Waggoner found a similarly false "leveling of the playing field" in her analysis of the CDC's preconception campaigns, arguing that, "if every woman is optimized and every risk anticipated, certain populations still will be at disproportionate risk due to other underlying causes, such as pollution, structural racism, lack of access to quality, stable health care, family planning services, or nutritional food."[72] Owlet and the other makers of wearable monitors are private companies, not influential government agencies, and thus are clearly held to a different standard; they are not tasked with promoting the health of the nation. However, the rhetoric produced by these companies becomes part of a larger health discourse in which the social determinants of health are downplayed in favor of personal responsibility and individual choice-making. And, of course, buying the right products is the purview of individual mothers.

Normalizing (Maternal) Anxiety

Worry and anxiety about infant safety are gendered as specifically maternal tasks in contemporary American culture. That is not to say, of course, that fathers do not worry (or that all families consist of a mother and a father), but rather that American society is set up in a way that encourages mothers to be physically and emotionally tied to the infant stage of childrearing. Feminist theorists have written extensively on the economic, political, and cultural forces that contribute to the social construction of motherhood, including essentialist views that frame women as inherently caring, empathetic, and self-sacrificial.[73] As Sharon Hays argues, even as women take on greater responsibilities outside of the home, they are expected to engage in "intensive mothering" that is expensive, all-encompassing, and informed by expert advice.[74] Susan Douglas and Meredith Michaels term this the "new momism," which romanticizes motherhood as a totalizing and fulfilling identity, while upholding expectations that no mother could ever achieve.[75] Tasha Dubriwny ties gendered expectations of motherhood to health, arguing that neoliberalism and postfeminism intersect such that women are framed as both vulnerable *and* empowered, although the form that this empowerment takes is consistently tied to traditional gender roles of wife, daughter, or mother.[76] Infant wearable monitors are an extension of intensive mothering and the new momism because they situate infant sleep as an activity that mothers must constantly attend to, gather data on, analyze, and perfect.

As this suggests, wearable monitors have the potential to extend women's physical and emotional labor; users and critics note the work involved in attending to the positioning and placement of the monitor, troubleshooting technological issues, and adjudicating false alarms.[77] There is also the time commitment and emotional labor of assessing the data that are compiled by the device itself. Owlet's app provides parents with extensive information about their infant's sleep history, including the total hours of sleep, the number of times the baby woke, and color-coded graphs of when the baby was in light versus deep sleep. Parents can view the infant's average heart rate and oxygen levels, as well as the highs and lows for both 24 hours and a one-month period. The app offers graphs that detail the time and duration of "red notifications," or an alert of high or low heart rate, or low oxygen saturation. A male voice on a video on the company's website instructs parents to "review this data and make adjustments in your routines as necessary" over the image of a woman intently scrolling through information on her smartphone. On "red notifications," the video admits that "these notifications can be scary, but now you can analyze the events that led up to the notification and react accordingly," this time over the image of a different mother holding a baby in one arm while calmly perusing the red notification data with her other manicured hand.

While the model moms who have already adopted the Smart Sock are represented as stress-free, the marketing of Owlet normalizes "worry" as any mother's natural state of mind. In a video advertisement for the Owlet 2, released in March 2017, an actor (and one of the few Black individuals in Owlet's marketing materials) introduces the device while holding a five-month-old baby girl, stating "she should be falling asleep right about . . . now. But there's no need to worry." Despite this assurance, the ad situates sleep as risk—at some point, all babies will sleep, thus all babies will be at risk. Indeed, this ad performatively *constitutes* worry through the unquestioned assumption that a sleeping baby should reflexively spark parental anxiety. "Worry" can only be mitigated through purchase of the Owlet Smart Sock 2. The video also relies on scientistic (as opposed to scientific) visuals—tracing the pathway of the infant's pulse and heartbeat from her body, to sock, to smartphone—that imbue the Smart Sock device (which is not particularly techie-looking) with technoscientific authority.

Men are part of the audience for the product but are less of a central presence than the ever-present concerned mother. Owlet's website, for example, uses gendered stereotypes to market its product to dads, such as a blog post titled "Why This 'Tech Head' Dad Purchased the Smart Sock." The app video also includes two men—one tattooed, hipster dad scrolls through the app while holding his baby, and a male doctor, seated at his desk, peruses a printout of the data. While it is entirely possible that both mothers and fathers would utilize the app, Wilson and Yochim argue that an effect of neoliberalism is the focused pressure on mothers to act as the "security guards" of their families, in charge of the "worry work," often by relentlessly seeking out information, advice, and opinions that will purportedly keep their children safe.[78] Mothers already use digital media like parenting websites, mommy blogs, or social media as sources that they hope will provide reassurance (although they often intensify anxiety instead); wearable data offer another avenue for this "infoglut" of intimate knowledge. The sheer amount of data provided by the Owlet app assumes that a parent will undertake the emotional labor and time necessary to "respond accordingly" to changes in the rhythm of their child's sleep or the beating of their heart. The constant stream of data and updates produced by the device reinforces women's socially constructed responsibility for infant health, and their primary role as mothers.[79]

The seeming imperative to utilize these devices is reminiscent of early twentieth-century "scientific motherhood," in which mothers track, measure, weigh, and record data about their children, but rely on scientific and medical experts to assess the meaning of this information.[80] In this case, the experts are technological rather than human; as the Owlet website contends, "We build products to tell parents what their babies can't." Unlike scientific mothers of the late nineteenth and early twentieth centuries, however, contemporary scientific parents are offered "peace of mind" by technology that also amasses their children's biodata and makes it available for corporate data-mining. Scientific motherhood was followed by theories of maternal attachment that implied that a mother's every reaction (or lack thereof) to her child could have lasting consequences.[81] The idea that the slightest parental misstep could lead to stunted development, or even death, aligns neatly with the marketing of infant wearables, which suggest that parents need to know their baby's heart rate and pulse in "real time," as well as "historical analytics and trends."[82]

This information is framed as empowering, utilizing a postfeminist appropriation of the term. Postfeminism "appropriates the language of feminism as it undermines feminism's radical impulse toward structural transformation," while it also "makes women exclusively responsible for ongoing structural inequities."[83] Owlet makers take up the language of feminism and other social justice movements, as in their mission statement, "empowering parents with the right information at the right time," or their tagline, "Join the movement." This strategy is not new; as sociologists Josée Johnston and Judith Taylor have demonstrated, companies ranging from Virginia Slims to Dove have linked their products to notions of empowerment, social responsibility, and emancipation, regardless of their true transformative potential.[84]

Feminist empowerment, however, is driven by collective action and social change. The empowerment offered by products like these is inherently individual and reflective of postfeminist consumerism. As Safiya Noble argues in *Algorithms of Oppression*, "new, neoliberal conceptions of individual freedom (especially in the realm of technology use) are over-supported in direct opposition to protections realized through large-scale organizing to ensure collective rights."[85] The imagined future of infant wearables is not conditioned on interdependence, movement-building, or collective organizing for structural change, but rather on individual, consumer-based "protection" stratified by class access. Monitors create a façade of insulation between the individual child and the environmental and social determinants of health. The baby is pried apart from the data, while the data benefit no one outside of the individual family. Parents who use digital biometrics to protect their children provide no "herd immunity" to the community at large. And while this may be true of dozens of decisions that parents make or products that they buy, not all apply a feigned veneer of social justice.

At the same time that mothers are encouraged to "join the movement" for safe sleep, a backlash against the over-surveillance of children is clearly present online. In addition to the dozens of "best of" baby monitor lists online are also numerous articles that mock mothers who shell out for expensive devices; as a writer on *Mashable* observes, "It's worth remembering that babies have their own built-in technology for telling you they're awake or need your attention—it's called screaming."[86] This position is echoed on other websites and blogs; *Popsugar* answers the question, "You know what's a good baby monitor?" with the tongue-in-cheek response, "a baby." The writer concludes that if you put your baby to bed and then continue to watch your baby on a video monitor, "you've truly failed."[87] As with many other facets of motherhood, women are simultaneously taught that they are individually responsible for maintaining the welfare of their child, and should spare nothing to do so, while also ridiculed as "helicopter," "lawnmower," or "snowplow" parents when they comply.

Within this Catch-22 of motherhood, the "bad mommy" of films like *Bad Moms* and *A Bad Moms Christmas* emerges—she lets her kids eat sugar cereal, she swears, she drinks (within reason), and she has a life outside of her child. As Tasha Dubriwny notes, however, our cultural construction of the "bad mommy" (or what Dubriwny terms "risky motherhood") is not the same as the "bad mom." The bad mom is poor, often a woman of color, and a potential danger to her children; the "bad mommy" is irreverent and imperfect, but ultimately devoted to her children. The "bad mommy" in the *Popsugar* article, for example, can mock intensive motherhood by dismissing the need for a high-tech monitor, but she also reports racing to her infant's room when she hears the baby being sick, and wondering if the monitor would have allowed her to respond faster. Women with higher social status can playfully adopt the "bad mommy" persona, given that race, class, and heterosexual privilege offer leeway that other women do not have. However, as Dubriwny finds in her analysis of mommy blogs, even "bad mommys" ultimately return to "the myth of the good mother: women are first and foremost mothers, and mothering is fulfilling and natural."[88] Within this context, wearable monitors up the ante for parents who can afford the steep price tag. Mothers are expected to feel anxious if they do not have the latest technology, but also a bit guilty at their own overzealousness if they do.

Technology and Surveillance: Where Do the Data Go?

Managing risk also means accepting and even encouraging surveillance in constantly evolving ways. Such monitoring has been termed "intimate surveillance," or "the purposeful and routinely well-intentioned surveillance of young people by parents."[89] Intimate surveillance *produces* data, or "dataveillance," which is accessible to the corporation as well as the parent.[90] In *The Quantified Self*, sociologist Deborah Lupton differentiates what she calls "self-tracking" from other forms of "covert surveillance." Self-tracking, she argues, "involves practices in which people knowingly and purposively collect information about themselves, which they can review and consider applying to the conduct of their lives."[91] Coercive surveillance, in contrast, results "in data sets to which the subjects of monitoring do not have access."[92] The kind of tracking undertaken by infant wearable devices seems to be a merger of the two. Parents are collecting information about their children that they are able to review and then utilize to make informed decisions, but that information also becomes part of a larger data set that neither children nor parents can fully access.

Owlet's privacy policy (which many users likely agree to without ever reading) stipulates that user information is non-confidential, and all data are tracked, collected, and stored by the company.[93] The data collected include personal information, like the infant's blood and heart rate measurement whenever the Sock is used, as well as usage and device information, like IP address (which essentially tracks the user's physical location), browser settings and preferences, dates and time spent on the Owlet website, pages viewed, and more.[94] According to the privacy policy, users' data may also be used for both internal and external research, and may be shared with third party researchers in anonymized or aggregate form. As Leaver argues in "Intimate Surveillance," this collection of data essentially allows Owlet to profit twice from a single product; first, through the purchase of the device itself, then again through the "insights and analytics produced from the aggregated and analyzed data."[95] Their user agreement also notes that Owlet products are not "covered health services" and thus do not fall under the Health Insurance Probability and Accountability Act (HIPAA), meaning that data provided to Owlet are not considered "protected health information."[96] Owlet states that they are collecting the largest data set about infant sleep, health, and wellness that has ever existed, and will use it to find causes and cures for disease.[97]

Critics of digital surveillance, however, question the uses to which such data will be put. Journalist Jacob Silverman refers to the forces that control such digital technologies as the "invasive other," which objectifies individuals into a "data source capable of being parsed, scanned, assessed, and monetized by other, invasive interests."[98] Wearable monitors allow private corporations to begin collecting biometric data about individuals at birth, which could continue throughout the lifespan with fitness trackers, "smart" watches, and more. Information about an infant's sleep patterns, pulse, or heart rate may seem innocuous, but if combined with other data, such as medical records, could create "such potential harms as discriminatory profiling, manipulative marketing, and security breaches."[99] While Owlet claims that the data it collects will be anonymized and used to promote infant health, technology experts have warned that much of the data gathered by our smart devices are vulnerable to hacking, and in 2015, hackers livestreamed the feeds of over 1,000 video baby monitors online.[100] Owlet attempts to reassure parents concerning the possibility of hacking, noting that "Owlet's app uses a secure, encrypted connection to Wi-Fi, so you can feel confident only you and your family are watching, streaming, and receiving notifications."[101] Their user agreement, however, also notes that "no security measures are perfect or impenetrable and thus we cannot and do not guarantee the security of your information."[102] Owlet's makers are clearly aware that parents harbor privacy concerns about their camera's video feed and data access, and attempt to allay those concerns while also protecting themselves should a data breach occur.

Government regulators and the technology industry have argued that individuals are responsible for "privacy self-management," or ensuring for themselves that they have carefully read, assessed, and made an informed choice about whether handing over their data (or in this case, their child's data) is worth the potential loss of privacy.[103] This concept again returns to the notion of personal responsibility and individual choice rather than oversight or regulation. As Montgomery, Chester, and Kopp argue, the problem of safeguards for children "is particularly acute in the wearable field, as children might find themselves at the first line of data collection, in many occasions as the result of deliberate decisions or actions of their parents."[104] If a parent believes that a wearable monitor has the potential to save the life of their child, they may sacrifice one form of security for another. And children are being subjected to data collection to which they did not and cannot consent, without anyone's full knowledge of how it will be used in the future.

While the marketing for wearable monitors does not directly address SIDS or accidental suffocation, instead foregrounding wellness and "peace of mind," parents are clearly motivated to purchase infant monitoring products to tamp down anxieties about unexpected infant death. Parents fear that their baby's face will get covered by a blanket or swaddle, that they will roll over onto their stomachs, or just stop breathing for no reason at all. When parents evaluate their fears about infant mortality, it is unlikely that their own arrest or prosecution comes to mind. And this is of course for good reason, as most cases of Sudden Unexpected Infant Death are determined to be natural or accidental, and no one is deemed responsible for the outcome. However, based on the database in chapter 4, caregivers who do not fit socially constructed paradigms of "good parents"—especially those who are low-income or chemically dependent—are viewed with more suspicion when their children die in what is considered an unsafe sleep environment. Poor and justice-involved parents may have limited access to expensive safety equipment, while also facing greater scrutiny and state intervention into their parenting practices.

While infant wearables have not yet become the norm or expected standard of care, we can already find examples of how technology or the failure to use it is weaving its way into the law. Chapter 4 analyzed 29 cases in which the co-sleeping death of an infant led to criminal charges for a parent or caregiver—one such case indicates how monitors may impact the perception of a parent's culpability for unexpected infant death. The mother in that case was a white woman initially charged with involuntary manslaughter, endangering the welfare of a child, and recklessly endangering another person after her five-month-old daughter died in her sleep. The parents had been instructed to use a breathing monitor on the infant because they had previously lost a twenty-seven-day-old infant son, presumably to Sudden Infant Death Syndrome. As previously mentioned, breathing monitors have been roundly criticized as an ineffective tool in reducing rates of SIDS, and the AAP has stated that the efficacy of breathing monitors for siblings of SIDS babies is unproven.[105] In other words, there is no evidence to suggest that the use of the monitor would have had any impact on the baby's survival. The involuntary manslaughter charges were later dropped, and the other charges had the potential to be dismissed upon the completion of a probation program designed for first-time offenders. In this case, the defendant's lack of criminal history aided in keeping her out of jail, given the severity of the initial charges.

However, the focus on the defendant's decision not to use the prescribed breathing monitor sets an ominous precedent for parents whose children succumb to unexpected infant death. When a local news channel posted about the case on the social media site Facebook, over 100 comments included notes of sympathy and understanding, but also posts calling the mother a baby killer, and stating that she should be put on death row or be hung, with several citing the fact that she had not used the prescribed monitor. Nationwide, community and law enforcement responses to parental behavior differ widely by factors such as gender, socioeconomic status, and race, with some parents being arrested for letting their children play alone in the park, eat in a mall food court unsupervised, or wait in the car with an iPad. Should products like infant wearable monitors become the norm, will the "failure" to monitor one's otherwise healthy infant be considered a strike against grieving parents? Historical evidence reinforces this concern; Cowgill found that when cardiorespiratory monitors failed to prevent infant deaths in the 1970s and '80s, it was not uncommon for blame to fall on the parents, particularly if they were poor, unmarried, lacked health insurance, or were parents of color.[106]

While a breathing monitor is intended (successfully or not) to alert a parent if their child is in danger, politicians more recently have proposed using technology to monitor the parents. In Maryland, for example, a 2018 House bill linked substance abuse to risky co-sleeping, with technological surveillance of parents as the proposed solution. Parents suspected of substance abuse would be required to utilize a not-yet-existent phone app called "I'm Alive Today"; the app would generate automated daily messages that the parent must reply to in order to ensure that she is "conscious and able to care for" the child.[107] While the language of the bill does not mention co-sleeping, the delegate who proposed the legislation told media that he feared substance-abusing parents would co-sleep and suffocate their children. Delegate Mike McKay acknowledged that a parent "doesn't wake up in the morning and say, 'You know what, I'm going to get high and I'm going to kill my baby today,'" but that "if we can get a heads up on a daily basis that parents are unable to make good decisions today, we might be able to save some of those babies who have been dying at the hands of their parents."[108] The bill, which later died in committee, was opposed by the Maryland State Medical Association and the Maryland chapters of the American Academy of Pediatrics and the American Congress of Obstetricians and Gynecologists—those organizations raised concerns in part because the bill assumed an unproven correlation between opioid possession and child endangerment.[109]

As with the Arkangel technology in the episode of *Black Mirror*, infant wearables offer individual parents a sense of security and the impression of managing risk. The episode offers a cautionary tale about the price of peace of mind and the pitfalls of a technological solution for broader social problems. In our contemporary society, poor parents and justice-involved parents are being exposed to technology in punitive ways, while more privileged parents are urged to invite biometric surveillance directly into their homes, their nurseries, and their phones, and are promised that their privacy and data are a fair exchange for their peace of mind. Both groups of parents experience intensive responsibility to individually manage risk, but an individualized, consumer-oriented response to safe sleep obscures the patterns that reflect structural and systemic inequality between groups. An individualistic ethos encourages parents to think narrowly about the choices they can make to protect their children, even if those choices do not extend beyond their own nursery to their neighborhoods or broader communities.[110] The commodification of sleep safety reinforces the idea that risk is and should be manageable through private resources. It places increased pressure on mothers, relying upon and reinforcing gendered expectations of women's caretaking roles. Moreover, a neoliberal safe sleep agenda promotes the myth that health and safety are themselves commodities, race- and class-neutral, and equally accessible by all.

Conclusion

Rethinking the Safe Sleep Environment

The final chapters of *Losing Sleep* were written in 2020, amidst the ongoing COVID-19 pandemic. In addition to wearing masks and practicing good hygiene, Americans are urged to "slow the curve" of the disease by working from home, social distancing, avoiding crowded public transportation, having our groceries delivered, and perhaps paying an educator to teach our children in a closed "pod," to name just a few of the risk reduction strategies that are highly stratified by socioeconomic status. Despite the maxim that the virus does not discriminate, data show that people of color are testing positive and dying from COVID at rates that far exceed their white counterparts.[1] The fissures in public health that have been implicated throughout this book are laid entirely bare by the pandemic; many of the same conditions that correlate with high rates of infant mortality—residential segregation, environmental hazards, inadequate access to health care, poor housing conditions, overcrowding—are being identified as predictors of the spread and lethality of the coronavirus, especially in multiply marginalized communities. The United States was primed for a poor pandemic response, public health experts explain, because while the country spends excessively on medical care, "it spends less on the social drivers of health, such as supportive housing, education, early childhood care, public safety, the environment, and public health practice itself."[2] The result has been a country whose population is at higher risk for COVID, and an uneven spread of the disease through the population.

Women and children are being impacted by the coronavirus pandemic in ways that reflect gender roles and resource distribution. As many feminist public intellectuals have already pointed out, the intersections of race and class with gender are already glaringly obvious in this pandemic, with women shouldering the majority of increased child- and elder-care responsibilities without reprieve from paid work,[3] paired with conservative resistance to the extension of federal unemployment subsidies that they see as incentivizing people to stay home from work.[4] Leading health organizations like UNICEF and the World Health Organization warn that while children are at lower risk for serious illness from coronavirus, the global health implications of the disease on children's health are potentially massive. Pregnant and postpartum women are experiencing disruptions in healthcare access as a result of the pandemic, and children are receiving fewer vaccinations and checkups.[5] Early research suggests that COVID-related shutdowns may have reduced the number of premature births, which may lower infant mortality rates—but potentially only for mothers who had the resources and stability to stay home without experiencing major financial stressors.[6] Modeling by Johns Hopkins University has estimated that COVID-based disruptions in health care could lead to the additional deaths of 6,000 children around the world per day; the disease is not only wreaking havoc on the systems that support women's and children's health, but revealing the vast inequities that were already in place before the pandemic struck.[7]

While the federal government fails to take decisive action to mitigate the effects of COVID, Boston University epidemiologist Ellie Murray tells the *New York Times* that "it seems like they're passing off the responsibility for controlling the outbreak to individuals and individual choices."[8] Unsurprisingly, given the context provided throughout this book, the rhetoric of individual choice and personal responsibility has emerged forcefully in the discourse surrounding COVID. As with infant sleep safety, there is of course a role for personal responsibility and a mandate for individuals to do their part in ensuring the health of those around them. However, the focus on individual responsibility similarly serves to shift attention from underlying inequalities that create different levels of risk for different communities; as Murray also noted, "A pandemic is more a failure of the system than the failure of individual choices."[9] COVID-19 underscores the significance of recognizing and challenging neoliberal responses to health crises wherever they emerge.

* * *

This book has considered infant sleep safety from a variety of perspectives, including how the social construction of sleep safety has changed over time, who defines sleep safety and how, the ways that safe sleep is surveilled and policed in different communities, and how it is packaged and sold to us as consumers. Much of this research starts from a relatively well-established assumption that sleep safety is about infant survival—that a safe sleep environment is one in which risks for serious injury or death are reduced. Indeed, mainstream infant sleep safety research has moved increasingly toward models that focus on external risk factors and how to reduce or eliminate them.

This is in part reflected in the "diagnostic shift," in which Sudden Infant Death Syndrome has been increasingly replaced by diagnoses that focus on the sleep environment like accidental suffocation or strangulation in bed. These diagnoses differ from SIDS, I argue, in that they suggest an agent or a "doer" at cause for the death. In contrast, while parents of SIDS babies have undoubtedly experienced blame and guilt for the death of their infants, SIDS retains its association with the unexplained or unpreventable. As I argued in chapter 4, "Everybody Loses," the diagnostic shift may also have an unintended consequence of casting a criminal shadow over parents whose babies are diagnosed as having suffocated, even when suffocation deaths are physiologically indistinguishable from SIDS deaths. In addition, some evidence suggests that the diagnosis of SIDS versus accidental suffocation may be racialized; a national survey in the 1970s found that white babies were two times more likely to have their deaths attributed to SIDS than were Black families, who were four times more likely to receive a diagnosis of suffocation.[10] In other words, and as a feminist science studies perspective would suggest, investigations occur within a broader culture in which class and race inform beliefs about parenting and culpability.

As racial disparities in SUID remain entrenched, notably with Black and American Indian/Alaskan Native infants remaining more than twice as likely to die from SUID than white infants,[11] the definition of the condition has evolved in ways that put greater emphasis on personal responsibility and parental culpability. Put differently, the risk of unexpected infant death has shifted from "unexplained" to "modifiable" or "preventable" at the same time that the problem of SIDS continues to be perceived as a racialized one. As *Losing Sleep* demonstrates, this diagnostic shift has real-world implications for the development of educational outreach to families, the way safety is marketed to parents, and the criminal justice response to unexpected infant death. This book has argued throughout that health disparities and the social determinants of health complicate the notion that parents can virtually eliminate sleep-related infant death, because some children are much more vulnerable *before they go to sleep*, and even before they are born. This conclusion takes that seriously and uses a reproductive justice framework to consider what a different vision of safe sleep might look like, one with a lens far broader than the interior of a baby's crib.

Learning from Reproductive Justice

Reproductive justice scholars and activists take a human rights–based approach to health that does not begin and end with pregnancy, and that calls for interventions to ensure access to equitable resources. As Loretta Ross, Lynn Roberts, and the other editors of *Radical Reproductive Justice* argue, reproductive justice examines the causes of reproductive oppression, not just the symptoms.[12] It also says to "look beyond resistance and survival to create conditions of thriving," as Zakiya Luna argues in *Reproductive Rights as Human Rights*.[13] While infant sleep safety is not typically understood within the context of reproductive health, the framework of reproductive justice illuminates how social structure and political ideology work together to stratify access to the foundations of infant sleep safety while masking this stratification with the rhetoric of personal responsibility.[14] In the case of infant sleep safety, the first step may be acknowledging that reproductive oppression is a significant factor in determining sleep safety, not the individual actions of parents. Infant mortality rates, including sleep-related infant death, are higher for certain racial groups (notably Black and indigenous people) that experience ongoing, systemic racism impacting the health of their pregnancies and the communities in which they live. Many issues that reproductive justice scholars have drawn attention to—issues that address the full scope of pregnancy and parenting beyond abortion or contraception— are factors that impact infant sleep safety and unexpected infant death.

Incarceration, for example, has been clearly articulated as a reproductive justice issue in recent years.[15] A study of Black women giving birth at two hospitals in Chicago found that 16 percent of their partners were incarcerated during their pregnancy, the life stress of which contributes to negative birth outcomes that are risk factors for unexpected infant death.[16] As chapter 4 demonstrates, a criminal justice response is also utilized in some cases of infant deaths that occur while bed-sharing, and in ways that disproportionately impact low-income parents and those who have histories of drug or alcohol use. Incarcerating parents whose children die while bed-sharing, or pushing them toward plea deals and burdening them with fines and fees, is rarely an appropriate or just response to the circumstances in which these accidents occur. This is particularly chilling given that evidence of having received safe sleep education was used *against* parents in some cases; while mandatory safe sleep education in medical settings is initiated with the stated goal of reducing sleep-related infant deaths and empowering parents to make healthy choices, it has the potential to be weaponized.

Reproductive justice theorizing also underscores how the physical and mental health of an individual is inseparable from the community or social context and is not solely a matter of individual "choice."[17] As Arline Geronimus articulates in her theory of "weathering," the "premature health deterioration among African American women may not be alleviated—and in fact may be exacerbated—by working hard, fulfilling responsibilities, and striving to make a better life" because this "high effort coping" alongside stress takes an extreme toll on the body and mind.[18] The stress of poverty is frequently implicated in premature birth and its correlative, low birth weight, but Dána-Ain Davis makes the important corrective that for Black women, education and income do not protect against this negative birth outcome the same way they do for white women. Davis also argues that for pregnant women, experiences of racism in the healthcare setting are not always explicit or overt; women may have positive experiences with their providers, yet still suffer negative birth outcomes as a cumulative result of bias and physician error.[19]

A growing body of research suggests that the experience of racial discrimination is a risk factor for premature birth among Black women.[20] Black infants in the United States are born at low birth weight at more than two times the rate of white infants, and low birth weight is a leading cause of infant death,[21] including a heightened risk of SIDS death.[22] As demonstrated in chapter 3, "What's Best for Baby?" the problems of premature birth and low birth weight are complicated, multifaceted, and deeply entrenched in our country's failing healthcare system; while public health officials undoubtedly acknowledge and seek to address these factors that impact racial disparities in infant mortality, they have also at times been tempted by the "low-hanging fruit" of co-sleeping and individual responsibility. In sum, reproductive oppression, including the effects of historical and contemporary racism, is undeniably a factor influencing infant sleep safety.

Yet, as we saw in chapter 5, "Advertising Infant Safety," one purported solution to sleep-related infant death is sold to parents in the form of technologies that monitor infants in their cribs. While the developers of such devices tend to make modest claims (like offering "peace of mind" rather than prevention), they capitalize on and arguably invigorate parents' fears about sleep safety. And given the price point at which most biometric monitors are sold, access to even this limited peace of mind is available only to those who can afford it. The implications of such devices are troubling in that they suggest that the most dedicated, careful parent can reduce the risk of unexpected infant death through the use of technology, the scope of which only continues to grow. Owlet, the makers of the Sleep Sock, has since developed a product that intervenes on health earlier in the life cycle, called the Owlet Band. They describe the band as "the world's first consumer pregnancy monitor"; it is made up of a stretchy material meant to be worn around a woman's pregnant belly to track contractions, heart rate, even the kicks of the "unborn baby."[23] As I argue elsewhere,[24] this device is indicative of the type of enhanced pregnancy surveillance that not only reinforces fetal personhood, but normalizes the criminalization of women for pregnancy behaviors and both fetal and infant health outcomes. In the case of both the Band and the Smart Sock, the "environment" is cast as potentially dangerous, yet within the control of the "good" parent.

A consumer-oriented approach to infant sleep safety valorizes market-based solutions that stratify access by class. Public health interventions have at times over-emphasized the role of individual behavior change, and have done so without sufficient collaboration with the communities they target. Safe sleep education that is mandated by hospitals or by law has the potential unintended consequence of being used against parents should they be swept into the criminal justice system.

Centralizing reproductive justice in our analysis of infant sleep safety would involve looking toward both the structural drivers of infant mortality as well as the community-oriented solutions. The next step in rethinking safe sleep, which is also influenced by reproductive justice principles, involves expanding a definition of the safe sleep environment that is broader than the physical layout of the sleep location.

Expanding the Safe Sleep Environment

This starts with a reconsideration of what we might mean by a safe sleep environment. To recap, a safe sleep environment is defined by the American Academy of Pediatrics as "supine positioning, the use of a firm sleep surface, room-sharing without bed-sharing, and the avoidance of soft bedding and overheating."[25] Per this description, the environment extends from the microcosm of the sleep surface only as far as the parameters of the caregiver's bedroom. The sleep environment is understood as a combination of physical objects (a firm mattress, temperature-appropriate clothing) and an individual's interaction with these physical objects (putting the infant down in a supine position, keeping the crib in the parent's room, removing soft objects from the crib). Within this framing, the ability to control the sleep environment is individualized, and is a matter of compliance with evidence-based guidelines.

Beyond safe sleep, the term "environment" has been used in a variety of ways that pertain to pregnancy and early childhood. Environment often encompasses modifiable risk factors that pregnant people or parents can hypothetically control, and our understanding of where the environment begins and ends (both physically and temporally) may shift along with changing science and policy. In the last several decades, women's bodies have been discursively positioned as a reproductive environment earlier and earlier in the life cycle. This has reinforced notions of maternal responsibility and the long-standing belief that "to govern risk was to govern women."[26] The view of sex as a dualism has then contributed to the perception of male bodies as non-reproductive, largely excluding men's contributions to pregnancy from the reproductive "environment," despite evidence that men's health impacts children's health in a wide variety of ways.[27]

A robust field of feminist scholarship analyzes the construction of the pregnant body as a fetal environment and the related production of a maternal/fetal conflict that has contributed to the rise of fetal person-hood as a basis for policy and legislation.[28] Natali Valdez adds to this discussion by noting that the very definition of an environment changes depending on what one is studying, yet a category like the "maternal environment" is frequently examined as if the body of a pregnant woman is separate from "home environments or toxic atmospheric environments," which are in turn impacted by social environments of violence, poverty, or racism.[29] In her ethnographic study of women targeted for weight-based pregnancy interventions, Valdez found that pregnant women's understanding of the maternal environment was significantly different than that of researchers; pregnant women prioritized housing, safety, mental health, and income, while researchers focused on caloric intake and exercise.[30] Their environment was more holistic, and more significantly influenced by external factors.

As Valdez's research suggests, guidance based on a narrowly defined safe sleep environment may fail to adequately consider why caregivers make the choices that they do. For example, when researchers or public health officials focus on eliminating a practice like co-sleeping because of the risk of accidental suffocation, they may be over-emphasizing a risk that, while real, is far less immediate to some mothers that they are targeting than is the sound of gunshots, the lack of heat, or the threat of pests that motivate mothers to keep their child in arm's reach. I offer these examples not to dramatize the reasons parents eschew some safe sleep guidelines—as discussed in chapters 3 and 4, they are explanations derived from research[31] and expressed by individuals who work in public and community health. They demonstrate that the environment of safe sleep extends significantly beyond the crib, mattress, or infant sleeper in which a baby is placed, especially for multiply marginalized parents who are most surveilled for their parenting practices. Most parents are making sleep-related choices for their infants based on their own best assessment of risk in their environment, and for many that includes not only the sleep surface, but also other individuals within their place of residence, the safety and security of that residence and neighborhood, and potentially their own sense of self-efficacy in responding to these risks. A narrow focus on the safe sleep environment as extending only so far as the sleeping area over-emphasizes or "molecularizes"[32] individual factors in ways that place exclusive responsibility for infant sleep safety on the family. While the safe sleep environment is frequently framed as a modifiable risk factor impacting infant sleep safety, modifying the broader social environment will necessitate more significant investment in structural change.

By restricting the safe sleep environment to sleep positioning, sleep surface, or the room in which sleep occurs, public health education efforts are failing to consider significant historical and social factors that impact infant mortality. As discussed throughout this book, factors like housing, neighborhood safety, and access to safe and affordable childcare, all of which are affected by race and class, make certain infants more vulnerable to sleep-related infant death and also influence how parents manage the micro-level environment. Following a reproductive justice framework, it is imperative to consider what structural factors influence sleep-related infant mortality, and how they can be addressed in ways that recognize the agency and capabilities of the communities most affected. While existing safe sleep guidance from public health campaigns, professional organizations, and media call on parents to make individual-level changes to the sleep environment or positioning, they largely omit demands for government-level policymaking and regulation that would protect all infants from the upstream drivers of infant mortality.[33]

Turning to Community Leaders

Another key component of reproductive justice activism is that it is crucial to trust and support the ability of communities to identify, analyze, and organize around the issues that impact them. According to feminist anthropologist Patricia Zavella, this includes utilizing strategies to recruit and organize community members, such as thinking critically about what language to use, where events will be located, transportation, and childcare.[34] The inclusion of community members is also imperative for safe sleep education. Local organizations led by people of color have recognized the broader issues that influence infant sleep safety and have been working to address them within their communities. Chapter 3 discussed the organizing efforts of the Black Health Coalition of Wisconsin, which, according to President Patricia McManus, had begun its own education and outreach addressing safe sleep in Milwaukee prior to the controversial campaign initiated by the City of Milwaukee Health Department. I return again to the work of this organization and my interview with Dr. McManus to highlight how community-based organizing can create safe sleep education that derives from the knowledge and needs of the community, and puts safe sleep within a much broader context of health disparities.

As McManus explained, the efforts her organization undertook around infant sleep safety in Milwaukee were based on focus groups within the African American, Hispanic, and Hmong communities. For McManus, this type of organizing begins by respecting what people already know, listening even when you disagree, and taking part in back and forth processes that gives people time to critically assess the information; in her words, "you have to have a belief that the community has something to offer."[35] This only works, she notes, when trust has been established and when the voices of those directly affected are centralized. Getting that input is an intensive process—McManus reports that she's been asked how the BHCW draws such large attendance at community meetings. Part of this answer is recognizing potential barriers to participation including transportation, time of day, and childcare and making sure those barriers are addressed with transportation stipends, after-work meetings, food, and places for kids to do their homework. As McManus says, "It's not rocket science. It really is, to me this is just another example of it, to try to get better outcomes, they've got to be included."[36]

Because the Black Health Coalition of Wisconsin had built trust with the community, the safe sleep materials that they created were developed based on what had been learned through focus groups. This included the fact that many parents saw positive advantages to co-sleeping and reflected this with language like "how to keep your baby sleeping safe with you," which acknowledges the reality of co-sleeping and offers tips for how and when to do so safely. Meeting parents where they are honors the idea that parents are actively making choices that they believe are best for their children, which stands in sharp contrast to some other anti–bed-sharing messaging in the media that has scapegoated parents as being lazy or indifferent to their children's lives. McManus also put the BHCW's work directly within the broader context and history of racial disparities in Milwaukee, including the lack of Section 8 housing in Milwaukee's suburbs and its effects on segregation, differential access to housing stock, lack of public transportation, the placement and quality of juvenile detention centers, disparities in educational quality, and environmental hazards like exposure to lead in water pipes.

The safe sleep "environment," in this conceptualizing, encompasses historical inequities and their contemporary effects, as well as the day-to-day lived realities that impact the decisions made by individuals and communities. The way the safe sleep environment is defined is crucial, because the determination of what constitutes the environment also impacts the interventions that will be attempted and the assessment of responsibility. In other words, if the safe sleep environment is narrowly defined as the sleep surface, positioning, and presence or absence of physical items, then interventions are likely to narrowly focus on the responsibility of the caregiver for maintaining that space. What if, as Valdez inquires, researchers or public health educators asked targeted individuals what they need and want?[37] What if they were considered collaborators or knowledge producers, rather than participants (at best) and at worst, vectors of risk?

Losing Sleep has argued that our understanding of infant sleep safety in the United States is socially constructed—although that makes its effects no less real—and its contemporary iterations are shaped in part by neoliberal ideologies and policies that prioritize personal responsibility for health outcomes. In effect, the end result of ensuring safe sleep is understood to be a matter of parental decision making; it is one that is largely divorced from the broader structural factors that shape the agency of parents and the health of both caregivers and infants throughout the life cycle, not only during their sleep. This conclusion has argued that although modifications to the traditional safe sleep environment, such as positioning infants on their backs and removing soft items from sleep surfaces, have been successful in reducing infant death—although not evenly across all demographics, this definition of the environment is insufficient to create true safe sleep equity. As the activism of community health advocates demonstrates, however, there are alternative approaches to outreach and education that utilize the evidence on how to reduce risk, but also honor and incorporate the knowledge and intentions of those communities that are most impacted by unexpected infant death today. This path forward, that rethinks and expands upon the safe sleep environment and is led by the communities most affected, offers a vision in which all babies are born with access to sleep safely.

ACKNOWLEDGMENTS

As I write these acknowledgments with the sound of children's television in the background, I am reminded to begin by thanking everyone involved in the education and childcare of my daughters. Thank you to my parents, Craig Harrison and Patricia DiMartino, my parents-in-law, Marcy and Larry Anderson, and all of our dear friends in Mankato who help love and care for our children; I appreciate you more than you know. Thank you especially to my mother, who stepped up to take on much more childcare than she ever bargained for during the pandemic, in addition to resuming a new version of her teaching career at home with the girls during their long stretches of involuntary home schooling. Thank you also to my husband, Timothy Anderson, who did not run away when I would say "listen to this!" as he walked in the door for his lunch break, even when the research topic was incredibly dark (and thanks for reminding me to censor my answers to "what are you writing about?" at parties). Tim, you are the best pandemic work-from-home partner, husband, and father to our daughters that I could ever hope for, and I am incredibly grateful to you. A big thanks to my daughters, Ada and Clara, who seem pretty proud that I wrote another book, even though I'm still not an author *and* illustrator. I can't wait to see what you write someday.

Thank you to the many graduate assistants who assisted in the research for this book, and to the smart and thoughtful feminist students at MSU, Mankato, who helped me to think about reproductive rights, feminist science studies, and feminist activism in new and exciting ways. Thank you to everyone who read drafts of these chapters, including the core members of my writing group at Minnesota State University, Mankato, particularly Ry Marcattilio-McCracken, Chad McCutchen, Angela Jill Cooley, Justin Biel, Rachael Hanel, and Lori Lahlum. Thanks for letting this non-historian join the club. Several chapters of this book were greatly improved by meticulous feedback from a reader in the field of public health who generously and tirelessly guided my understanding of unexpected infant death and the role of public health—thank you, thank you, thank you. A special thanks to Danielle Haque, who has definitely read every word of this book, probably twice. Your feedback made this better, and your encouragement helped make it finished. I also appreciate the valuable feedback I received from two anonymous readers of the manuscript; the book is stronger based on your thoughtful comments. An earlier version of chapter 3 appeared in *Frontiers: A Journal of Women's Studies* 39 (3): 63–95 in 2018, and I benefited immensely from the reviewer feedback of Laury Oaks on the initial draft.

Thank you to MSU, Mankato for the opportunity to take a full year of sabbatical to write and research, and to my colleagues in the Department of Gender and Women's Studies for your support. A special thank you to my wonderful friend and colleague, Maria Bevacqua, who has taught me so much about feminist teaching and life in academia. I also continue to benefit from the wisdom and support of my friend and mentor, Suzanna Walters, even from afar. I would also like to thank the editors and staff at NYU Press who assisted in this publication—thank you in particular to Ilene Kalish and Sonia Tsuruoka. While there is never enough time and space for a sufficient expression of my thanks, the network of support around me has made this possible, and I am deeply grateful.

NOTES

INTRODUCTION

1   Waggoner, *The Zero Trimester*.
2   Bombard et al., "Vital Signs."
3   Kirkland and Metzl, *Against Health*.
4   Gold, "Sleeping Like a Baby."
5   Fernandes, *Feminists Rethink the Neoliberal State*.
6   Fentiman, *Blaming Mothers*.
7   "About SUIDS and SIDS," Centers for Disease Control and Prevention, last accessed August 28, 2018, www.cdc.gov.
8   Matthews, MacDorman, and Thoma, "Infant Mortality Statistics."
9   Fentiman, *Blaming Mothers*.
10 Walls et al., "Implications of Structure," 56.
11 Asphyxia is a general term referring to a death that results from a lack of oxygen; asphyxia can result from multiple mechanisms, including smothering, choking, or aspiration. The CDC uses the category "accidental suffocation or strangulation in bed" to describe asphyxia deaths in infants, thus I use the term "suffocation" when referring to asphyxia deaths in an unsafe sleep environment.
12 See Wolf-Meyer, *The Slumbering Masses*.
13 Anecdotally, it seems that adherence to some safe sleep guidance is more strictly policed among parents and pediatricians than are others. For example, the AAP recommends that parents room-share with their infant for the first 12 months, but much popular guidance recommends that infants begin sleep training in their own rooms far earlier. Choosing not to room-share does not seem as closely aligned with risky sleep as does co-sleeping, even though guidance on room-sharing and guidance against co-sleeping are both measures meant to reduce SIDS risk.
14 American Academy of Pediatrics Task Force on Sudden Infant Death Syndrome, "SIDS and Other Sleep-Related Infant Deaths."
15 Byard, "Sudden Infant Death Syndrome: Definitions," 4.
16 Ibid., 5.
17 "Sudden Unexpected Infant Death and Sudden Infant Death Syndrome," Centers for Disease Control and Prevention, last accessed May 17, 2019, www.cdc.gov.
18 "Infographic: Accidental Suffocation and Strangulation," National Institute of Child Health and Human Development, last accessed October 3, 2019, https://safetosleep.nichd.nih.gov.

19 Shapiro-Mendoza et al., "Classification System."

20 Goldstein et al., "Overall Postneonatal Mortality"; Shapiro-Mendoza et al., "Classification System."

21 Russell Jones, "Sudden Infant Death."

22 Obladen, "Cot Death."

23 Cowgill, *Rest Uneasy*.

24 Byard, "Sudden Infant Death Syndrome: Definitions"; Filiano and Kinney, "A Perspective."

25 Duncan and Byard, "Sudden Infant Death Syndrome."

26 See Cowgill, *Rest Uneasy*; Duncan and Byard, "Sudden Infant Death Syndrome"; Miller et al., "Consequences of the 'Back to Sleep' Program in Infants"; American Academy of Pediatrics Task Force on Sudden Infant Death Syndrome, "The Changing Concept of Sudden Infant Death Syndrome"; Centers for Disease Control and Prevention, "Sudden Unexpected Infant Death and Sudden Infant Death Syndrome"; National Institutes of Health, "NIH Expands Safe Sleep Outreach Effort."

27 Goldstein et al., "Overall Postneonatal Mortality"; Shapiro-Mendoza et al., "Classification System."

28 Shapiro-Mendoza et al., "The Epidemiology of Sudden Infant Death Syndrome"; US Department of Health and Human Services Office of Minority Health, "Minority Population Profiles."

29 Cowgill, *Rest Uneasy*.

30 Kendall-Tackett, "Don't Sleep with Big Knives."

31 Young and Shipstone, "Shared Sleeping Surface.".

32 Colson et al., "Trends and Factors."

33 American Academy of Pediatrics, "Safe Sleep: Recommendations," last accessed August 28, 2020, www.aap.org.

34 Stewart, *Co-Sleeping*.

35 Krouse et al., "Bed-sharing Influences"; Stewart, *Co-Sleeping*.

36 See Ward and Ngui, "Factors Associated with Bed-Sharing"; Colson et al., "Trends and Factors"; Joyner et al., "Where Should My Baby Sleep?"

37 Joyner et al., "Where Should My Baby Sleep?"

38 American Academy of Pediatrics Task Force on Sudden Infant Death Syndrome, "SIDS and Other Sleep-Related Infant Deaths."

39 Beck, *Risk Society*; Lupton, *The Imperative of Health*.

40 Nichter, "Harm Reduction."

41 Cossman, "Anxiety Governance."

42 Fernandes, *Feminists Rethink the Neoliberal State*, 11.

43 Fernandes, *Feminists Rethink the Neoliberal State*.

44 Duggan, *The Twilight of Equality?*

45 Harvey, *A Brief History of Neoliberalism*, 65.

46 Lupton, *The Imperative of Health*, 78.

47 Lupton, *The Imperative of Health*, 80.

48 American Academy of Pediatrics Task Force on Sudden Infant Death Syndrome, "SIDS and Other Sleep-Related Infant Deaths: Updated 2016 Recommendations."

49 Lupton, *The Imperative of Health.*

50 Joyner et al., "Where Should My Baby Sleep?"

51 Nelkin, "Foreword."

52 Clarke et al., "Biomedicalization: Technoscientific Transformations."

53 Abramson, "This Is What Postpartum Anxiety Feels Like."

54 Faircloth, "Intensive Parenting and the Expansion of Parenting."

55 "Data and Statistics," Centers for Disease Control and Prevention, last accessed April 8, 2020, www.cdc.gov.

56 Macvarish, "Babies' Brains and Parenting Policy," 168.

57 Cosman, "Anxiety Governance." See also Cairns et al., "Feeding the 'Organic Child.'"

58 Nelkin, "Foreword."

59 Fixmer-Oraiz, *Homeland Maternity.*

60 Waggoner, *The Zero Trimester.*

61 Fixmer-Oraiz, *Homeland Maternity*, 17.

62 Gilman, "Feminism."

63 See Fentiman, *Blaming Mothers* for analyses of the McKnight, Beltran, and Shuai cases. McKnight spent eight years in prison before the South Carolina Supreme Court overturned her conviction based on ineffective counsel. Shuai pled guilty to reckless endangerment, and was sentenced to time served (189 days in jail). See Fixmer-Oraiz, *Homeland Maternity*, for an analysis of the Purvi Patel case. Patel's case was overturned by the Indiana Court of Appeals, and she was resentenced to 18 months on a lesser felony charge of neglect of a dependent, which was less time than she had already served. See also "Judge Says Purvi Patel Should Be Freed Immediately After Feticide Conviction Overturned," *The Guardian*, September 1, 2016, www.theguardian.com.

64 Reints, "These Are the States."

65 Eckholm, "Case Explores Rights of Fetus Versus Mother."

66 Mills, "Opponents of Wisconsin's 'Cocaine Mom' Law Continue Fight."

67 Eckholm, "Case Explores Rights of Fetus Versus Mother."

68 Mills, "Opponents of Wisconsin's 'Cocaine Mom' Law Continue Fight." For more on the Loertscher case, see Fixmer-Oraiz, *Homeland Maternity.*

69 Mills, "Opponents of Wisconsin's 'Cocaine Mom' Law Continue Fight."

70 Golden, *Message in a Bottle.*

71 Hays, *The Cultural Contradictions of Motherhood.*

72 Collins, *Making Motherhood Work*, 209.

73 Douglas and Michaels, *The Mommy Myth*; Lareau, *Unequal Childhoods*; Nelson, *Parenting Out of Control*; Wolf, *Is Breast Best?*

74 Douglas and Michaels, *The Mommy Myth*, 5.

75 Villalobos, *Motherload*, 9.

76 Ginsburg and Rapp, "Introduction."

77 Oaks, *Giving Up Baby*.
78 Denbow, *Governed Through Choice*, 3.
79 Armstrong, "Lessons in Control."
80 Waggoner, *The Zero Trimester*, 88.
81 Dubriwny, *The Vulnerable Empowered Woman*, 30; Waggoner, *The Zero Trimester*.
82 Mansfield, "Gendered Biopolitics of Public Health," 597.
83 Armstrong, "Lessons in Control."
84 Oaks, *Giving Up Baby*.
85 Ross et al., "Introduction," 11–12.
86 Zavella, *The Movement for Reproductive Justice*.
87 See Ross et al., *Radical Reproductive Justice*; Roberts, *Killing the Black Body*; Nelson, *Women of Color*; Silliman et al., eds., *Undivided Rights*; Price, "What Is Reproductive Justice?"; Luna and Luker, "Reproductive Justice"; Gurr, *Reproductive Justice*; Zavella, *The Movement for Reproductive Justice*; Luna, *Reproductive Rights as Human Rights*.

CHAPTER 1. "SLEEP LIKE A BABY" AND OTHER HISTORICAL FALLACIES

1 *The Bible*, 21st Century King James Version, 1 Kings 3:16–28.
2 Oskar and O'Connor, "Children's Sleep."
3 See Degler, *At Odds*.
4 Stearns, Rowland, and Giarnella, "Children's Sleep."
5 Vandenberg-Daves, *Modern Motherhood*.
6 Johnson and Quinlan, *You're Doing It Wrong*.
7 Degler notes that most advice literature reached urban parents (and necessarily white parents) primarily through the nineteenth century, and these parents made up a minority of Americans. He concludes that "historians know relatively little about the intimate details of working-class families . . . principally because the traditional written sources are lacking." See Degler, *At Odds, 82*.
8 Cowgill, *Rest Uneasy*.
9 Åström, "A Narrative of Fear."
10 Hardyment, *Dream Babies*; Cott, *The Bonds of Womanhood*.
11 Kukla, *Mass Hysteria*.
12 Cowgill, *Rest Uneasy*.
13 Norvenius, "Some Medico-Historic Remarks on SIDS."
14 Högberg and Bergström, "Suffocated Prone."
15 Obladen, "Cot Death."
16 Anders and Taylor, "Babies and Their Sleep Environment"; Hardyment, *Dream Babies*.
17 Hardyment, *Dream Babies*.
18 Kukla, *Mass Hysteria*, 48.
19 Anders and Taylor, "Babies and Their Sleep Environment."
20 Kukla, *Mass Hysteria*, 66.
21 Solinger, *Pregnancy and Power*, 48.
22 Stearns, Rowland, and Giarnella, "Children's Sleep."

23 Anders and Taylor, "Babies and Their Sleep Environment."

24 Denbow, "Good Motherhood Before Birth."

25 Degler, *At Odds.*

26 Cott, *The Bonds of Womanhood.*

27 Buskens, "The Impossibility of 'Natural Parenting'," 86.

28 Eyer, *Mother-Infant Bonding.*

29 Kukla, *Mass Hysteria.*

30 Hardyment, *Dream Babies.*

31 Cott, *The Bonds of Womanhood*, 84.

32 Kukla, *Mass Hysteria.*

33 Cott, *The Bonds of Womanhood*, 87.

34 Zelizer, *Pricing the Priceless Child.*

35 Duncan and Byard, "Sudden Infant Death Syndrome."

36 Russell-Jones, "Sudden Infant Death."

37 Russell-Jones, "Sudden Infant Death," 279; Obladen, "Cot Death," 163.

38 Duncan and Byard, "Sudden Infant Death Syndrome."

39 Federici, *Caliban and the Witch*, 88.

40 Davis, *Reproductive Injustice.*

41 Roberts, *Killing the Black Body.*

42 Johnson, "Smothered Slave Infants."

43 Ibid.

44 Kemkes, "'Smothered' Infants."

45 Morgan, *Laboring Women.* For more on the history and continuing effects of "reproductive slavery," see Weinbaum, *The Afterlife of Reproductive Slavery.*

46 Cowgill, *Rest Uneasy*; Johnson, "Smothered Slave Infants;" Roberts, *Killing the Black Body.* Historian Caitlin Rosenthal argues that slaveowners even influenced the length of time between an enslaved woman's pregnancies based on how long they were allowed to nurse their children and how soon they returned to hard labor after giving birth. Enslaved women resisted by continuing to breastfeed against orders, or using methods to prevent pregnancy, but could not avoid "planters' frequent and often violent efforts to manipulate reproductive life." Rosenthal, *Accounting for Slavery*, 131.

47 Hemphill, "Driven to the Commission of This Crime," 445.

48 Kemkes, "'Smothered' Infants," 393.

49 Collins, *Black Feminist Thought.*

50 Roberts, "Racism and Patriarchy."

51 Smalls, *Our Babies, Ourselves.*

52 Anders and Taylor, "Babies and Their Sleep Environments"; Hardyment, *Dream Babies.*

53 Wolf-Meyer, *The Slumbering Masses*, 141.

54 Stearns, Rowland, and Giarnella, "Children's Sleep."

55 Holt, *The Care and Feeding of Children*, 180.

56 Hinds, *A Cultural History of Twin Beds*, 51.

57 Smalls, *Our Babies, Ourselves.*
58 Gross-Loh, *Parenting Without Borders*; Tomori, *Nighttime Breastfeeding.*
59 Atkinson, "Shifting Sands."
60 Lee, "Experts and Parenting Culture"; Meckel, *Save the Babies.*
61 See Wolf-Meyer, *The Slumbering Masses.*
62 Meckel, *Save the Babies.*
63 Theobold, *Reproduction on the Reservation.*
64 Ehrenreich and English, *For Her Own Good.*
65 Meckel, *Save the Babies.*
66 Ibid.
67 Vandenberg-Daves, *Modern Motherhood*, 80.
68 Meckel, *Save the Babies*; Zelizer, *Pricing the Priceless Child.*
69 Theobold, *Reproduction on the Reservation*; Meckel, *Save the Babies.*
70 Golden, *Babies Made Us Modern.*
71 Meckel, *Save the Babies*, 100.
72 Golden, *Babies Made Us Modern*; Meckel, *Save the Babies.*
73 Casper and Moore, *Missing Bodies.*
74 Meckel, *Save the Babies*, 158.
75 Buskens, "The Impossibility of Natural Parenting."
76 Apple, "Constructing Mothers," 91; Golden, *Babies Made Us Modern.*
77 Vandenberg-Daves, *Modern Motherhood*; Golden, *Babies Made Us Modern.*
78 Apple, "Constructing Mothers."
79 Vandenberg-Daves, *Modern Motherhood.*
80 Golden, *Babies Made Us Modern.*
81 Ehrenreich and Engels, *For Her Own Good*, 191.
82 Hulbert, *Raising America*, 36.
83 Meckel, *Save the Babies.*
84 Hardyment, *Dream Babies.*
85 Apple, "Constructing Mothers"; Meckel, *Save the Babies.*
86 Apple, *Perfect Motherhood.*
87 Theobold, *Reproduction on the Reservation*; Gurr, *Reproductive Justice.*
88 Theobold, *Reproduction on the Reservation*, 44.
89 Golden, *Babies Made Us Modern.*
90 Apple, "Constructing Mothers."
91 Atkinson, "Shifting Sands."
92 Meckel, *Save the Babies.*
93 US Department of Labor, Children's Bureau, *Infant Care*, 56. Notably, the admonition concerning suffocation was removed from the 1929 version of *Infant Care*, arguably leaving the impression that solo sleep was largely a matter of infant comfort rather than safety.
94 Atkinson, "Shifting Sands," 134.
95 US Department of Labor, *Infant Care*, 57.
96 Atkinson, "Shifting Sands."

97 Eyer, *Mother-Infant Bonding.*
98 Pawluch, "Transitions in Pediatrics."
99 Meckel *Save the Babies,* 47.
100 Eyer, *Mother-Infant Bonding.*
101 Tomori, *Nighttime Breastfeeding.*
102 Ibid.
103 Golden, *Babies Made Us Modern*; Apple, *Perfect Motherhood.*
104 Eyer, *Mother-Infant Bonding*; Hardyment, *Dream Babies.*
105 Watson, *Psychological Care of Infant and Child,* 79.
106 Watson, *Psychological Care of Infant and Child,* 120.
107 Golden, *Babies Made Us Modern.*
108 Kessen, "The American Child," 819.
109 Plant, *Mom.*
110 Apple, *Perfect Motherhood.*
111 Golden, *Babies Made Us Modern.*
112 Eyer, *Mother-Infant Bonding.*
113 Hulbert, *Raising America,* 226.
114 Apple, *Perfect Motherhood.*
115 Atkinson, "Shifting Sands."
116 McKenna, Ball, and Gettler, "Mother-Infant Co-Sleeping."
117 Eyer, *Mother-Infant Bonding.*
118 Wall, "Mothers' Experiences."
119 Eyer, *Mother-Infant Bonding*; Lee, "Experts in Parenting Culture."
120 Eyer, *Mother-Infant Bonding.*
121 Ehrenreich and English, *For Her Own Good,* 227.
122 Hulbert, *Raising America.*
123 Lee, "Experts in Parenting Culture," 60.
124 Randall, *Dreamland.*
125 Kenyon, "Sleep Habits."
126 Felder, "Your Baby After Dark."
127 Cowgill, *Rest Uneasy.*
128 Martucci, *Back to the Breast,* 14.
129 Hardyment, *Dream Babies.*
130 Martucci, *Back to the Breast.*
131 "Margaret Ribble, Psychoanalyst, 80," *New York Times,* July 21, 1971, 38.
132 Martucci, "Why Breastfeeding?"
133 Weiner, "Reconstructing Motherhood"; Apple, *Perfect Motherhood.*
134 Martucci, "Why Breastfeeding?"
135 See Martucci's *Back to the Breast* for an overview of these debates.
136 Apple, *Perfect Motherhood.*
137 Ibid.
138 Ibid.
139 Eyer, *Mother-Infant Bonding.*

140 Ibid., 178.

141 Ibid.

142 Nelson, *More Than Medicine*, 6.

143 Cowgill, *Rest Uneasy*.

144 Ibid.

145 Meckel, *Save the Babies*.

146 Bridges, *Reproducing Race*.

147 Cowgill, *Rest Uneasy*, 78.

148 Ibid.

149 Roberts, *Killing the Black Body*.

150 Goodwin, *Policing the Womb*.

151 Hardyment, *Dream Babies*.

152 Hardyment, *Dream Babies*; Liedloff, *The Continuum Concept*, 22.

153 Sears et al., *The Baby Book*, 341.

154 Sears and Sears, *The Attachment Parenting Book*, 91.

155 Matchar, *Homeward Bound*.

156 Moore and Abetz, "'Uh Oh. Cue the [New] Mommy Wars.'"

157 Sears et al., *The Baby Book*.

158 Pickert, "The Man Who Remade Motherhood."

159 National Institutes of Child Health and Human Development, "Key Moments."

160 Duncan and Byard, "Sudden Infant Death Syndrome"; Miller et al., "Consequences of the 'Back to Sleep' Program in Infants"; Goldstein et al., "Overall Postneonatal Mortality." See also the American Academy of Pediatrics Task Force on Sudden Infant Death Syndrome, "The Changing Concept of Sudden Infant Death Syndrome"; Centers for Disease Control and Prevention, "Sudden Unexpected Infant Death and Sudden Infant Death Syndrome."

161 See National Institutes of Health, "NIH Expands Safe Sleep Outreach Effort."

162 Shapiro-Mendoza et al., "The Epidemiology of Sudden Infant Death Syndrome"; Tanabe and Hauck, "A United States Perspective."

163 Sidebotham et al., "Preventive Strategies for Sudden Infant Death Syndrome."

164 Ibid.

165 Pickett, Luo, and Lauderdale, "Widening Social Inequalities." See also Ray et al., "Infant Sleep Position Instruction and Parental Practice."

166 Moon et al., "Qualitative Analysis of Beliefs and Perceptions."

167 Colson et al., "Barriers to Following the Supine Sleep Recommendation."

168 Washington, *Medical Apartheid*.

169 Gamble, "Under the Shadow of Tuskegee."

170 Bridges, *Reproducing Race*.

171 Washington, *Medical Apartheid*. See also Owens, *Medical Bondage*.

172 Abdou and Fingerhut, "Stereotype Threat Among Black and White Women in Healthcare Settings."

173 Davis, *Reproductive Injustice*.

CHAPTER 2. MAKING AND UNMAKING A SAFE SLEEP ENVIRONMENT

1 Meckel, *Save the Babies*, 47.

2 See Korneva, "20 Common Questions."

3 Eyer, *Mother-Infant Bonding*.

4 Pearson, "The American Pediatric Society."

5 American Academy of Family Physicians, "About the American Academy of Pediatrics," last accessed December 18, 2019, www.aafp.org; American Academy of Pediatrics, "Advocacy," last accessed September 14, 2020, www.aap.org.

6 Earp and Shaw, "Cultural Bias in American Medicine."

7 The AAP does not include the 1992 or 1996 policy statements in its AAP Policy Collection by the Task Force on Sudden Infant Death Syndrome, but given that both were authored by the Task Force and published in *Pediatrics*, I am including them in this analysis. See https://pediatrics.apppublications.org.

8 American Academy of Pediatrics Task Force on Sudden Infant Death Syndrome, "Positioning and SIDS."

9 American Academy of Pediatrics Task Force on Sudden Infant Death Syndrome, "The Changing Concept of Sudden Infant Death Syndrome."

10 Cowgill, *Rest Uneasy*.

11 American Academy of Pediatrics Task Force on Sudden Infant Death Syndrome, "The Changing Concept of Sudden Infant Death Syndrome."

12 American Academy of Pediatrics Task Force on Sudden Infant Death Syndrome, "SIDS and Other Sleep-Related Infant Deaths."

13 American Academy of Pediatrics Task Force on Sudden Infant Death Syndrome, "Positioning and Sudden Infant Death Syndrome (SIDS): Update."

14 Cowgill, *Rest Uneasy*, 142.

15 Cowgill, *Rest Uneasy*.

16 Ibid.

17 American Academy of Pediatrics Task Force on Sudden Infant Death Syndrome, "Changing Concepts of Sudden Infant Death Syndrome: Implications for Infant Sleeping Environment and Sleep Position."

18 In 1999, the US Consumer Product Safety Commission (CPSC) published a study in the *Archives of Pediatric and Adolescent Medicine* that specifically addressed concerns about babies sleeping in adult beds. The CPSC, as discussed later in this chapter, is an independent federal regulatory agency that develops both voluntary and mandatory standards for consumer products, researches hazardous products, and oversees product recalls. This report identified 64 deaths per year of children put to sleep in adult beds, waterbeds, and daybeds, and attributes these deaths to a combination of suffocation, mechanical asphyxiation (overlay), and entrapment. While the CPSC's report was not cited in the AAP's subsequent recommendations, released in 2005, it seems to have foreshadowed the direction that the updated recommendations would take. See the CPSC's website at www.cpsc.gov. See also Nakamura, Wind, and Danello, "Review of Hazards."

19 American Academy of Pediatrics Task Force on Sudden Infant Death Syndrome, "Changing Concepts of Sudden Infant Death Syndrome."

20 American Academy of Pediatrics Task Force on Sudden Infant Death Syndrome, "The Changing Concept of Sudden Infant Death Syndrome."

21 American Academy of Pediatrics Task Force on Sudden Infant Death Syndrome, "The Changing Concept of Sudden Infant Death Syndrome," 1252.

22 American Academy of Pediatrics Task Force on Sudden Infant Death Syndrome, "SIDS and Other Sleep-Related Infant Deaths," 1030.

23 Ibid.

24 American Academy of Pediatrics Task Force on Sudden Infant Death Syndrome, "SIDS and Other Sleep-Related Infant Deaths."

25 Ibid.

26 Kendall-Tackett, Cong, and Hale, "Mother-Infant Sleep Locations."

27 Kendall-Tackett, "Don't Sleep with Big Knives."

28 Ibid., 10.

29 Duncan and Byard, "Sudden Infant Death Syndrome."

30 Colson et al., "Trends and Factors."

31 Bombard et al., "Vital Signs."

32 Doucleff, "Is Sleeping with Your Baby as Dangerous as Doctors Say?"

33 Blair et al., "Bed-Sharing in the Absence of Hazardous Circumstances," 2.

34 Blair et al., "Bed-Sharing in the Absence of Hazardous Circumstances," 6.

35 Centers for Disease Control and Prevention, "Safe Sleep for Babies," last accessed October 13, 2020, www.cdc.gov; Moon, "How to Keep Your Sleeping Baby Safe."

36 Moon, "How to Keep Your Sleeping Baby Safe."

37 Miller and Carrol, "Should Your Baby Really Sleep in the Same Room as You?"

38 Ibid.

39 Paul et al., "Mother-Infant Room-Sharing and Sleep Outcomes in the INSIGHT Study." In a response to Paul et al.'s paper, Rachel Moon and Fern Hauck (Moon chairs the AAP Task Force on SIDS and Hauck is a member) point out that consolidated sleep may have its own hazards, given that the failure to arouse is a risk factor for SIDS. See Moon and Hauck, "Are There Long-Term Consequences of Room-Sharing During Infancy?"

40 Paul et al., "Mother-Infant Room-Sharing and Sleep Outcomes in the INSIGHT Study."

41 Teti et al., "Sleep-Arrangements."

42 Stewart, Co-Sleeping.

43 Lee, "Introduction."

44 Faircloth, "Intensive Parenting and the Expansion of Parenting."

45 Lee, "Experts and Parenting Culture."

46 For more, see Jan Macvarish's discussion of "neuroparenting" in "Babies' Brains and Parenting Policy."

47 Ball, Tomori, and McKenna, "Toward an Integrated Anthropology of Infant Sleep."

48 McKenna, "An Anthropological Perspective on the Sudden Infant Death Syndrome (SIDS)."

49 Ball, "Reasons to Bed-Share."

50 McKenna, "An Anthropological Perspective on the Sudden Infant Death Syndrome (SIDS)." McKenna only briefly discusses the role of breastfeeding in this essay, noting that its preventative role at the time of that essay was still under debate. Later works would foreground the connection between breastfeeding, co-sleeping, and SIDS reduction; see McKenna and McDade, "Why Babies Should Never Sleep Alone."

51 Bartick, Tomori, and Ball, "Babies in Boxes and the Missing Links on Safe Sleep."

52 McKenna, Ball, and Gettler, "Mother-Infant Co-Sleeping."

53 McKenna, "Night Waking Among Breastfeeding Mothers and Infants."

54 Anders and Taylor, "Babies and Their Sleep Environment."

55 Bartick, Tomori, and Ball, "Babies in Boxes and the Missing Links on Safe Sleep."

56 McKenna, Ball, and Gettler, "Mother-Infant Co-Sleeping."

57 Wolf et al., "Parental Theories," 366.

58 McKenna and McDade, "Why Babies Should Never Sleep Alone."

59 McKenna, Ball, and Gettler, "Mother-Infant Co-Sleeping."

60 Pryor and Huggins, *Nursing Mother, Working Mother- Revised*, 82; Tomori, *Nighttime Breastfeeding*, 73.

61 Fetherston and Leach, "Analysis of the Ethical Issues in the Breastfeeding and Bedsharing Debates," 10.

62 Fetherston and Leach, "Analysis of the Ethical Issues in the Breastfeeding and Bedsharing Debates," 12.

63 Lawrence, "Solomon's Wisdom," 279.

64 Lawrence, "Solomon's Wisdom."

65 Darnall, Goodstein, Hauck, and Moon, "American Academy of Pediatrics' Task Force."

66 La Leche League International, "The Safe Sleep Seven."

67 Ibid.

68 Sears et al., *The Baby Book*.

69 Fleming, Blair, and McKenna, "New Knowledge, New Insights, and New Recommendations."

70 Ibid.

71 Hsu, "Fisher-Price Recalls Rock 'n Play Sleeper Linked to Infant Deaths"; Committee on Oversight and Reform, "Infant Deaths in Inclined Sleepers: Fisher-Price's Rock 'n Play Reveals Dangerous Flaws in US Product Safety," June 2021, www.oversight.house.gov.

72 Peachman, "Government Moves Closer to Stopping the Sale of Dangerous Baby Sleep Products."

73 Hsu, "Fisher-Price Recalls Rock 'n Play Sleeper Linked to Infant Deaths."

74 In Re: Rock'n Play Sleeper Marketing, Sales Practices, and Products Liability Litigation, 1:19-md-2903 US (2019); Committee on Oversight and Reform, "Infant

Deaths in Inclined Sleepers: Fisher-Price's Rock 'n Play Reveals Dangerous Flaws in US Product Safety."

75 "Media Statement on the US Consumer Product Safety Commission–Fisher-Price Joint Security Alert Released on April 5, 2019," *Mattel Newsroom*, April 5, 2019, https://news.mattel.com. The response by Fisher-Price was echoed several years later by the fitness company Peloton, when their at-home treadmill was linked to the death of one child and the injury of dozens more children, as well as pets. Peloton CEO John Foley responded to the child's death in an open letter in March 2021 acknowledging the tragedy, but minimizing the "small number of incidents" that had been reported. He downplayed Peloton's safety role, stating that the company does their part but that to prevent accidents, especially during the COVID-19 pandemic, "we need your help." The letter directed readers to keep children and pets away from the treadmill, and to store the safety key (needed to activate the machine) out of reach of children. The safety reminders and direct address to users shifted safety responsibility away from Peloton and back to the consumer, suggesting that resulting accidents were due to pandemic-frazzled parents failing to take basic precautions. The CPSC warned consumers to stop using the treadmill in April 2021 after numerous small children and pets were "entrapped, pinned, and pulled under" the machine. Consumer Product Safety Commission, "CPSC Warns Consumers: Stop Using the Peloton Tread+," April 17, 2021, www.cpsc.gov. Peloton released a statement describing the CPSC's report as "inaccurate and misleading," and reiterated that such incidents could be avoided if consumers followed safety instructions. They offered tips to parents such as exercising while their child naps, when a partner or spouse can supervise the child, or blocking access to the treadmill with a baby gate. "Peloton Refutes Consumer Product Safety Commission Claims," April 17, 2021, www.onepeloton.com. However, by May 5, 2021, Peloton and the CPSC agreed to issue a voluntary recall of the Tread+, and Foley apologized in a call to Wall Street analysts in response to an estimated $165 million in potential recall costs. Kate Gibson, "Peloton CEO Apologizes for Not Recalling Deadly Treadmills Sooner," May 7, 2021, www.cbsnews.com. Both the Fisher-Price and Peloton responses indicate that even in the face of severe injury and death of children, corporations weaponize personal and parental responsibility to downplay their own accountability for consumer safety.

76 Hsu, "Before Fisher-Price's Rock 'n Play Recall"; Frankel, "Fisher-Price Invented a Popular Baby Sleeper"; Committee on Oversight and Reform, "Infant Deaths in Inclined Sleepers."

77 Committee on Oversight and Reform, "Infant Deaths in Inclined Sleepers."

78 Hsu, "Before Fisher-Price's Rock 'n Play Recall."

79 In Re: Rock'n Play Sleeper Marketing, Sales Practices, and Products Liability Litigation, 1:19-md-2903 US (2019).

80 Tyko, "Kids II Recalls 700,000 Baby Sleepers."

81 Hsu, "Before Fisher-Price's Rock 'n Play Recall."

82 Holiday, Densley, and Norman, "Influencer Marketing Between Mothers."

83 Peachman, "While They Were Sleeping."

84 Committee on Oversight and Reform, "Infant Deaths in Inclined Sleepers."

85 Peachman, "Inclined Sleeper Deaths."

86 In Re: Rock'n Play Sleeper Marketing, Sales Practices, and Products Liability Litigation, 1:19-md-2903 US (2019).

87 "Fisher-Price Rock 'n Play Lawsuit," *ConsumerNotice.org*, last accessed September 16, 2020, www.consumernotice.org.

88 Hsu, "Before Fisher-Price's Rock 'n Play Recall."

89 In Re: Rock'n Play Sleeper Marketing, Sales Practices, and Products Liability Litigation, 1:19-md-2903 US (2019).

90 Peachman, "Fisher-Price Rock 'n Play Sleeper Should be Recalled."

91 Committee on Oversight and Reform, "Infant Deaths in Inclined Sleepers."

92 US Consumer Product Safety Commission, "Who We Are—What We Do For You."

93 Committee on Oversight and Reform, "Infant Deaths in Inclined Sleepers."

94 Friedman, "Chemical Industry Executive Nominated."

95 Peachman, "Fisher-Price Rock 'n Play Sleeper Should Be Recalled."

96 Nancy A. Cowles et al., "Comments of Kids in Danger."

97 Frankel, "Fisher-Price Invented a Popular Baby Sleeper."

98 In Re: Rock'n Play Sleeper Marketing, Sales Practices, and Products Liability Litigation, 1:19-md-2903 US (2019).

99 Cowles et al., "Comments of Kids in Danger."

100 MacKendrick, *Better Safe Than Sorry*.

101 "About Fisher-Price," last accessed September 16, 2020, www.fisher-price.com.

102 Frankel, "Fisher-Price Invented a Popular Baby Sleeper."

103 Peachman, "Government Moves Closer to Stopping the Sale of Dangerous Baby Sleep Products."

104 "Fisher-Price Recalls Rock 'n Play Amid Pressure for AAP," *AAP News*, April 12, 2019, www.aappublications.org.

105 In Re: Rock'n Play Sleeper Marketing, Sales Practices, and Products Liability Litigation, 1:19-md-2903 US (2019).

106 *Evan Amber Overton and John Keenan Overton v. Fisher-Price, Inc. and Mattel Inc.*, 1:2019cv00751, US District Court for the Eastern District of Virginia, 2019.

107 Committee on Oversight and Reform, "Infant Deaths in Inclined Sleepers."

108 Amy Haneline, "Rock 'n Play Recall."

109 "Grieving Family Wants Fisher-Price Sleeper Recalled," *CNN*, YouTube Video, April 11, 2019, www.youtube.com/watch?v=E5_tHF3uOzA. Dozens of comments on the YouTube video of the story blamed the parents, several with racist remarks about Black women and motherhood.

110 Fentiman, *Blaming Mothers*.

111 Peterson, "Fisher-Price Is Giving Away Refunds."

112 Peachman, "While They Were Sleeping."

113 Hsu, "Why a Fisher-Price Sleeper Linked to Infant Deaths Hasn't Been Recalled."

114 Friedman, "Chemical Industry Executive Nominated."

115 US Congress, Senate, *Safe Sleep For Babies Act of 2019*, HR 3172, 116th Congress, 1st sess., referred in Senate December 17, 2019, www.congress.gov.

116 "Consumer Reports: Congress Should Pass 'Lifesaving' Safe Sleep For Babies Act," May 13, 2021, www.consumerreport.org.

117 Peachman, "While They Were Sleeping."

118 Committee on Oversight and Reform, "Infant Deaths in Inclined Sleepers."

119 Todd C. Frankel, "House Panel Grills Executives."

120 Peachman, "Government Moves Closer to Stopping the Sale of Dangerous Baby Sleep Products."

121 "Statement of Commissioner Dana Baiocco on Final Rule for Infant Sleep Products," www.cpsc.gov.

122 Peachman, "Government Moves Closer to Stopping the Sale of Dangerous Baby Sleep Products."

123 "Statement of Commissioner Dana Baiocco on Final Rule for Infant Sleep Products," www.cpsc.gov.

124 Stewart, *Co-Sleeping*.

125 In a questionnaire completed by 250 mothers who identified as attachment parents, almost 80% of parents reported that their babies slept in the same bed as them for the first six months; of these 250 parents, 230 identified as white. Greene and Groves, "Attachment Parenting: An Exploration of Demographics and Practices."

126 The gendering of infant care even colored the response of CPSC commissioners—in a footnote to her statement, Commissioner Baiocco remarks that she found it "ironic that my three male colleagues summarily dismissed the views and concerns of the only mother on this Commission."

CHAPTER 3. WHAT'S BEST FOR BABY?

1 "Safe Sleep Campaign," Milwaukee Health Department, accessed October 15, 2020, http://city.milwaukee.gov.

2 According to the City of Milwaukee's Safe Sleep Campaign website, the campaign was rolled out in late 2009/early 2010. Personal communication with the City of Milwaukee's Health Communications Officer described the specific advertising campaign analyzed in this chapter as beginning in 2010 and rolling out new messages through 2012. The website lists January 2010 as the date attached to the "Tombstone" billboards (discussed later in this article) and two 30-second radio spots titled "Helpless" and "News." The same website links to a Wisconsin Radio Network interview with Anna Benton, Milwaukee Health Department's Family and Community Health Services Director from December 30, 2009, which discusses the Tombstone ads and the goals of the campaign. The last efforts listed on the Safe Sleep Campaign's website are advertising materials from July 2012 marketing the message that babies should always sleep in a crib. See http://city.milwaukee.gov for all Safe Sleep Campaign advertising materials.

3   See Fu, Moon, and Hauck, "Bed-Sharing Among Black Infants."

4   Matthews, Ely, and Driscoll, "State Variations in Infant Mortality."

5   Interview with Milwaukee public health official.

6   Matthews, Ely, and Driscoll, "State Variations in Infant Mortality."

7   Colen, "'Like a Mother to Them."

8   Ginsburg and Rapp, *Conceiving the New World Order*.

9   Gurr, *Reproductive Justice*.

10 Oaks, *Giving Up Baby*; Miller, and Griffin, "Safe Haven Laws as Crime Control Theater."

11 Australian Breastfeeding Association, "Analysis of the Ethical Issues in the Breast-feeding and Bedsharing Debate."

12 For more on the ways that institutional racism is masked by a focus on individual or familial "pathology," see Roberts, *Fatal Invention*, among her other work.

13 Roberts, "Race, Gender, and Genetic Technologies."

14 Feminist theorists have similarly argued that anti-abortion rhetoric has at times utilized the discourse of saving "babies" from their mothers, or saving women from irrational choice making. See Denbow, *Governed Through Choice*.

15 For more on how the decision making of poor women and women of color is cast as reckless or uninformed, see Solinger, *Beggars and Choosers*; Roberts, *Killing the Black Body*; Bridges, *Reproducing Race*; Oaks, *Giving Up Baby*.

16 Interview with Milwaukee public health official. The Health Department would later revise this assessment and acknowledge that bed-sharing was a much more difficult behavior to change than they had first assumed.

17 This connection between the safety of an infant and the safety/danger posed by a vehicle is reminiscent of Janelle Taylor's analysis of an early 1990s Volvo commercial. The commercial was dominated by an ultrasound image of a fetus in the womb, with the tagline "Is something inside telling you to buy a Volvo?" Taylor describes this as the equation "of the image of fetus with endangered childhood in need of parental protection," which "drew upon public cultural deployments of fetal imagery in antiabortion materials." See Taylor, *The Public Life of the Fetal Sonogram*, 2–3. The Safe Sleep radio piece likewise plays upon parental anxiety about safety and risk, but in this case the parent is positioned as an embodied threat to the child, rather than a consumer for whom safety is a commodity.

18 Swain, "Birth Outcomes in Milwaukee and Wisconsin: What Can Policymakers Do?"

19 Herzog and Stephenson, "Ad Campaign Unveiled." As of 2016, the Black infant mortality rate was 13.6/1000, leading the *Milwaukee Journal Sentinel* to describe the health department's goal as "all but unachievable." Stephenson, "Milwaukee's Infant Mortality Numbers Improve, but the Racial Disparity Is Still Wide."

20 "Community Health Needs Assessment," Children's Hospital of Wisconsin, 2013, www.chw.org.

21 Herzog and Stephenson, "Ad Campaign Unveiled."

22 Herzog, "Milwaukee Sets Goal."

23 US Census Bureau, "State and County Quick Facts."
24 Downs, "Why Is Milwaukee So Bad for Black People?"
25 Losen et al., "Are We Closing the School Discipline Gap?"
26 Beck, "National Report Card."
27 Losen et al., "Are We Closing the School Discipline Gap?"
28 Downs, "Why Is Milwaukee So Bad for Black People?"
29 Span, "Black Milwaukee's Challenge," 617.
30 Schmid and Crowe, "An Intractable Problem."
31 Schmid, "From Generation to Generation."
32 Byrd, Remington, and Katcher, "Reducing Black Infant Mortality in Wisconsin."
33 Waggoner, *The Zero Trimester*.
34 The majority of "natural" infant deaths in Milwaukee are a result of complications of premature birth (60%) and birth defects (20%). See Milwaukee Health Department, "Infant Mortality."
35 Ngui et al., "City of Milwaukee Fetal Infant Mortality Review Report."
36 David and Collins, "Disparities in Infant Mortality."
37 Ngui et al., "City of Milwaukee Fetal Infant Mortality Review Report."
38 Stephenson, "Milwaukee's Infant Mortality Numbers Improve, but the Racial Disparity Is Still Wide."
39 Centers for Disease Control and Prevention, "Premature Births and the Environment."
40 Jackson et al., "Examining the Burdens of Gendered Racism"; David and Collins, "Differing Birth Weight."
41 Ngui et al., "City of Milwaukee Fetal Infant Mortality Review Report."
42 Wisconsin Department of Health Services, "Wisconsin PRAMS 2016–2017 Surveillance Report," October 2019, www.dhs.wisconsin.gov.
43 FIMR selects roughly 20% of all infant deaths to be reviewed by an interdisciplinary team of social workers, physicians, and public health officials to identify the factors that contributed to the death, and to find ways to improve systems that support pregnant women, families, and children. Ngui et al., "City of Milwaukee Fetal Infant Mortality Review Report."
44 Davis, *Reproductive Injustice*, 204.
45 Davis, *Reproductive Injustice*.
46 Roberts Jr., *Infectious Fear*; David and Collins, "Disparities in Infant Mortality."
47 See Conis, *Vaccine Nation*; Roberts Jr., *Infectious Fear*.
48 Sorgi, "Barrett Starts Six Year Campaign to Drop Infant Mortality Rates."
49 Milwaukee Health Department, "Safe Sleep Campaign."
50 Ibid.
51 Swain, "Birth Outcomes in Milwaukee and Wisconsin."
52 The Safe Sleep Campaign incorporates the AAP's successful "back to sleep" message in its marketing materials by instructing parents to put children to sleep on their backs, and in materials rolled out in July 2012, with three ads representing babies of varying ethnicities sleeping in safe sleep environments—in cribs, on

their backs, with no blankets, pillows, or toys, and the message "Babies should always sleep in a crib" followed by "If you can't afford a crib, please call [phone number]." It is possible that these marketing materials, far less controversial than the "Knife" or "Tombstone" ads, were more measured in response to the media and community backlash against the earlier ads. Milwaukee's campaign builds beyond "back to sleep," however, by specifically targeting bed-sharing in relation to SIDS.

53 Swain, "Birth Outcomes in Milwaukee and Wisconsin."
54 Ibid.
55 Blabey and Gessner, "Infant Bed-Sharing Practices."
56 Milwaukee Health Department, "Safe Sleep Summit Questions and Answers."
57 Doucleff, "Is Sleeping With Your Baby as Dangerous as Doctors Say?"
58 McKenna and McDade, "Why Babies Should Never Sleep Alone"; Sobralske and Gruber, "Risks and Benefits of Parent/Child Bed Sharing."
59 "A Final Resting Place," *Milwaukee Journal Sentinel*, December 29, 2009, www.jsonline.com.
60 Docter, "Should Co-Sleeping that Results in Death Be Criminalized?"
61 Tsing, "Monster Stories," 282. See also Ladd-Taylor and Umansky, *"Bad" Mothers*.
62 Bridges, *Reproducing Race*, 16.
63 Davis, *Reproductive Injustice*, 8.
64 Lee, "Introduction," 16.
65 This event was later rebranded Strong Baby Sabbath, seemingly when the Safe Sleep Campaign phased out and the I Want a Strong Baby campaign began.
66 As of January 2019, nine of the links were active and were therefore included in the analysis of the campaign.
67 Personal communication with Serve Marketing.
68 Serve Marketing.
69 Serve Marketing, "Co-Sleeping."
70 Serve Marketing, "Pregnant Boys." For an analysis of this campaign, see Tanner, "Queering Teenage Pregnancy Prevention." Conference paper presented at the National Women's Studies Association, 2015. Tanner argues that the campaign utilizes shame and disgust toward the specter of male pregnancy to further stigmatize teen mothers in ways that are deeply classed, gendered, and racialized.
71 Interview with Milwaukee Health Department official.
72 Ibid.
73 Clear Channel Outdoor, email message to author, September 19, 2013.
74 Milwaukee Health Department, "Safe Sleep Campaign."
75 Moon, Hauck, and Colson, "Safe Infant Sleep Interventions."
76 Jaggar, *Just Methods*.
77 Mullings and Schulz, "Intersectionality and Health," 4.
78 Lupton, *The Imperative of Health*, 92.
79 Ibid.; Jaggar, *Just Methods*.
80 Moran, *Governing Bodies*, 2.

81 Lupton, *The Imperative of Health*, 61.

82 Dennis, "Does Milwaukee's Ad Campaign Against Sleeping with Babies Go Too Far?"

83 Milwaukee Health Department, "Safe Sleep Campaign."

84 Stephenson, "Safe Sleep Campaign Hits the Streets."

85 Milwaukee Health Department, "Safe Sleep Campaign."

86 Oliviero, *Vulnerability Politics*.

87 The "Helpless" PSA can be found on Serve Marketing's website, at http://serve-marketing.org. The "what she's up against" phrasing may also be a play on words, given that the newborn is literally "up against" the parent in terms of physical proximity while co-sleeping. Similar to the "Knife" and "Rollover" PSAs, in this framing the parent stands in for the deadly force that could suffocate the child.

88 MacKendrick and Cairns, "The Polluted Child."

89 Oaks, "Smoke-filled Wombs," 63.

90 Oaks, "Smoke-filled Wombs."

91 Mansfield, "Gendered Biopolitics of Public Health."

92 See MacKendrick and Cairns, "The Polluted Child"; Oaks, "Smoke-filled Wombs"; Waggoner, "Cultivating the Maternal Future."

93 Waggoner, "Cultivating the Maternal Future," 954.

94 Personal communication with Serve Marketing.

95 Green, "Is Sleeping With Your Baby as Dangerous as Doctors Say?"; McKenna, Ball, and Gettler, "Mother-Infant Co-Sleeping."

96 Young and Shipstone, "Shared Sleeping Surfaces"; Kendall-Tackett, Cong, and Hale, "Mother-Infant Sleep Locations."

97 Milwaukee Health Department, "Infant Mortality."

98 See Ladd-Taylor and Umansky, *"Bad" Mothers*; Douglas and Michaels, *The Mommy Myth*; Warner, *Perfect Madness*.

99 Briggs, *Somebody's Children*, 9.

100 Milwaukee Health Department, "Cribs for Kids Program."

101 Richman, "Controversial Posters."

102 Ward, "Group Donates Cribs."

103 "City of Milwaukee Safe Sleep Program Background," email communication to author, March 4, 2015.

104 Bridges, *Reproducing Race*.

105 Roberts, *Shattered Bonds*.

106 Lahr, Rosenberg, and Lapidus, "Maternal-Infant Bedsharing."

107 Chu, Hackett, andKaur, "Exploring Caregiver Behavior."

108 Ateah and Hamelin, "Maternal Bedsharing Practices."

109 Toner, "Co-Sleeping Deaths Persist in Milwaukee. "

110 Lahr et al., "Maternal- Infant Bed-Sharing."

111 Moon, Hauck, and Colson, "Safe Infant Sleep Interventions."

112 Bornstein, *Handbook of Parenting*.

113 Milwaukee Health Department, "Safe Sleep Campaign."

114 Geiger, "Health Disparities," 261–288.

115 Bridges, *Reproducing Race*, 135.

116 Daniels and Schulz, "Constructing Whiteness."

117 Polcyn and Watson, "'I Just Don't Want Any Baby to Die.'"

118 Bornstein, *Handbook of Parenting*, 3.

119 See Davis, *Women, Race, and Class*; Roberts, *Killing the Black Body*.

120 Reilly, "Wisconsin Has Yet to Implement Drug Screening Requirements." The FoodShare Wisconsin Handbook, released August 3, 2020, states that individuals convicted of a drug felony must test negative for that substance to become eligible for FoodShare, and that a FoodShare applicant must report whether they or any member of their "food unit" has been convicted of felony possession, use, or distribution of a controlled substance. See www.emhandbooks.wisconsin.gov.

121 Gurr, *Reproductive Justice*, 5.

122 Gurr, *Reproductive Justice*, 50.

123 Oaks, "Smoke-filled Wombs."

124 Gurr, *Reproductive Justice*.

125 "B'More for Healthy Babies," Johns Hopkins Center for Communication Programs, accessed January 25, 2019, https://ccp.jhu.edu.

126 Annie E. Casey Foundation, "B'More for Healthy Babies."

127 Moon, Hauck, and Colson, "Safe Infant Sleep Interventions."

128 "B'More for Healthy Babies: About the Initiative," Baltimore Health, accessed January 25, 2019, www.baltimorehealth.org.

129 "B'More for Healthy Babies."

130 Moon, Hauck, and Colson, "Safe Sleep Interventions."

131 Chu, Hackett, and Kaur, "Exploring Caregiver Behavior."

132 Other videos are directed toward caregivers of infants and fathers, featuring "safe sleep ambassadors" who espouse the importance of the message. In one safe sleep ambassador video, Black fathers interact with their children at home and at work, while explaining the significant role that men play in enabling safe sleep, including talking to other men and educating older siblings about sleep safety. See http://healthybabiesbaltimore.com for videos.

133 Meredith Cohn, "Ads to Use Moms Who Lost their Children."

134 Casper and Moore, *Missing Bodies*, 62.

135 Casper and Moore, *Missing Bodies*, 67.

136 "Safe Sleep," accessed October 16, 2020, http://healthybabiesbaltimore.com/safe-sleep/.

137 "About B'More for Healthy Babies," Healthy Babies Baltimore, accessed February 11, 2019, www.healthybabiesbaltimore.com.

138 "Innovations in American Government Awards," Harvard Kennedy School Ash Center for Democratic Governance and Innovation, accessed February 11, 2019, https://ash.harvard.edu.

139 Luthern, "Medical Examiner." This headline is seemingly misleading; while it states that half of infant deaths were related to unsafe sleep, the reporter is

referring to the number of infant deaths that were investigated by the medical examiner's office. The medical examiner may not investigate deaths that occur in a hospital rather than at home, which suggests that the number of infant deaths involving unsafe sleep is unlikely to be near 50%.

140 Ngui et al., "City of Milwaukee Fetal Infant Mortality Review Report."
141 Fox 6 Now Milwaukee, "Is Milwaukee's Anti-Co-Sleeping Campaign Working?"
142 Annie E. Casey Foundation, "B'More for Healthy Babies," 11.
143 Waggoner, The Zero Trimester, 175.
144 "Babies Sleeping Safely: Co-Sleeping With Your Baby," produced by the Black Health Coalition of Wisconsin.
145 Interview with Dr. Patricia McManus.
146 Personal communication with Serve Marketing.
147 Interview with Dr. Patricia McManus.
148 Toner, "Co-Sleeping Deaths Persist in Milwaukee."
149 Interview with Milwaukee Health Department official.
150 Ibid.
151 Spicuzza and Johnson, "Milwaukee Health Commissioner Bevan Baker Out"; Quirmbach, "Milwaukee Officials Hope Lead Controversy Brings Positive Change"; State of Wisconsin Department of Health Services, "Report."
152 Interview with Milwaukee Health Department official.

CHAPTER 4. "EVERYBODY LOSES"

1 Polcyn and Watson, "'I Just Don't Want Any Baby to Die.'"
2 Stephenson, "Wisconsin Bill Would Make Some Co-sleeping Deaths a Felony."
3 State of Wisconsin 2015–2016 Legislature, "2015 Senate Bill 46," https://docs.legis.wisconsin.gov.
4 Swain, "Co-Sleeping Deaths"; Jessica Gathirimu, Testimony Before the Wisconsin Senate Committee on Health and Human Services, April 1, 2016.
5 Swain, "Co-Sleeping Deaths."
6 Michael, "New Bill Would Make Some Co-Sleeping Deaths Felony."
7 Swain, "Co-Sleeping Deaths."
8 Gathirimu, Testimony Before the Wisconsin Senate.
9 Michael, "New Bill Would Make Some Co-Sleeping Deaths Felony."
10 American Academy of Pediatrics Task Force on Sudden Infant Death Syndrome, "SIDS and Other Sleep-Related Infant Deaths," 1033.
11 Chen, Oster, and Williams, "Why Is Infant Mortality Higher in the United States than in Europe?"; Stewart, Co-Sleeping.
12 Cowgill, Rest Uneasy; Centers for Disease Control and Prevention, "About SUID and SIDS"; Stewart, Co-Sleeping.
13 Centers for Disease Control and Prevention, "Sudden Unexpected Infant Death and Sudden Infant Death Syndrome."
14 American Academy of Pediatrics, "Positioning and SIDS."
15 Goldstein et al., "Overall Postneonatal Mortality."

16 Hunt, Darnall, McEntire, and Hyma, "Assigning Cause for Sudden Unexpected Infant Death."

17 Duncan and Byard, "Sudden Infant Death Syndrome."

18 Hunt et al., "Assigning Cause for Sudden Unexpected Infant Death"; Cowgill, *Rest Uneasy.*

19 Cowgill, *Rest Uneasy.*

20 Goldstein et al., "Overall Postneonatal Mortality"; Moon and Hauck, "SIDS Risk"; Shapiro-Mendoza et al., "Classification System."

21 American Academy of Pediatrics Task Force on Sudden Infant Death Syndrome, "The Changing Concept."

22 Cowgill, *Rest Uneasy.*

23 Byard, "Sudden Infant Death Syndrome: Definitions," 4.

24 Duncan and Byard, "Sudden Infant Death Syndrome."

25 Cowgill, *Rest Uneasy.*

26 Byard, "Sudden Infant Death Syndrome," 4.

27 Hunt et al., "Assigning Cause for Sudden Unexpected Infant Death."

28 Shapiro-Mendoza et al., "Classification System." Shapiro-Mendoza et al. note that the International Classification of Diseases-10, which is used to classify the cause of death for a death certificate, does not offer a unique coding category for SUID. As a result, SUID deaths are often coded as SIDS, even if SIDS was not the cause of death that the medical examiner concluded. These death certificates are used to monitor SUID estimates, which causes problems in gathering accurate data.

29 Shapiro-Mendoza et al., "Classification System."

30 Shapiro-Mendoza et al., "The Epidemiology of Sudden Infant Death Syndrome."

31 Goldstein et al., "Overall Postneonatal Mortality"; Shapiro-Mendoza et al., "Classification System and Sudden Unexpected Infant Deaths."

32 Hunt et al., "Assigning Cause"; Shapiro-Mendoza et al., "The Epidemiology of Sudden Infant Death Syndrome"; Cowgill, *Rest Uneasy.*

33 Sidebotham, Marshall, and Garstang, "Responding to Unexpected Child Deaths."

34 Duncan and Byard, "Sudden Infant Death Syndrome."

35 Centers for Disease Control and Prevention, "SUIDI Reporting Form," accessed April 25, 2019, www.cdc.gov.

36 Shapiro-Mendoza et al., "The Epidemiology of Sudden Infant Death Syndrome."

37 Malloy and MacDorman, "Changes in the Classification of Sudden Unexpected Infant Deaths."

38 Shapiro-Mendoza et al., "The Epidemiology of Sudden Infant Death Syndrome."

39 Shapiro-Mendoza et al., "Classification System."

40 Duncan and Byard, "Sudden Infant Death Syndrome," 17.

41 Shapiro-Mendoza et al., "The Epidemiology of Sudden Infant Death Syndrome."

42 Cowgill, *Rest Uneasy*; Moon and Hauck, "SIDS Risk." The ambiguity in defining unexpected infant deaths is well known to SIDS advocates, who are careful to differentiate SIDS from other forms of sudden unexpected infant death (SUID) such as accidental suffocation; the American SIDS Institute notes that SIDS results

from an "unknown medical abnormality or vulnerability" and is a "natural" death, while the other results from "full or partial airway obstruction" and is an accidental death.

43 I am referring to each individual or family as one case. For example, even when both parents are prosecuted separately for the death of a child or children, that family is referred to as one case. A total of 35 total adults were charged in this data set.

44 Accidental asphyxia may also be referred to as accidental suffocation and strangulation in bed (ASSB).

45 The American Academy of Pediatrics defines a safe sleep environment as including "supine positioning, the use of a firm sleep surface, room-sharing without bed-sharing, and the avoidance of soft bedding and overheating." See American Academy of Pediatrics, "SIDS and Other Sleep-Related Infant Deaths: Updated 2016 Recommendations."

46 Flavin and Paltrow, "Arrests of and Forced Interventions on Pregnant Women in the United States," 333.

47 Bazelon, *Charged*.

48 Street addresses were determined in a variety of ways, including media coverage of the cases, on court documents, and in children's obituaries. These street addresses were entered into the database Simply Analytics, which provided the median household income for the block on which each address was located.

49 Goodwin, *Policing the Womb*.

50 Flavin and Paltrow, "Arrests of and Forced Interventions on Pregnant Women in the United States."

51 Collins, "Crime and Parenthood."

52 Eubanks, *Automating Inequality*.

53 Fentiman, *Blaming Mothers*.

54 Ibid.

55 Cunliffe, *Murder, Medicine, and Motherhood*, 37.

56 Cunliffe, *Murder, Medicine and Motherhood*.

57 The number of infant deaths does not match the number of cases because in two cases the parents were charged with the death of two children, respectively. In one case, both children died at the same time, and in another case, the parents were retroactively charged with the death of their first child after their second child died in a similar manner.

58 The location of death was determined using media reports and/or legal documents. If a document did not specifically identify the location as a bed, but used the term "bed-sharing," then the location was coded as a bed. In one case the reporting identified "co-sleeping" but did not specify a location, and therefore location could not be coded.

59 A small number of cases described the sleep surface as a mattress on the floor; these were coded as a bed because the risk factor for a mattress is similar whether on the floor or in a bed frame.

60 Couches and chairs are considered particularly dangerous locations for co-sleeping because of the increased likelihood of entrapment between cushions, or "overlay" by an adult. American Academy of Pediatrics Task Force on Sudden Infant Death Syndrome, "SIDS and Other Sleep-Related Infant Deaths."

61 Bazelon, *Charged*.

62 Of the three cases remaining, all three had either been previously counseled and/or already lost a baby to SIDS/accidental suffocation.

63 Centers for Disease Control and Prevention, "Understanding the Epidemic," last accessed April 29, 2019, www.cdc.gov.

64 Rummans, Burton, and Dawson, "How Good Intentions Contributed to Bad Outcomes."

65 Knight, *Addicted. Pregnant. Poor.*

66 American Civil Liberties Union, "Words from Prison"; Campbell, *Using Women*.

67 Paltrow, "Punishment and Prejudice."

68 Raphael, *Freeing Tammy*, 41.

69 Flavin, *Our Bodies, Our Crimes*, 184.

70 Fixmer-Oraiz, *Homeland Maternity*, 13.

71 Reich, *Fixing Families*.

72 Wolf, *Is Breast Best?*

73 New York Times Editorial Board, "A Woman's Right, Part 4" ; Roberts, *Killing the Black Body*.

74 Washington, *Medical Apartheid*, 214–215.

75 Amnesty International, "Criminalizing Pregnancy."

76 New York Times Editorial Board, "A Woman's Right, Part 4."

77 Guttmacher Institute, "Substance Use During Pregnancy."

78 Hunt et al., "Assigning Cause for Sudden Unexpected Infant Death."

79 Fentiman, *Blaming Mothers*.

80 New York Times Editorial Board, "A Woman's Right"; National Advocates for Pregnant Women, "Victory in Texas!"

81 Bridges, *The Poverty of Privacy Rights*.

82 Reich, *Fixing Families*.

83 Gurr, *Reproductive Justice*.

84 Eubanks, *Automating Inequality*, 162.

85 Cowgill, *Rest Uneasy*.

86 Fentiman, *Blaming Mothers*.

87 Khazan, "Into the Body of Another"; Kunins et al., "The Effect of Race on Provider Decisions." Kunins et al. do temper their findings of a disproportionate testing of Black women and babies by noting that had they been able to control for other factors like clinical behavior or a history of substance abuse, the connection between race and drug testing may have disappeared.

88 Bazelon, *Charged*.

89 Leverentz, *The Ex-Prisoners Dilemma*, 7.

90 Goodwin, *Policing the Womb*.

91 Illinois General Assembly, "Illinois Compiled Statutes."

92 Hager, "Six States Where Felons Can't Get Food Stamps"; Knight, *Addicted. Pregnant. Poor.*

93 Stone, "Pregnant Women and Substance Use"; Knight, *Addicted. Pregnant. Poor.*

94 Fentiman, *Blaming Mothers*; Stone, "Pregnant Women and Substance Use."

95 Gurr, *Reproductive Justice.*

96 To maintain the privacy of individuals in this data set, I will not be citing sources for court documents or media coverage of the cases in the published edition of the book.

97 Lupton, *The Imperative of Health*, 85.

98 Campbell, *Using Women*, 3.

99 Fixmer-Oraiz, *Homeland Maternity.*

100 National Conference of State Legislatures, "Sudden Unexpected Infant Death Legislation."

101 Cribs for Kids, "The National Safe Sleep Hospital Certification."

102 B'More for Healthy Babies, "B'More for Healthy Babies: Achievements and Results 2010–2013."

103 Krugman and Cumpsty-Fowler, "A Hospital-Based Initiative."

104 Moreover, co-sleeping is remarkably commonplace—a large, population-based study in Oregon found that 20.5% of women reported that they "always" bed-shared with their infants, 14.7% said that they "almost always" co-slept, and 41.4% reported that they sometimes shared a bed. In other words, the parents being prosecuted in this study are engaging in a practice that more than 75% of parents are also doing. Lahr, Rosenberg, and Lapidus, "Maternal Infant Bed-sharing."

105 Reich, *Fixing Families*, 12.

106 State of Wisconsin 2015–2016 Legislature, "2015 Senate Bill 46," https://docs.legis.wisconsin.gov/2015/related/proposals/sb46.pdf.

107 Reich, *Fixing Families*, 172.

108 Cosman, "Anxiety Governance."

109 Mounk, *The Age of Responsibility*, 22.

110 Sankaran, "Child Welfare's Scarlet Letter."

111 Roth, "No New Babies?"

112 Ibid.

113 Information from "Erin's" arrest affidavit.

114 Brush, "Work and Love in the Gendered U.S. Insecurity State."

115 Cowgill, *Rest Uneasy*, 78.

116 Chemaly, *Rage Becomes Her.*

117 Reich, *Fixing Families.*

118 Wendling, "SIDS Risk Up Fourfold."

119 Duncan and Byard, "Sudden Infant Death Syndrome."

120 American Academy of Pediatrics Task Force on Sudden Infant Death Syndrome, "The Changing Concept of Sudden Infant Death Syndrome," 1251.

121 Cunliffe, *Murder, Medicine, and Motherhood*.

122 Moon and Hauck, "SIDS Risk."

123 Obladen, "Cot Death."

124 Cowgill, *Rest Uneasy*, 90.

125 Shapiro-Mendoza et al., "Classification System."

126 Bridges, *The Poverty of Privacy Rights*.

127 Goodwin, *Policing the Womb*; Roberts, *Killing the Black Body*.

CHAPTER 5. ADVERTISING INFANT SAFETY

1 *Black Mirror*, Season 4, Episode 2, "Arkangel," director Jodie Foster, aired on December 29, 2017, Netflix, www.netflix.com.

2 Peck, "Baby Monitor 2.0 Is Born."

3 "Owlet Launches Entirely Redesigned Smart Sock."

4 Centers for Disease Control and Prevention, "Infant Mortality."

5 Transportation Security Administration, "TSA Releases Roadmap."

6 Magnet, *When Biometrics Fail*, 8. While Owlet's technology gathers and tracks data, rather than necessarily using them to identify individuals, the company defines what they does as a form of biometrics on its website, stating that the smart sock and sensor "work to collect heart rate, oxygen, and other biometric data for parents." http://blog.owletcare.com.

7 Lupton, *The Quantified Self*.

8 Magnet, *When Biometrics Fail*.

9 Consumers may be rightly wary of biometric technologies that seem to promise too much due to the recent scandal surrounding the company Theranos. Theranos was founded by in 2003 by nineteen-year-old Elizabeth Holmes, who contended that she had invented a blood-testing device that could process hundreds of tests with just the prick of a finger. The company was valued at $9 billion before investigations revealed that its testing was often unreliable and inaccurate, and did not perform as well as competing alternatives. The company has since declared bankruptcy, and its founder is facing criminal charges. Laurel Wamsley, "Theranos."

10 Gold, "Sleeping Like a Baby."

11 Michaels and Douglas argue that working mothers became a market in the 1970s, and that an emphasis on child safety was key to advertising this "new" demographic. See Douglas and Michaels, *The Mommy Myth*.

12 Wilson and Yochim, *Mothering Through Precarity*.

13 MacKendrick, *Better Safe Than Sorry*.

14 Onion, "The World's First Baby Monitor."

15 Catlin, "After the Tragic Lindbergh Kidnapping."

16 Stearns, *Anxious Parents*.

17 Renfro, "Keeping Children Safe Is Good Business"; Stearns, *Anxious Parents*, 34.

18 Renfro, "Keeping Children Safe Is Good Business."

19 Ibid.; Green, "Kiddie Alert: Sad Commentary on Life."

20 Markoff, "Fight of the (Next) Century." Notably, this article pits Sony and Microsoft as key players in the forthcoming "smart" technology battle, which would come to be dominated by corporations like Apple, Amazon, and Google.

21 Biggs, "Keeping an Eye on the Little One via a Video Feed."

22 Nelson, *Parenting Out of Control.*

23 Nichter, "Harm Reduction," 18.

24 Nelson, "Watching Children," 224.

25 Cowgill, *Rest Uneasy.*

26 Ibid., 115.

27 Ibid., 126.

28 King, "Marketing Wearable Home Baby Monitors"; American Academy of Pediatrics, "Apnea, Sudden Infant Death Syndrome, and Home Monitoring."

29 Canal, "This Company Makes Wearable Devices for Babies."

30 Toompas, "16 High Tech Baby Monitors."

31 Nelkin, "Foreword," viii.

32 "Wearable Technology Is New Top Fitness Trend for 2019, According to ACSM Survey," *BusinessWire*, December 5, 2018, www.businesswire.com.

33 Blei, "The False Promises of Wellness Culture."

34 Blei, "The False Promises of Wellness Culture"; Ehrenreich, *Natural Causes.*

35 Lupton, *The Quantified Self.*

36 Elman, "'Find Your Fit,'" 3761.

37 White, "Infant Wearables"; Bonafide, Localio, and Ferro, "Accuracy of Pulse Oximetry-Based Home Baby Monitors."

38 CBS News, "Experts Warn Smartphone Baby Monitors May Do More Harm Than Good."

39 Magnet, *When Biometrics Fail*, 12.

40 Lupton, *The Quantified Self.*

41 Dangerfield, Ward, Davidson, and Adamian, "Initial Experience and Usage Patterns."

42 Mamo and Fosket, "Scripting the Body."

43 "Terms and Conditions," Owlet Baby Care, last updated May 8, 2019, https://owletcare.com.

44 Dangerfield et al., "Initial Experience and Usage Patterns."

45 Metzl and Kirkland, "Introduction: Why Against Heath?", 9.

46 Ibid., 4.

47 Conrad, "Wellness as Virtue," 387.

48 This sponsored content was posted by the users ohlafemmeblog, thismamaloveslife, and vitafamblog on Instagram as of July 1, 2019, and were just a few of the posts about Owlet that contained the hashtag #sponsored or #ad.

49 Leaver, "Intimate Surveillance."

50 Farkas, "'Tons of Useful Stuff.'"

51 Clarke et al., *Biomedicalization.*

52 Clarke et al., *Biomedicalization*, 48.

53 Clarke et al., *Biomedicalization*.

54 King, "Marketing Wearable Home Baby Monitors"; Bonafide, Jamison, and Foglia, "The Emerging Market."

55 Callahan, "New Type of Baby Monitors."

56 Bonafide, Jamison, and Foglia, "The Emerging Market."

57 Ibid.

58 Bonafide, Localio, and Ferro, "Accuracy of Pulse Oximetry-Based Home Baby Monitors."

59 CBS News, "Experts Warn Smartphone Baby Monitors May do More Harm Than Good."

60 McCullough, "Why That Wearable Baby Monitor Could Do Your Baby More Harm Than Good."

61 Fernandes, *Feminists Rethink the Neoliberal State*.

62 See Frankel, "Fisher-Price Invented a Popular Baby Sleeper."

63 American Academy of Pediatrics Task Force on Sudden Infant Death Syndrome, "SIDS and Other Sleep-Related Infant Deaths."

64 Thompson, "Pediatricians Say No to Wearable Smartphone Baby Monitors."

65 Callahan, "New Type of Baby Monitors Offer 'Peace of Mind' But May Deliver Just the Opposite."

66 Elliott, "Pharmaceutical Propaganda."

67 Mamo, Nelson, and Clark, "Producing and Protecting Risky Girlhoods."

68 Lupton, *The Quantified Self*, 54.

69 Waggoner, *The Zero Trimester*, 92.

70 Centers for Disease Control and Prevention, "Infant Mortality."

71 Centers for Disease Control and Prevention, "Sudden Unexpected Infant Death and Sudden Infant Death Syndrome."

72 Waggoner, *The Zero Trimester*, 132.

73 DiQuinzio, *The Impossibility of Motherhood*, xiii.

74 Hays, *The Cultural Contradictions of Motherhood*.

75 Douglas and Michaels, *The Mommy Myth*. See also Warner, *Perfect Madness*.

76 Dubriwny, *The Vulnerable Empowered Woman*.

77 Swearingen, "Making My Baby A Smart Baby Was a Mistake"; Callahan, "New Type of Baby Monitors"; Paul, "These 'Extreme Baby Monitors.'"

78 Wilson and Yochim, *Mothering Through Precarity*.

79 For more on the how women's "master status" as mothers is reinforced by health and medical discourse, see Miranda Waggoner's *The Zero Trimester*.

80 Apple, *Perfect Motherhood*.

81 Wilson and Yochim, *Mothering Through Precarity*.

82 Owlet Baby Care, https://owletcare.com.

83 Fixmer-Oraiz, *Homeland Maternity*, 12.

84 Johnston and Taylor, "Feminist Consumerism and Fat Activists."

85 Noble, *Algorithms of Oppression*, 165.

86 Murdoch, "Finally There's a Baby Monitor That Can Constantly Scare the Crap Out of You."

87 Schweitzer, "Why I Ditched the Baby Monitor." Interestingly, the stock photo that goes along with this article is of a pair of white hands holding a video monitor, which shows a baby sleeping on their stomach, in an unsafe sleep environment (with blankets, stuffed animals, and other items in the crib). See also Walker, "Why I Don't Use a Baby Monitor."

88 Dubriwny, *The Vulnerable Empowered Woman*, 81; Fixmer-Oraiz, *Homeland Maternity*.

89 Leaver, "Intimate Surveillance."

90 Ibid.

91 Lupton, *The Quantified Self*, 2.

92 Ibid., 2.

93 Owlet Baby Care, "Owlet Care Privacy Policy."

94 Ibid.

95 Leaver, "Intimate Surveillance," 3.

96 Owlet Baby Care, "Terms and Conditions."

97 Leaver, "Intimate Surveillance."

98 Silverman, "Privacy Under Surveillance Capitalism."

99 Montgomery, Chester, and Kopp, "Health Wearable Devices," 2.

100 Todd, "Baby Monitors."

101 Owlet Baby Care, https://owletcare.com.

102 Owlet Baby Care, "Owlet Care Privacy Policy."

103 Montgomery et al., "Health Wearable Devices."

104 Ibid., 109.

105 American Academy of Pediatrics, "Apnea, Sudden Infant Death Syndrome, and Home Monitoring."

106 Cowgill, *Rest Uneasy*.

107 "Family Law—Opioid–Exposed Newborns and Parents Addicted to Opioids—Mobile Application," Maryland House Bill 1271 (2018), http://mgaleg.maryland.gov.

108 Wolford, "Legislation Would Help Monitor Newborn Children of Drug Addicts."

109 Ibid. The original drafting of the bill included a requirement that women who have been charged with possession of a controlled substance are referred to social services, even if the infant is not born exposed. In Maryland, the state currently does not mandate such referrals even if women or their infants have a positive toxicology report; the bill would have gone even further to link charges of opioid possession with child endangerment, and in the mind of its author, with co-sleeping deaths.

110 For more on this, see work by feminist scholars on vaccine resistance, such as Jennifer Reich, *Calling the Shots*; and Elena Conis, *Vaccine Nation*.

CONCLUSION

1   Adhikari et al., "Assessment of Community-Level Disparities."
2   Rollston and Galea, "COVID-19 and the Social Determinants of Health," 687.
3   See Chemaly, "Coronavirus Could Hurt Women the Most."
4   Tankersley and Casselman, "Here's How."
5   World Health Organization, "COVID-19 Could Reverse Decades of Progress."
6   Preston, "Did Lockdowns Lower Premature Birth?"
7   World Health Organization, "COVID-19 Could Reverse Decades of Progress."
8   Mandavilli, "Small Social Gatherings Aren't Driving the Virus Surge (So Far)."
9   Ibid.
10 Cowgill, *Rest Uneasy*.
11 Centers for Disease Control and Prevention, "Sudden Unexpected Infant Death and Sudden Infant Death Syndrome."
12 Ross et al., "Introduction."
13 Luna, *Reproductive Rights as Human Rights*, 15.
14 See also Gurr, *Reproductive Justice*.
15 Roth, "'She Doesn't Deserve to Be Treated Like This.'"
16 David and Collins Jr., "Disparities in Infant Mortality."
17 Ross and Solinger, *Reproductive Justice*.
18 Geronimus, "Understanding and Eliminating Racial Inequalities," 135.
19 Davis, *Reproductive Injustice*.
20 Collins Jr. et al., "Very Low Birthweight in African American Infants"; Chaterjee and Davis, "How Racism May Cause Black Mothers to Suffer the Death of Their Infants."
21 Womack, Rossen, and Martin, "Singleton Low Birthweight Rates."
22 Ostfeld et al., "Prematurity and Sudden Infant Death in the United States."
23 Owlet Baby Care, "The Owlet Baby Band Tracker."
24 Harrison, "How Pregnancy Monitoring Technology Contributes to the War on Women."
25 American Academy of Pediatrics, "SIDS and Other Sleep-Related Infant Deaths," 2.
26 Waggoner, *The Zero Trimester*, 176.
27 Almeling, *GUYnecology*.
28 See Casper, *The Making of the Unborn Patient*; Dubow, *Ourselves Unborn*; Martin, *The Woman in the Body*; Oaks, *Smoking and Pregnancy*; Flavin and Paltrow, "Arrests of and Forced Interventions on Pregnant Women in the United States"; Petchesky, "Fetal Images"; Rapp, *Testing Women, Testing the Fetus*; Taylor, *The Public Life of the Fetal Sonogram*; Hartouni, *Cultural Conceptions*.
29 Valdez, "The Redistribution of Reproductive Responsibility."
30 Ibid.
31 Joyner et al., "Where Should My Baby Sleep?"
32 See Valdez, "The Redistribution of Reproductive Responsibility."

33 Almeling makes a similar argument regarding the messages about paternal effects
    on children's health; the focus on individualized risk, she argues, assumes that
    all men have the resources to modify their behaviors, and sidelines the role of
    environmental or structural factors that contribute to health risks. See Almeling,
    GUYnecology.
34 Zavella, *The Movement for Reproductive Justice.*
35 Interview with Dr. Patricia McManus.
36 Ibid.
37 Valdez, "The Redistribution of Reproductive Responsibility."

REFERENCES

Abdou, Cleopatra M., and Adam W. Fingerhut. "Stereotype Threat Among Black and White Women in Healthcare Settings." *Cultural Diversity and Ethnic Minority Psychology* 20, no. 3 (2014): 316–323.

Abramson, Ashley. "This Is What Postpartum Anxiety Feels Like." *New York Times*, April 15, 2020. https://parenting.nytimes.com.

Adhikari, Samrachana, Nicholas Pantaleo, Justin Feldman, Olugbenga Ogedegbe, Lorna Thorpe, and Andrea Troxel. "Assessment of Community-Level Disparities in Coronavirus Disease 2019 (COVID-19) Infections and Deaths in Large US Metropolitan Areas." *JAMA Network Open* 3, no. 7 (2020): e2016938.

Almeling, Rene. *GUYnecology: The Missing Science of Men's Reproductive Health.* Berkeley: University of California Press, 2020.

American Academy of Pediatrics. "Positioning and SIDS." *Pediatrics* 89, no. 6 (1992): 1120–1126.

——. "Apnea, Sudden Infant Death Syndrome, and Home Monitoring." *Pediatrics* 11, no. 4 (2003): 914–917.

——. "Fisher-Price Recalls Rock 'n Play Amid Pressure from AAP." *AAP News*, April 12, 2019. www.aappublications.org.

——. "AAP Urges US Consumer Product Safety Commission to Recall Fisher-Price Rock 'n Play Sleeper." April 9, 2019. www.aap.org.

American Academy of Pediatrics Task Force on Sudden Infant Death Syndrome. "Positioning and SIDS." *Pediatrics* 89, no. 6 (1992): 1120–1126.

——. "Positioning and Sudden Infant Death Syndrome (SIDS): Update." *Pediatrics* 98, no. 6 (1996): 1216–1218.

——. "Changing Concepts of Sudden Infant Death Syndrome: Implications for Infant Sleeping Environment and Sleep Position." *Pediatrics* 105, no. 3 (2000): 650–656.

——. "The Changing Concept of Sudden Infant Death Syndrome: Diagnostic Coding Shifts, Controversies Regarding the Sleeping Environment, and New Variables to Consider in Reducing Risk." *Pediatrics* 116, no. 5 (2005): 1245–1255.

——. "SIDS and Other Sleep-Related Infant Deaths: Expansion of Recommendations for a Safe Infant Sleeping Environment." *Pediatrics* 128, no. 5 (2011): 1030–1039.

——. "SIDS and Other Sleep-Related Infant Deaths: Updated 2016 Recommendations for a Safe Infant Sleeping Environment." *Pediatrics* 138, no. 5 (2016): 1–12.

American Civil Liberties Union. "Words from Prison: Drug Policy, Race, and Women's Incarceration." Accessed May 23, 2019. www.aclu.org.

Amnesty International. "Criminalizing Pregnancy: Policing Pregnant Women Who Use Drugs in the USA." 2017. www.amnesty.org.

Anders, Thomas F., and Teresa R. Taylor. "Babies and Their Sleep Environment." *Children's Environments* 11, no. 2 (Summer 1994): 123–134.

Annie E. Casey Foundation. "B'More for Healthy Babies: A Collaborative Funding Model to Reduce Infant Mortality in Baltimore." 2018. www.aecf.org.

Apple, Rima. "Constructing Mothers: Scientific Motherhood in the Nineteenth and Twentieth Centuries." In *Mothers and Motherhood: Readings in American History*, edited by Rima Apple and Janet Golden, 90–110. Columbus: Ohio State University Press, 1997.

———. *Perfect Motherhood: Science and Childrearing in America*. New Brunswick, NJ: Rutgers University Press, 2006.

Armstrong, Elizabeth. "Lessons in Control: Prenatal Education in the Hospital." *Social Problems* 47, no. 4 (2000): 583–605.

Åström, Berit. "A Narrative of Fear: Advice to Mothers." *Literature and Medicine* 33, no. 1 (Spring 2015): 113–131.

Ateah, Christine, and Kathy Hamelin. "Maternal Bedsharing Practices, Experiences, and Awareness of Risks." *Journal of Obstetric Gynecologic & Neonatal Nursing* 37, no. 3 (2008): 274–281.

Atkinson, V. Sue. "Shifting Sands: Professional Advice to Mothers in the First Half of the Twentieth Century." *Journal of Family History* 42, no. 2 (2017): 128–146.

Australian Breastfeeding Association. "Analysis of the Ethical Issues in the Breastfeeding and Bedsharing Debate." *Breastfeeding Review* 20, no. 3 (2012): 7–17.

Ball, Helen. "Reasons to Bed-Share: Why Parents Sleep with Their Infants." *Journal of Reproductive and Infant Psychology* 20, no. 4 (2002): 207–221.

Ball, Helen, Cecília Tomori, and James McKenna. "Toward an Integrated Anthropology of Infant Sleep." *American Anthropologist* 121, no. 3 (2019): 596–612.

Baltimore Health. "B'More for Healthy Babies: About the Initiative." Accessed January 25, 2019. www.baltimorehealth.org.

Bartick, Melissa, Cecília Tomori, and Helen L. Ball. "Babies in Boxes and the Missing Links on Safe Sleep: Human Evolution and Cultural Revolution." *Maternal and Child Nutrition* 14, no. 2 (2018): e12544.

Bazelon, Emily. *Charged: The New Movement to Transform American Prosecution and End Mass Incarceration*. New York: Random House, 2019.

Beck, Molly. "National Report Card: Wisconsin's Achievement Gap Worst in Nation." *Wisconsin State Journal*, November 8, 2013. http://host.madison.com.

Beck, Ulrich. *Risk Society: Toward a New Modernity*. London: Sage, 1992.

The Bible. 21st Century King James Version. Deuel Enterprises, 1994.

Biggs, John. "Keeping an Eye on the Little One via a Video Feed." *New York Times*, October 4, 2007. www.nytimes.com.

Blabey, Margaret H., and Bradford D. Gessner. "Infant Bed-Sharing Practices and Associated Risk Factors Among Births and Infant Deaths in Alaska." *Public Health Reports* 124, no. 4 (2009): 527–534.

Blair, Peter, Peter Sidebotham, Anna Pease, and Peter Fleming. "Bed-Sharing in the Absence of Hazardous Circumstances: Is There a Risk of Sudden Infant Death Syndrome? An Analysis from Two Case Control Studies Conducted in the UK." *PLOS One* 9, no. 9 (2014): e107799.

Blei, Daniela. "The False Promises of Wellness Culture." *JSTOR Daily*, January 4, 2017. https://daily.jstor.org.

B'More for Healthy Babies. "B'More for Healthy Babies: Achievements and Results 2010–2013." Accessed December 31, 2018. https://health.baltimorecity.gov.

Bombard, Jennifer, Katherine Kortsmit, Lee Warner, Carrie Shapiro-Mendoza, Shanna Cox, Charlan Kroelinger, Sharyn Parks, Deborah Dee, Denise D'Angelo, Ruben Smith, et al. "Vital Signs: Trends and Disparities in Infant Safe Sleep Practices—United States, 2009–2015." *Morbidity and Mortality Weekly Report* 67, no. 1 (2018): 39–46.

Bonafide, Christopher, David T. Jamison, and Elizabeth E. Foglia. "The Emerging Market of Smartphone-Integrated Infant Physiologic Monitors." *Journal of the American Medical Association* 317, no. 4 (Winter 2017): 353–354.

Bonafide, Christopher, Russell Localio, and Daria Ferro. "Accuracy of Pulse Oximetry-Based Home Baby Monitors." *Journal of the American Medical Association* 320, no. 7 (2018): 717–719.

Bornstein, Marc H. *Handbook of Parenting: Volume Four Social Conditions and Applied Parenting.* New York: Routledge, 2002.

Bridges, Khiara. *Reproducing Race: An Ethnography of Pregnancy as a Site of Racialization.* Berkeley: University of California Press, 2011.

———. *The Poverty of Privacy Rights.* Stanford, CA: Stanford University Press, 2017.

Briggs, Laura. *Somebody's Children: The Politics of Transnational and Transracial Adoption.* Durham, NC: Duke University Press, 2012.

Brooker, Charlie, writer. *Black Mirror.* Season 4, Episode 2, "Arkangel." Directed by Jodie Foster. Aired December 29, 2017 on Netflix. www.netflix.com.

Brush, Lisa D. "Work and Love in the Gendered U.S. Insecurity State." In *Gender, Violence, and Human Security: Critical Feminist Perspectives,* edited by Aili Mari Tripp, Myra Marx Ferree, and Christina Ewig, 109–131. New York: NYU Press, 2013.

Business Wire. "Wearable Technology Is New Top Fitness Trend for 2019, According to ACSM Survey." *BusinessWire,* December 5, 2018. www.businesswire.com.

Buskens, Petra. "The Impossibility of 'Natural Parenting' for Modern Mothers: On Social Structure and the Formation of Habit." *Journal for the Association of Research on Mothering* 3, no. 1 (2001): 75–86.

Byard, Roger W. "Sudden Infant Death Syndrome: Definitions." In *Sudden Infant and Early Childhood Death: The Past, Present, and Future,* edited by Jhodie Duncan and Roger Byard, 1–14. Adelaide, Australia: University of Adelaide Press, 2018.

Byrd, DeAnnah R., Patrick L. Remington, and Murray L. Katcher. "Reducing Black Infant Mortality in Wisconsin: Best Practices and Model Programs." *Wisconsin Public Health and Health Policy* 6, no. 3 (2005).

Cairns, Kate, Josée Johnston, and Norah MacKendrick. "Feeding the 'Organic Child': Mothering Through Ethical Consumption." *Journal of Consumer Culture* 13, no. 2 (2013): 97–118.

Callahan, Alice. "New Type of Baby Monitors Offer 'Peace of Mind' but May Deliver Just the Opposite." *Washington Post*, May 6, 2017. www.washingtonpost.com.

Campbell, Nancy. *Using Women: Gender, Drug Policy, and Social Justice.* New York: Routledge, 2000.

Canal, Emily. "This Company Makes Wearable Devices for Babies so Their Parents Can Sleep Better." *Inc.* December 4, 2018. www.inc.com.

Casper, Monica. *The Making of the Unborn Patient: A Social Anatomy of Fetal Surgery.* New Brunswick, NJ: Rutgers University Press, 1998.

Casper, Monica, and Lisa Jean Moore. *Missing Bodies: The Politics of Visibility.* New York: NYU Press, 2009.

Catlin, Roger. "After the Tragic Lindbergh Kidnapping, Artist Isamu Noguchi Designed the First Baby Monitor." *The Smithsonian.com*, December 20, 2016. www.smithsonianmag.com.

CBS News. "Experts Warn Smartphone Baby Monitors May Do More Harm Than Good." *CBS This Morning*, January 25, 2017. www.cbsnews.com.

Centers for Disease Control and Prevention. "About SUIDS and SIDS." Page last reviewed June 15, 2021. www.cdc.gov.

———. "Data and Statistics." Page last reviewed April 28, 2021. www.cdc.gov.

———. "Infant Mortality." Page last reviewed September 8, 2021. www.cdc.gov.

———. "Premature Births and the Environment." Page last reviewed December 3, 2021. https://ephtracking.cdc.gov.

———. "Safe Sleep for Babies." Page last reviewed January 9, 2018. www.cdc.gov.

———. "Sudden Unexpected Infant Death and Sudden Infant Death Syndrome." Page last reviewed December 31, 2020. www.cdc.gov.

———. "SUIDI Reporting Form." Page last reviewed March 18, 2021. www.cdc.gov.

———. "Understanding the Epidemic." Page last reviewed March 12, 2021. www.cdc.gov.

Chaterjee, Rhitu, and Rebecca Davis. "How Racism May Cause Black Mothers to Suffer the Death of Their Infants." *National Public Radio*, December 20, 2017. www.npr.org.

Chemaly, Soraya. *Rage Becomes Her: The Power of Women's Anger.* New York: Atria Books, 2018.

———. "Coronavirus Could Hurt Women the Most." *NBC News*, April 20, 2020. www.nbcnews.com.

Chen, Alice, Emily Oster, and Heidi Williams. "Why Is Infant Mortality Higher in the United States than in Europe?" *American Economic Journal: Economic Policy* 8, no. 2 (May 2016): 89–124.

Children's Hospital of Wisconsin. "Community Health Needs Assessment." 2013. www.chw.org.

Chu, Tracy, Martine Hackett, and Navpreet Kaur. "Exploring Caregiver Behavior and Knowledge About Unsafe Sleep Surfaces in Infant Injury Death Cases." *Health Education and Behavior* 42, no. 3 (2015): 293–301.

Clarke, Adele, Laura Mamo, Jennifer Fosket, Jennifer Fishman, Janet Shim, eds., *Biomedicalization: Technoscience, Health, and Illness in the US*. Durham, NC: Duke University Press, 2010.

Clarke, Adele, Janet Shim, Laura Mamo, Jennifer Ruth Fosket, and Jennifer Fishman. "Biomedicalization: Technoscientific Transformations of Health, Illness, and US Biomedicine." In *Biomedicalization: Technoscience, Health, and Illness in the US*, edited by Adele Clarke et al., 48–87. Durham, NC: Duke University Press, 2010.

CNN. "Grieving Family Wants Fisher-Price Sleeper Recalled." *CNN*, April 11, 2019. YouTube Video. https://www.youtube.com/watch?v=E5_tHF3uOzA.

Cohn, Meredith. "Ads to Use Moms Who Lost Their Children to Promote Safe Sleeping Practices for Babies." *Baltimore Sun*. Accessed February 11, 2019. www.nwsids.org.

Colen, Shellee. "'Like a Mother to Them: Stratified Reproduction and West Indian Childcare Workers and Employers in New York." In *Conceiving the New World Order: The Global Politics of Reproduction*, edited by Faye Ginsburg and Rayna Rapp. Berkeley: University of California Press, 1995.

Collins, Caitlyn. *Making Motherhood Work: How Women Manage Careers and Caregiving*. Princeton, NJ: Princeton University Press, 2019.

Collins, James W. Jr., Richard J. David, Arden Handler, Stephen Wall, and Steven Andes. "Very Low Birthweight in African American Infants: The Role of Maternal Exposure to Interpersonal Racial Discrimination." *American Journal of Public Health* 94, no. 12 (2004): 2132–2138.

Collins, Jennifer. "Crime and Parenthood: The Uneasy Case for Prosecution of Negligent Parents." *Northwestern University Law Review* 100, no. 2 (Winter 2006): 807–855.

Collins, Patricia Hill. *Black Feminist Thought: Knowledge, Consciousness, and the Politics of Empowerment*. New York: Routledge, 1990.

Colson, Eve R., Suzette Levenson, Denis Rybin, Catharine Calianos, Amy Margolis, Theodore Colton, George Lister, and Michael J. Corwin. "Barriers to Following the Supine Sleep Recommendation Among Mothers at Four Centers for the Women, Infants, and Children Program." *Pediatrics* 118, no. 2 (2006): 243–250.

Colson, Eve R., Marian Willinger, Denis Rybin, Timothy Heeren, Lauren Smith, George Lister, and Michael Corwin. "Trends and Factors Associated with Infant Bedsharing, 1993–2010, the National Infant Sleep Position Study." *JAMA Pediatric* 167, no. 11 (2013): 1032–1037.

Conis, Elena. *Vaccine Nation: America's Changing Relationship with Immunization*. Chicago: University of Chicago Press, 2015.

Conrad, Peter. "Wellness as Virtue: Morality and the Pursuit of Health." *Culture, Medicine, and Psychiatry* 18 (1994): 385–401.

ConsumerNotice.org. "Fisher-Price Rock 'n Play Lawsuit." *ConsumerNotice.org*. Accessed September 16, 2020. www.consumernotice.org.

"Consumer Reports: Congress Should Pass 'Lifesaving' Safe Sleep For Babies Act." May 13, 2021, www.consumerreport.org.

Cossman, Brenda. "Anxiety Governance." *Law & Social Inquiry* 38, no. 4 (Fall 2013): 892–919.

Cott, Nancy. *The Bonds of Womanhood: "Woman's Sphere" in New England, 1780–1835.* New Haven, CT: Yale University Press, 1977.

Cowgill, Brittany. *Rest Uneasy: Sudden Infant Death Syndrome in Twentieth-Century America.* New Brunswick, NJ: Rutgers University Press, 2018.

Cowles, Nancy A., Rachel Weintraub, William Wallace, Joan Muratore, Remington A. Gregg, and Edmund Mierzwinski. "Comments of Kids in Danger, Consumer Federation of America, Consumers Union, Public Citizen, and US PIRG to the US Consumer Product Safety Commission on the Notice of Proposed Rulemaking 'Safety Standard for Inclined Sleep Products.'" June 21, 2017. www.citizen.org.

Cribs for Kids. "The National Safe Sleep Hospital Certification." Accessed December 31, 2018. https://cribsforkids.org.

Cunliffe, Emma. *Murder, Medicine, and Motherhood.* Oxford: Hart Publishing, 2011.

Dangerfield, Michelle, Kenneth Ward, Luke Davidson, and Milena Adamian. "Initial Experience and Usage Patterns with the Owlet Smart Sock Monitor in 47,495 Newborns." *Global Pediatric Health* 4 (2017): 1–8.

Daniels, Jesse, and Amy Schulz. "Constructing Whiteness in Health Disparities Research." In *Gender, Race, Class, and Health*, edited by Leith Mullings and Amy J. Schulz, 89–130. San Francisco: Jossey-Bass, 2006.

Darnall, Robert A., Michael H. Goodstein, Fern R. Hauck, and Rachel Y. Moon. "American Academy of Pediatrics' Task Force on SIDS Fully Supports Breastfeeding." *Breastfeeding Medicine* 9, no. 9 (2014): 486–487.

David, Richard, and James Collins. "Differing Birth Weight Among Infants of U.S.-Born Blacks, African-Born Blacks, and U.S.-Born Whites." *New England Journal of Medicine* 337, no. 17 (1997): 1209–1214.

———. "Disparities in Infant Mortality: What's Genetics Got to Do With It?" *American Journal of Public Health* 97, no. 7 (2007): 1191–1197.

Davis, Angela. *Women, Race, and Class.* New York: Vintage Books, 1983.

Davis, Dána-Ain. *Reproductive Injustice: Racism, Pregnancy, and Premature Birth.* New York: NYU Press, 2019.

Degler, Carl N. *At Odds: Women and the Family in America from the Revolution to the Present.* New York: Oxford University Press, 1980.

Denbow, Jennifer. *Governed Through Choice: Autonomy, Technology, and the Politics of Reproduction.* New York: NYU Press, 2015.

———. "Good Motherhood Before Birth: Measuring Attachment and Ultrasound as an Affective Technology." *Engaging Science, Technology, and Society* 5 (2019): 1–20.

Dennis, Latoya. "Does Milwaukee's Ad Campaign Against Sleeping with Babies Go Too Far?" National Public Radio. November 30, 2011. www.npr.org.

DiQuinzio, Patrice. *The Impossibility of Motherhood: Feminism, Individualism, and the Problem of Mothering.* New York: Routledge, 1999.

Docter, Cary. "Should Co-Sleeping that Results in Death Be Criminalized?" Fox News 6, September 26, 2013. http://fox6now.com.

Doucleff, Michaeleen. "Is Sleeping with Your Baby as Dangerous as Doctors Say?" *Maine Public Radio*. May 21, 2018. www.mainepublic.org.

Douglas, Susan J., and Meredith W. Michaels. *The Mommy Myth: The Idealization of Motherhood and How It Has Undermined All Women*. New York: Free Press, 2004.

Downs, Kenya. "Why Is Milwaukee So Bad for Black People?" *National Public Radio*. March 5, 2015. www.npr.org.

Dubow, Sara. *Ourselves Unborn: A History of the Fetus in Modern America*. Oxford: Oxford University Press, 2010.

Dubriwny, Tasha. *The Vulnerable Empowered Woman: Feminism, Postfeminism, and Women's Health*. New Brunswick, NJ: Rutgers University Press, 2013.

Duggan, Lisa. *The Twilight of Equality? Neoliberalism, Cultural Politics, and the Attack on Democracy*. Boston: Beacon Press, 2003.

Duncan, Jhodie R., and Roger W. Byard. "Sudden Infant Death Syndrome: An Overview." In *Sudden Infant and Early Childhood Death: The Past, The Present and The Future*, edited by Jhodie R. Duncan and Roger W. Byard, 15–50. Adelaide, Australia: University of Adelaide Press, 2018.

Earp, Brian, and David Shaw. "Cultural Bias in American Medicine: The Case of Infant Male Circumcision." *Journal of Pediatrics* 1, no. 1 (2017): 8–26.

Eckholm, Erick. "Case Explores Rights of Fetus Versus Mother." *New York Times*. October 23, 2013. www.nytimes.com.

Ehrenreich, Barbara. *Natural Causes: An Epidemic of Wellness, The Certainty of Dying, and Killing Ourselves to Live Longer*. New York: Twelve, 2018.

Ehrenreich, Barbara, and Deirdre English. *For Her Own Good: Two Centuries of the Experts' Advice to Women*. New York: Anchor Books, 2005.

Elliott, Carl. "Pharmaceutical Propaganda." In *Against Health: How Health Became the New Morality*, edited by Jonathan Metzl and Anna Kirkland, 93–104. New York: NYU Press, 2010.

Elman, Julie Passanante. "'Find Your Fit': Wearable Technology and the Cultural Politics of Disability." *New Media & Society* 20, no. 10 (2018): 3760–3777.

Eubanks, Virginia. *Automating Inequality: How High-Tech Tools Profile, Police, and Punish the Poor*. New York: St. Martin's Press, 2017.

Eyers, Diane. *Mother-Infant Bonding: A Scientific Fiction*. New Haven, CT: Yale University Press, 1993.

Faircloth, Charlotte. "Intensive Parenting and the Expansion of Parenting." In *Parenting Culture Studies*, edited by Ellie Lee, Jennie Bristow, Charlotte Faircloth, and Jan Macvarish, 25–50. London: Palgrave Macmillan, 2014.

Farkas, Carol-Ann. "'Tons of Useful Stuff': Defining Wellness in Popular Magazines." *Studies in Popular Culture* 33, no. 1 (Fall 2010): 113–132.

Federici, Silvia. *Caliban and the Witch*. Brooklyn, NY: Autonomedia, 2004.

Felder, Eleanor K. "Your Baby After Dark." *McCall's* 80 (1953): 114–115.

Fentiman, Linda C. *Blaming Mothers: American Law and the Risks to Children's Health*. New York: NYU Press, 2017.

Fernandes, Leela. *Feminists Rethink the Neoliberal State: Inequality, Exclusion, and Change.* New York: NYU Press, 2018.

Fetherston, Catherine M., and J. Shaughn Leach. "Analysis of the Ethical Issues in the Breastfeeding and Bedsharing Debates." *Breastfeeding Review* 20, no. 3 (2012): 7–17.

Filiano, J. J., and H. C. Kinney. "A Perspective on Neuropathologic Findings in Victims of the Sudden Infant Death Syndrome: The Triple Risk Model." *Biology of the Neonate* 65, no. 3–4 (1994): 194–197.

Fisher-Price. "About Fisher-Price." Accessed September 16, 2020. www.fisher-price.com.

Fixmer-Oraiz, Natalie. *Homeland Maternity: US Security Culture and the New Reproductive Regime.* Chicago: Illinois University Press, 2019.

Flavin, Jeanne. *Our Bodies, Our Crimes: The Policing of Women's Reproduction in America.* New York: NYU Press, 2010.

Flavin, Jeanne, and Lynn Paltrow. "Arrests of and Forced Interventions on Pregnant Women in the United States, 1973–2005: Implications for Women's Legal Status and Public Health." *Journal of Health Politics, Policy, and Law* 38, no. 2 (April 2013): 299–343.

Fleming, Peter, Peter Blair, and James McKenna. "New Knowledge, New Insights, and New Recommendations." *Archives of Disease in Childhood* 91, no. 10 (2003): 799–801.

Fox 6 Now Milwaukee. "Is Milwaukee's Anti-Co-Sleeping Campaign Working?" Fox6News, February 21, 2012. http://fox6now.com.

Frankel, Todd C. "Fisher-Price Invented a Popular Baby Sleeper Without Medical Safety Tests and Kept Selling It, Even as Babies Died." *Washington Post*, May 30, 2019. www.washingtonpost.com

———. "House Panel Grills Executives Over Popular Fisher-Price Infant Sleeper Tied to More Than 90 Deaths." *Washington Post*, June 7, 2021. www.washingtonpost.com.

Friedman, Lisa. "Chemical Industry Executive Nominated to Lead Consumer Watchdog Agency." *New York Times*, March 20, 2020. www.nytimes.com.

Fu, Linda Y., Rachel Y. Moon, and Fern R. Hauck. "Bed-Sharing Among Black Infants and Sudden Infant Death Syndrome: Interactions with Other Known Risk Factors." *Academic Pediatrics* 10, no. 6 (2010): 376–382.

Gamble, Vanessa Northington. "Under the Shadow of Tuskegee: African Americans and Health Care." *American Journal of Public Health* 87, no. 11 (1997): 1773–1778.

Geiger, H. Jack. "Health Disparities." In *Gender, Race, Class, and Health*, edited by Leith Mullings and Amy J. Schulz, 261–288. San Francisco: Jossey-Bass, 2006.

Geronimus, Arline. "Understanding and Eliminating Racial Inequalities in Women's Health in the United States: The Role of the Weathering Conceptual Framework." *Journal of the American Medical Women's Association* 56, no. 4 (1972): 133–136.

Gilman, Michele Estrin. "Feminism, Democracy and the 'War on Women.'" *Law and Inequality* 32, no. 1 (Winter 2014): 1–30.

Ginsburg, Faye, and Rayna Rapp. *Conceiving the New World Order: The Global Politics of Reproduction.* Berkeley: University of California Press, 1995.

———. "Introduction: Conceiving the New World Order." In *Conceiving the New World Order: The Global Politics of Reproduction*, edited by Ginsburg and Rapp, 1–19.

Gold, Jenny. "Sleeping Like a Baby Is a $325 Million Industry." *Marketplace*, January 16, 2017. www.marketplace.org.

Golden, Janet. *Message in a Bottle: The Making of Fetal Alcohol Syndrome*. Cambridge, MA: Harvard University Press, 2005.

———. *Babies Made Us Modern: How Infants Brought America into the Twentieth Century*. Cambridge: Cambridge University Press, 2018.

Goldstein, Richard, Felicia Trachtenberg, Mary Ann Sens, Brian J. Harty, and Hannah Kinney. "Overall Postneonatal Mortality and Rates of SIDS." *Pediatrics* 137, no. 1 (2015). DOI: 10.1542/peds.2015-2298.

Goodwin, Michele. *Policing the Womb: Invisible Women and the Criminalization of Motherhood*. Cambridge: Cambridge University Press, 2020.

Green, Bob. "Kiddie Alert: Sad Commentary on Life." *Chicago Tribune*, February 18, 1985. www.chicagotribune.com.

Green, Katherine E., and Melissa M. Groves. "Attachment Parenting: An Exploration of Demographics and Practices." *Early Child Development and Care*, 178, no. 5 (2008): 513–525.

Gross-Loh, Christine. *Parenting Without Borders: Surprising Lessons Parents Around the World Can Teach Us*. New York: Avery, 2014.

Gurr, Barbara. *Reproductive Justice: The Politics of Health Care for Native American Women*. New Brunswick, NJ: Rutgers University Press, 2015.

Guttmacher Institute. "Substance Use During Pregnancy." Updated April 1, 2019. www.guttmacher.org.

Hager, Eli. "Six States Where Felons Can't Get Food Stamps." *The Marshall Project*, February 4, 2016. www.themarshallproject.org.

Hammond, Michelle, Monica K. Miller, and Timothy Griffin. "Safe Haven Laws as Crime Control Theater." *Child Abuse and Neglect* 34, no. 7 (2010): 545–552.

Haneline, Amy. "Rock 'n Play Recall and the Myth of 'Sleeping Through the Night': What Parents Should Know." *USA Today*, May 14, 2019. www.usatoday.com.

Hardyment, Christina. *Dream Babies: Childcare Advice from John Locke to Gina Ford*. London: Frances Lincoln, 1983.

Harrison, Laura. "How Pregnancy Monitoring Technology Contributes to the War on Women." *Washington Post*, July 9, 2019. www.washingtonpost.com.

Hartouni, Valerie. *Cultural Conceptions: On Reproductive Technologies and the Remaking of Life*. Minneapolis: University of Minnesota Press, 1997.

Harvard Kennedy School Ash Center for Democratic Governance and Innovation. "Innovations in American Government Awards." Accessed February 11, 2019. https://ash.harvard.edu.

Harvey, David. *A Brief History of Neoliberalism*. Oxford: Oxford University Press, 2005.

Hays, Sharon. *The Cultural Contradictions of Motherhood*. New Haven, CT: Yale University Press, 1996.

Hemphill, Katie. "'Driven to the Commission of This Crime': Women and Infanticide in Baltimore, 1835–1860." *Journal of the Early Republic* 32, no. 3 (2012): 437–461.

Herzog, Karen. "Milwaukee Sets Goal to Reduce Infant Mortality." *Milwaukee-Wisconsin Journal Sentinel*, November 8, 2011. www.jsonline.com.

Herzog, Karen, and Crocker Stephenson. "Ad Campaign Unveiled as Another Co-Sleeping Death Is Announced." *Milwaukee Journal Sentinel*, November 9, 2011. www.jsonline.com.

Hinds, Hilary. *A Cultural History of Twin Beds*. London: Bloomsbury Academy, 2019.

Högberg, Ulf, and Erik Bergström. "Suffocated Prone: The Iatrogenic Tragedy of SIDS." *American Journal of Public Health* 90, no. 4 (2000): 527–531.

Holiday, Steven, Rebecca L. Densley, and Mary S. Norman. "Influencer Marketing Between Mothers: The Impact of Disclosure and Visual Brand Promotion." *Journal of Current Issues and Research in Advertising*. DOI: 10.1080/10641734.2020.1782790.

Holt, L. Emmett. *The Care and Feeding of Children: A Catechism for the Use of Mothers and Children's Nurses*. New York: D. Appleton and Company, 1922.

Hsu, Tiffany. "Fisher-Price Recalls Rock 'n Play Sleeper Linked to Infant Deaths." *New York Times*, April 12, 2019. www.nytimes.com.

Hsu, Tiffany. "Before Fisher-Price's Rock 'n Play Recall, Safety Fears and Dubious Marketing." *New York Times*, April 19, 2019. www.nytimes.com.

Hulbert, Ann. *Raising America: Experts, Parents, and a Century of Advice About Children*. New York: Knopf, 2003.

Hunt, Carl, Robert Darnall, Betty McEntire, and Bruce Hyma. "Assigning Cause for Sudden Unexpected Infant Death." *Forensic Science, Medicine, and Pathology* 11, no. 2 (June 2015): 283–288.

Illinois General Assembly. "Illinois Compiled Statutes." Accessed April 30, 2019. www.ilga.gov.

Jackson, Fleda, Mona Taylor Phillips, Carol Hogue, and Tracy Curry Owens. "Examining the Burdens of Gendered Racism: Implications for Pregnancy Outcomes Among College-Educated African American Women." *Maternal and Child Health Journal* 5, no. 2 (2001): e329–336.

Jaggar, Alison. *Just Methods: An Interdisciplinary Feminist Reader*. Boulder, CO: Paradigm, 2013.

Johns Hopkins Center for Communication Programs. "B'More for Healthy Babies." Accessed January 25, 2019. https://ccp.jhu.edu.

Johnson, Bethany L., and Margaret M. Quinlan. *You're Doing It Wrong: Mothering, Media, and Medical Expertise*. New Brunswick, NJ: Rutgers University Press, 2019.

Johnson, Michael P. "Smothered Slave Infants: Were Slave Mothers at Fault?" *Journal of Southern History* 47, no. 4 (Fall 1981): 493–520.

Johnston, Josée, and Judith Taylor. "Feminist Consumerism and Fat Activists: A Comparative Study of Grassroots Activism and the Dove Real Beauty Campaign." *Signs* 33, no. 4 (2008): 941–966.

Joyner, Brandi, Rosalind Oden, Taiwo Ajao, and Rachel Moon. "Where Should My Baby Sleep? A Qualitative Study of African American Infant Sleep Location Decisions." *Journal of the National Medical Association* 102, no. 10 (2010): 881–889.

Kemkes, Ariane. "'Smothered' Infants—Neglect, Infanticide, or SIDS? A Fresh Look at the 19th Century Mortality Schedules." *Human Ecology* 37, no. 4 (2009): 393–405.

Kendall-Tackett, Kathleen. "Don't Sleep with Big Knives: Interesting (and Promising) Developments in the Mother-Infant Sleep Debate." *Clinical Lactation* 3, no. 1 (2012): 27–31.

Kendall-Tackett, Kathleen, Zhen Cong, and Thomas W. Hale. "Mother-Infant Sleep Locations and Nighttime Feeding Behavior: US Data from the Survey of Mothers' Sleep and Fatigue." *Clinical Lactation* 1, no. 1 (2010): 27–31.

Kenyon, Josephine H. "Sleep Habits." *Good Housekeeping* 128 (1949): 146–147.

Kessen, William. "The American Child and Other Cultural Inventions." *American Psychologist* 34, no. 10 (1979): 815–820.

Khazan, Olga. "Into the Body of Another." *The Atlantic*, May 8, 2015. Accessed December 21, 2018. www.theatlantic.com.

King, David. "Marketing Wearable Home Baby Monitors: Real Peace of Mind?" *BMJ*, November 18, 2014. www.bmj.com.

Kirkland, Anna, and Jonathan Metzl. *Against Health: How Health Became the New Morality.* New York: NYU Press, 2018.

Knight, Kelly Ray. *Addicted. Pregnant. Poor.* Durham, NC: Duke University Press, 2015.

Korneva, Julia. "20 Common Questions from New Parents, Answered by a Pediatrician." *Moms.* Accessed September 11, 2020. www.moms.com.

Krouse, Anne, Joanne Craig, Ursula Watson, Zannia Matthews, Gerald Kolski, and Kay Isola. "Bed-sharing Influences, Attitudes, and Practices: Implications for Promoting Safe Infant Sleep." *Journal of Child Healthcare* 16, no. 3 (2012): 274–283.

Krugman, Scott D., and Carolyn J. Cumpsty-Fowler. "A Hospital-Based Initiative to Reduce Postdischarge Sudden Unexpected Infant Deaths." *Hospital Pediatrics* 8, no. 7 (August 2018): 443–449.

Kukla, Rebecca. *Mass Hysteria: Medicine, Culture, and Mothers' Bodies.* Lanham, MD: Rowman & Littlefield, 2006.

Kunins, Hillary Veda, Eran Bellin, Cynthia Chazotte, Evelyn Du, and Julia Hope Arnsten. "The Effect of Race on Provider Decisions to Test for Illicit Drug Use in the Peripartum Setting." *Journal of Women's Health* 16, no. 2 (April 2010): 245–255.

La Leche League International. "The Safe Sleep Seven." November 28, 2018. www.llli. org.

Ladd-Taylor, Molly, and Laurie Umansky. *"Bad" Mothers: The Politics of Blame in the Twentieth Century.* New York: NYU Press, 1998.

Lahr, Martin B., Kenneth D. Rosenberg, and Jodi A. Lapidus. "Maternal-Infant Bed-sharing: Risk Factors for Bedsharing in a Population-Based Survey of New Mothers and Implications for SIDS Risk Reduction." *Maternal Child Health* 11, no. 3 (2007): 277–286.

Lareau, Annette. *Unequal Childhoods: Class, Race, and Family Life*. Berkeley: University of California Press, 2011.

Lawrence, Ruth A. "Solomon's Wisdom." *Breastfeeding Medicine* 9, no. 6 (2014): 279–280.

Leaver, Tama. "Intimate Surveillance: Normalizing Parental Monitoring and Mediation of Infants Online." *Social Media + Society* 3, no. 2 (2017): 1–10.

Lee, Ellie. "Experts and Parenting Culture." In *Parenting Culture Studies*, edited by Ellie Lee, Jennie Bristow, Charlotte Faircloth, and Jan Macvarish, 51–75. London: Palgrave Macmillan, 2014.

———. "Introduction." In *Parenting Culture Studies*, edited by Ellie Lee, Jennie Bristow, Charlotte Faircloth, and Jan Macvarish, 1–22. London: Palgrave Macmillan, 2014.

Leverentz, Andrea. *The Ex-Prisoner's Dilemma: How Women Negotiate Competing Narratives of Reentry and Desistance*. New Brunswick, NJ: Rutgers University Press, 2014.

Liedloff, Jean. *The Continuum Concept: In Search of Happiness Lost*. Boston: De Capo Press, 1986.

Losen, Daniel, Cheri Hodson, Michael A. Keith II, Katrina Morrison, and Shakti Belway. "Are We Closing the School Discipline Gap?" The Center for Civil Rights Remedies, February 23, 2015. http://civilrightsproject.ucla.edu.

Luna, Zakiya. *Reproductive Rights as Human Rights: Women of Color and the Fight for Reproductive Justice*. New York: NYU Press, 2020.

Luna, Zakiya, and Kristin Luker. "Reproductive Justice." *Annual Review of Law and Social Science* 9, no. 1 (2013): 327–352.

Lupton, Deborah. *The Imperative of Health: Public Health and the Regulated Body*. London: Sage, 1995.

———. *The Quantified Self*. Cambridge: Polity Press, 2016.

Luthern, Ashley. "Medical Examiner: Half of Infant Deaths in Milwaukee County in 2017 Related to Unsafe Sleep." *Milwaukee Journal Sentinel*, January 2, 2018. www.jsonline.com.

MacKendrick, Norah. *Better Safe Than Sorry: How Consumers Navigate Exposure to Everyday Toxics*. Berkeley: University of California Press, 2018.

MacKendrick, Norah, and Kate Cairns. "The Polluted Child and Maternal Responsibility in the US Environmental Health Movement." *Signs* 44, no. 2 (Winter 2019): 307–332.

Macvarish, Jan. "Babies' Brains and Parenting Policy: The Insensitive Mother." In *Parenting Culture Studies*, edited by Ellie Lee, Jennie Bristow, Charlotte Faircloth, and Jan Macvarish, 165–188. London: Palgrave Macmillan, 2014.

Magnet, Shoshana. *When Biometrics Fail: Gender, Race, and the Technology of Identity*. Durham, NC: Duke University Press, 2011.

Malloy, Michael H., and Marian MacDorman. "Changes in the Classification of Sudden Unexpected Infant Deaths: United States, 1992–2001." *Pediatrics* 115, no. 5 (2005): 1247–1253.

Mamo, Laura, and Jennifer Ruth Fosket. "Scripting the Body: Pharmaceuticals and the (Re)Making of Menstruation." *Signs* 34, no. 4 (2009): 925–949.

Mamo, Laura, Amber Nelson, and Aleia Clark. "Producing and Protecting Risky Girlhoods." In *Three Shots at Prevention: The HPV Vaccine and the Politics of Medicine's Simple Solutions*, edited by Keith Wailoo, Julie Livingston, Steven Epstein, and Robert Aronowitz, 121–145. Baltimore, MD: Johns Hopkins University Press, 2010.

Mandavilli, Apoorva. "Small Social Gatherings Aren't Driving the Virus Surge (So Far)." *New York Times*, November 23, 2020. www.nytimes.com.

Mansfield, Becky. "Gendered Biopolitics of Public Health: Regulation and Discipline in Seafood Consumption Advisories." *Environment and Planning* 30, no. 4 (2012): 588–602.

Markoff, John. "Fight of the (Next) Century: Converging Technologies Put Sony and Microsoft on a Collision Course." *New York Times*, March 7, 1999. www.nytimes.com.

Martin, Emily. *The Woman in the Body: A Cultural Analysis of Reproduction*. Boston: Beacon Press, 2001.

Martucci, Jessica. *Back to the Breast: Natural Motherhood and Breastfeeding in America*. Chicago: University of Chicago Press, 2015.

———. "Why Breastfeeding? Natural Motherhood in Post-War America." *Journal of Women's History* 27, no. 2 (2015): 110–133.

Matchar, Emily. *Homeward Bound: Why Women Are Embracing the New Domesticity*. New York: Simon & Schuster, 2013.

Matthews, T. J., Danielle M. Ely, and Anne K. Driscoll. "State Variations in Infant Mortality by Race and Hispanic Origin of Mother, 2013–2015." *NCHS Data Brief*, no. 295 (January 2018): 1–8.

Matthews, T. J., Marian MacDorman, and Marie Thoma. "Infant Mortality Statistics from the 2013 Period." *National Vital Statistics Report* 64, no. 9 (2015): 1–30.

Mattel. "Media Statement on the US Consumer Product Safety Commission–Fisher-Price Joint Security Alert Released on April 5, 2019." *Mattel Newsroom*, April 5, 2019. https://news.mattel.com.

McCullough, Marie. "Why That Wearable Baby Monitor Could Do Your Baby More Harm Than Good." *The Inquirer*, January 24, 2017. www.philly.com.

McKenna, James. "An Anthropological Perspective on the Sudden Infant Death Syndrome (SIDS): The Role of Parental Breathing Cues and Speech Breathing Adaptations." *Medical Anthropology* 10, no, 1 (Winter 1986): 9–53.

———. "Night Waking Among Breastfeeding Mothers and Infants: Conflict, Congruence, or Both?" *Evolution, Medicine, and Public Health*, no. 1 (2014): 40–47.

McKenna, James J., Helen L. Ball, and Lee T. Gettler. "Mother-Infant Co-Sleeping, Breastfeeding and Sudden Infant Death Syndrome: What Biological Anthropology Has Discovered About Normal Infant Sleep and Pediatric Sleep Medicine." *Yearbook of Physical Anthropology* 50 (2007): 133–161.

McKenna, James, and Thomas McDade. "Why Babies Should Never Sleep Alone: A Review of the Co-Sleeping Controversy in Relation to SIDS, Bedsharing and Breastfeeding." *Paediatric Respiratory Reviews* 6 (2005): 134–152.

Meckel, Richard. *Save the Babies: American Public Health Reform and the Prevention of Infant Mortality 1850–1929*. Baltimore:, MD Johns Hopkins University Press, 1990.

Metzl, Jonathan, and Anna Kirkland. "Introduction: Why Against Heath?" In *Against Health: How Health Became the New Morality*, edited by Jonathan Metzl and Anna Kirkland, 1–14. New York: NYU Press, 2010.

Michael, Olga. "New Bill Would Make Some Co-Sleeping Deaths Felony." WEAU 13 News, November 7, 2013. www.weau.com.

Miller, Claire Cain, and Aaron E. Carroll. "Should Your Baby Really Sleep in the Same Room as You?" *New York Times*, November 4, 2016. www.nytimes.com.

Miller, Lauren C., Arlene Johnson, Lisa Duggan, and Melissa Behm. "Consequences of the 'Back to Sleep' Program in Infants." *Journal of Pediatric Nursing* 26, no. 4 (2011): 364–368.

Mills, Shamane. "Opponents of Wisconsin's 'Cocaine Mom' Law Continue Fight." *Wisconsin Public Radio*, August 1, 2018. www.wpr.org.

Milwaukee Health Department. "Cribs for Kids Program." Accessed October 15, 2020. http://city.milwaukee.gov.

———. "Infant Mortality." Accessed October 15, 2020. http://city.milwaukee.gov.

———. "Safe Sleep Campaign." Accessed October 15, 2020. http://city.milwaukee.gov.

———. "Safe Sleep Summit Questions and Answers." Accessed October 15, 2020. http://city.milwaukee.gov.

Milwaukee Journal Sentinel. "A Final Resting Place." December 29, 2009. www.jsonline.com.

Montgomery, Kathryn, Jeff Chester, and Katharina Kopp. "Health Wearable Devices in the Big Data Era: Ensuring Privacy, Security, and Consumer Protection." Center for Digital Democracy, 2016. www.democraticmedia.org.

Moon, Rachel Y. "How to Keep Your Sleeping Baby Safe: AAP Policy Explained." *HealthyChildren.org*. Accessed September 14, 2020. www.healthychildren.org.

Moon, Rachel Y., and Fern Hauck. "SIDS Risk: It's More Than Just the Sleep Environment." *Pediatrics* 137, no. 1 (January 2016): e20153665.

———. "Are There Long-Term Consequences of Room-Sharing During Infancy?" *Pediatrics* 140, no. 1 (2017): e20171323.

Moon, Rachel Y., Fern R. Hauck, and Eve R. Colson, "Safe Infant Sleep Interventions: What Is the Evidence for Successful Behavior Change?" *Current Pediatric Review* 11, no. 12 (2016): 67–75.

Moon, Rachel Y., Rosalind P. Oden, Brandi L. Joyner, and Taiwo I. Ajao. "Qualitative Analysis of Beliefs and Perceptions about Sudden Infant Death Syndrome in African-American Mothers: Implications for Safe Sleep Recommendations." *Journal of Pediatrics* 157, no. 1 (2010): 92–97.

Moore, Julia, and Jenna Abetz. "'Uh Oh. Cue the [New] Mommy Wars': The Ideology of Combative Mothering in Popular US Newspaper Articles About Attachment Parenting." *Southern Communication Journal* 81, no. 1 (2016): 49–62.

Moran, Rachel Lousie. *Governing Bodies: American Politics and the Shaping of the Modern Physique*. Philadelphia: University of Pennsylvania Press, 2018.

Morgan, Jennifer. *Laboring Women: Reproduction and Gender in New World Slavery.* Philadelphia: University of Pennsylvania Press. 2004.

Mounk, Yascha. *The Age of Responsibility: Luck, Choice, and the Welfare State.* Cambridge, MA: Harvard University Press, 2017.

Mullings, Leith, and Amy J. Schulz. "Intersectionality and Health: An Introduction." In *Gender, Race, Class, and Health,* edited by Leith Mullings and Amy J. Schulz, 3–20. San Francisco: Jossey-Bass, 2006.

Murdoch, Cassie. "Finally There's a Baby Monitor That Can Constantly Scare the Crap Out of You." *Mashable,* February 18, 2017. https://mashable.com.

Nakamura, Suad, Marilyn Wind, and Mary Ann Danello. "Review of Hazards Associated with Children Placed in Adult Beds." *Archives of Pediatric and Adolescent Medicine* 153, no. 10 (1999): 1019–1023.

National Advocates for Pregnant Women. "Victory in Texas!" March 30, 2006. http://advocatesforpregnantwomen.org.

National Conference of State Legislatures. "Sudden Unexpected Infant Death Legislation." Accessed December 31, 2018. www.ncsl.org.

National Institute of Child Health and Human Development. "Key Moments in Safe to Sleep History: 1994–2003." Accessed December 31, 2018. https://safetosleep.nichd.nih.gov.

———. "Infographic: Accidental Suffocation and Strangulation." Accessed October 3, 2019. https://safetosleep.nichd.nih.gov.

National Institutes of Health. "NIH Expands Safe Sleep Outreach Effort." Accessed January 8, 2020. www.nichd.nih.gov.

Nelkin, Dorothy. "Foreword." In *Risk, Culture, and Health Inequality: Shifting Perceptions of Danger and Blame,* edited by Barbara Herr Harthorn and Laury Oaks, vi–xiii. Westport, CT: Praeger, 2003.

Nelson, Jennifer. *Women of Color and the Reproductive Rights Movement.* New York: NYU Press, 2003.

———. *More Than Medicine: A History of the Feminist Women's Health Movement.* New York: NYU Press, 2015.

Nelson, Margaret. "Watching Children." In *Who's Watching? Daily Practices of Surveillance Among Contemporary Families,* edited by Margaret K. Nelson and Anita Ilta Garey, 219–238. Nashville, TN: Vanderbilt University Press, 2009.

———. *Parenting Out of Control: Anxious Parents in Uncertain Times.* New York: NYU Press, 2010.

New York Times. "Margaret Ribble, Psychoanalyst, 80." July 21, 1971. www.nytimes.com.

New York Times Editorial Board. "A Woman's Right." *New York Times.* December 28, 2018. www.nytimes.com.

———. "A Woman's Right, Part 4: Slandering the Unborn." December 28, 2018. www.nytimes.com.

Ngui, Emmanuel, Karen Michalski, Erica LeCounte, and Anneke Mohr. "City of Milwaukee Fetal Infant Mortality Review Report: Status Report on 2012–2015 Stillbirths and Infant Deaths." January 31, 2017. https://city.milwaukee.gov.

Nichter, Mark. "Harm Reduction: A Core Concern for Medical Anthropology." In *Risk, Culture, and Health Inequality: Shifting Perceptions of Danger and Blame*, edited by Barbara Herr Harthorn and Laury Oaks, 13–33. Westport, CT: Praeger, 2003.

Noble, Safiya. *Algorithms of Oppression: How Search Engines Reinforce Racism*. New York: NYU Press, 2018.

Norvenius, S. G. "Some Medico-Historic Remarks on SIDS." *Acta Pædiatrica* 82 (1993): 3–9.

Oaks, Laury. "Smoke-filled Wombs and Fragile Fetuses: The Social Politics of Fetal Representation." *Signs* 26, no. 1 (Autumn 2000): 63–108.

———. *Smoking and Pregnancy: The Politics of Fetal Protection*. New Brunswick, NJ: Rutgers University Press, 2001.

———. *Giving Up Baby: Safe Haven Laws, Motherhood, and Reproductive Justice*. New York: NYU Press, 2015.

Obladen, Michael. "Cot Death: History of an Iatrogenic Disorder." *Sources of Neonatal Medicine* 113, no. 2 (2018): 162–169.

Oliviero, Katie. *Vulnerability Politics: The Uses and Abuses of Vulnerability Precarity in Political Debate*. New York: NYU Press, 2018.

Onion, Rebecca. "The World's First Baby Monitor: Zenith's 1937 'Baby Nurse.'" *Slate*, February 2, 2013. https://slate.com.

Oskar, Jenni, and Bonnie Blair O'Connor. "Children's Sleep: An Interplay Between Culture and Biology." *Pediatrics* 115 (February 2005): 204–216.

Ostfeld, Barbara M., Ofira Schwartz-Soicher, Nancy E. Reichman, Julien O. Teitler, and Thomas Hegyi. "Prematurity and Sudden Infant Death in the United States." *Pediatrics* 140, no. (2017): e20163334.

Owens, Dierdre Cooper. *Medical Bondage: Race, Gender, and the Origins of American Gynecology*. Athens: University of Georgia Press, 2018.

Owlet Baby Care. "Owlet Care Privacy Policy." Last updated May 14, 2019. https://owletcare.com.

———. "The Owlet Baby Band Tracker." Accessed December 3, 2020. https://owletcare.com.

———. "Terms and Conditions." Last updated May 8, 2019. https://owletcare.com.

"Owlet Launches Entirely Redesigned Smart Sock, Giving Canadian Parents What They Really Want—Peace of Mind." July 9, 2020. www.businesswire.com.

Paltrow, Lynn M. "Punishment and Prejudice: Judging Drug-Using Pregnant Women." Accessed December 31, 2018. http://advocatesforpregnantwomen.org.

Paul, Ian M., Emily E. Hohman, Eric Loken, Jennifer S. Savage, Stephanie Anzman-Frasca, Patricia Carper, Michele E. Marini, and Leann L. Birch. "Mother-Infant Room-Sharing and Sleep Outcomes in the INSIGHT Study." *Pediatrics* 140, no. 1 (2017): e20170122.

Paul, Kari. "These 'Extreme Baby Monitors' Claim to Track Your Child's Breathing, Heart Rate, and Every Movement." *Market Watch*, January 16, 2019. www.marketwatch.com.

Pawluch, Dorothy. "Transitions in Pediatrics: A Segmental Analysis." *Social Problems* 30, no. 4 (1983): 449–465.

Peachman, Rachel Rabkin. "Fisher-Price Rock 'n Play Sleeper Should Be Recalled, Consumer Reports Says." *Consumer Reports*. April 26, 2019. www.consumerreports. org.

———. "Inclined Sleeper Deaths Rise to 50 as Industry Continues to Sell the Products." *Consumer Reports*. June 20, 2019. www.consumerreports.org.

———. "While They Were Sleeping." *Consumer Reports*. December 30, 2019. www. consumerreports.org.

———. "Government Moves Closer to Stopping the Sale of Dangerous Baby Sleep Products." *Consumer Reports*. May 19, 2021. www.consumerreports.org.

Pearson, Howard A. "The American Pediatric Society." *Pediatrics* 95, no. 1 (1995): 147–151.

Peck, Sally. "Baby Monitor 2.0 Is Born: But Does It Spell the End of Maternal Instinct?" *The Telegraph*, April 24, 2014. www.telegraph.co.uk.

Petchesky, Rosalind. "Fetal Images: The Power of Visual Culture in the Politics of Reproduction." *Feminist Studies* 13, no. 2 (1987): 263–292.

Peterson, Hayley. "Fisher-Price Is Giving Away Refunds and Vouchers for All Rock 'n Play Sleepers." *Business Insider*, April 15, 2019. www.businessinsider.com.

Pickert, Kate. "The Man Who Remade Motherhood." *Time*, May 21, 2012. http://time. com.

Pickett, Kate, Ye Luo, and Diane Lauderdale. "Widening Social Inequalities in Risk for Sudden Infant Death Syndrome." *American Journal of Public Health* 95, no. 11 (2005): 1976–1981.

Plant, Rebecca Jo. *Mom: The Transformation of Motherhood in Modern America*. Chicago: University of Chicago Press, 2010.

Polcyn, Bryan, and Leann Watson. "'I Just Don't Want Any Baby to Die': Lawmakers Struggle for Consensus on Co-sleeping Legislation." *Fox6News*, January 25, 2015. http://fox6now.com.

Preston, Elizabeth. "Did Lockdowns Lower Premature Birth? A New Study Adds Evidence." *New York Times*, October 15, 2020. www.nytimes.com.

Price, Kimala. "What Is Reproductive Justice? How Women of Color Activists Are Redefining the Pro-Choice Paradigm." *Meridians* 10, no. 2 (2010): 42–65.

Pryor, Gale, and Kathleen Huggins. *Nursing Mother, Working Mother—Revised: The Essential Guide to Breastfeeding Your Baby Before and After Your Return to Work*. Boston: Harvard Common Press, 2007.

Quirmbach, Chuck. "Milwaukee Officials Hope Lead Controversy Brings Positive Change." *Wisconsin Public Radio*, January 17, 2018. www.wpr.org.

Randall, David K. *Dreamland: Adventures in the Strange Science of Sleep*. Norton, 2013.

Raphael, Jody. *Freeing Tammy: Women, Drugs, and Incarceration*. Boston: Northeastern University Press, 2007.

Rapp, Rayna. *Testing Women, Testing the Fetus*. Hove: Psychology Press, 1999.

Ray, Brenda J., Sharon C. Metcalf, Sofia M. Franco, and Charlene K. Mitchell. "Infant Sleep Position Instruction and Parental Practice: Comparison of a Private Pediatric Office and an Inner-City Clinic." *Pediatrics* 99, no. 5 (1997). DOI: 10.1542/peds.99.5.e12.

Reich, Jennifer. *Fixing Families: Parents, Power, and the Child Welfare System.* New York: Routledge, 2005.

Reilly, Briana. "Wisconsin Has Yet to Implement Drug Screening Requirements for Certain FoodShare Recipients." *The Cap Times*, October 22, 2019. https://madison.com.

Reints, Renae. "These Are the States That Passed 'Heartbeat Bills.'" *Fortune*, May 31, 2019. http://fortune.com.

Renfro, Paul Mokrzycki. "Keeping Children Safe Is Good Business: The Enterprise of Child Safety in the Age of Reagan." *Enterprise & Society*, 17, no. 1 (Spring 2016): 151–187.

Richman, Bonnie. "Controversial Posters of Babies Sleeping with Knives Aim to Reduce Co- Sleeping Deaths." *Time*, November 18, 2011. http://healthland.time.com.

Roberts, Dorothy. "Racism and Patriarchy in the Meaning of Motherhood." Faculty Scholarship at Penn Law. 1993.https://scholarship.law.upenn.edu.

———. *Killing the Black Body: Race, Reproduction, and the Meaning of Liberty.* New York: Pantheon Books, 1997.

———. *Shattered Bonds: The Color of Child Welfare.* New York: Basic Books, 2001.

———. *Fatal Invention: How Science, Politics, and Big Business Re-Create Race in the Twenty-first Century.* New York: New Press, 2012.

———. "Race, Gender, and Genetic Technologies: A New Reproductive Dystopia?" In *Feminist Surveillance Studies*, edited by Rachel E. Dubrofsky and Shoshana Magnet, 169–187. Durham, NC: Duke University Press, 2015.

Roberts Jr., Samuel Kelton. *Infectious Fear: Politics, Disease, and the Health Effects of Segregation.* Chapel Hill: University of North Carolina Press, 2009.

Rollston, Rebekah, and Sandra Galea. "COVID-19 and the Social Determinants of Health." *American Journal of Health Promotion* 34, no. 6 (2020): 687–689.

Rosenthal, Caitlin. *Accounting for Slavery: Masters and Management.* Cambridge, MA: Harvard University Press, 2018.

Ross, Loretta, Lynn Roberts, Erika Derkas, Whitney Peoples, and Pamela Bridgewater Toure. *Radical Reproductive Justice: Foundations, Theory, Practice, Critique.* New York: Feminist Press, 2017.

Ross, Loretta, Lynn Roberts, Erika Derkas, Whitney Peoples, and Pamela Bridgewater Toure. "Introduction." In *Radical Reproductive Justice: Foundations, Theory, Practice, Critique*, edited by Whitney Peoples, Erika Derkas, Lynn Roberts, Pamela D. Bridgewater, and Loretta Ross, 11–34.

Ross, Loretta, and Rickie Solinger. *Reproductive Justice: An Introduction.* Berkeley: University of California Press, 2017.

Roth, Rachel. "No New Babies? Gender Inequality and Reproductive Control in the Criminal Justice and Prison Systems." *Journal of Gender, Social Policy, and the Law* 12, no. 3 (2004): 391–425.

———. "'She Doesn't Deserve to Be Treated Like This': Prisons as Sites of Reproductive Injustice." In *Radical Reproductive Justice: Foundations, Theory, Practice, Critique*, edited by Whitney Peoples, Erika Derkas, Lynn Roberts, Pamela D. Bridgewater, and Loretta Ross, 285–301.

Rummans, Teresa, Caroline Burton, and Nancy Dawson. "How Good Intentions Contributed to Bad Outcomes: The Opioid Crisis." *Mayo Clinic Proceedings* 93, no. 3 (2018) 344–350.

Russell-Jones, D. L. "Sudden Infant Death in History and Literature." *Archives of the Disease in Childhood* 60, no. 3 (1985): 278–281.

Sankaran, Vivek S. "Child Welfare's Scarlet Letter: How a Prior Termination of Parental Rights Can Permanently Brand a Parent as Unfit." *NYU Review of Law and Social Change* 41, no. 4 (2017): 685–705.

Schmid, John. "From Generation to Generation." *Milwaukee Journal Sentinel*, March 23, 2017. www.jsonline.com.

Schmid, John, and Kevin Crowe. "An Intractable Problem." *Milwaukee Journal Sentinel*, March 27, 2017. www.jsonline.com.

Schweitzer, Kate. "Why I Ditched the Baby Monitor—And So Should You." *PopSugar*, April 15, 2018. www.popsugar.com.

Sears, William, and Martha Sears. *The Attachment Parenting Book: A Commonsense Guide to Understanding and Nurturing Your Baby*. Boston: Little, Brown, 2001.

Sears, William, Martha Sears, Robert Sears, and James Sears. *The Baby Book: Everything You Need to Know About Your Baby from Birth to Age Two (Revised and Updated Edition)*. Boston: Little, Brown, 2003.

Serve Marketing. Accessed December 14, 2020. http://servemarketing.org.

———. "Co-Sleeping." Accessed December 14, 2020. http://servemarketing.org.

———. "Pregnant Boys." Accessed December 14, 2020. http://servemarketing.org.

Shapiro-Mendoza, Carrie K., Lena Camperlengo, Rebecca Ludvigsen, Carri Cottengim, Robert N. Anderson, Thomas Andrew, Theresa Covington, Fern R. Hauck, James Kemp, and Marian MacDorman. "Classification System for the Sudden Unexpected Infant Death Case Registry and Its Application." *Pediatrics* 134, no. 1 (July 2014): e210–219.

Shapiro-Mendoza, Carrie K., Sharyn Parks, Alexa Erck Lambert, Lena Camperlengo, Carri Cottengim, and Christine Olson. "The Epidemiology of Sudden Infant Death Syndrome and Sudden Unexpected Infant Death: Diagnostic Shift and Other Temporal Changes." In *Sudden Infant and Early Childhood Death: The Past, The Present, and the Future*, edited by Jhodie Duncan and Roger Byard, 257–282. Adelaide, Australia: University of Adelaide Press, 2018.

Sidebotham, Peter, Francine Bates, Catherine Ellis, and Lucy Lyus. "Preventive Strategies for Sudden Infant Death Syndrome." In *Sudden Infant and Early Childhood Death: The Past, the Present, and the Future*, edited by Jhodie R. Duncan and Roger W. Byard, 217–256. Adelaide, Australia: University of Adelaide Press, 2018.

Sidebotham, Peter, David Marshall, and Joanna Garstang. "Responding to Unexpected Child Deaths." In *Sudden Infant and Early Childhood Death: The Past, The Present, and The Future*, edited by Jhodie R. Duncan and Roger W. Byard, 85–115. Adelaide, Australia: University of Adelaide Press, 2018.

Silliman, Jael, Marlene Gerber Fried, Loretta Ross, and Elena Gutierrez, eds. *Undivided Rights: Women of Color Organize for Reproductive Justice*. Chicago: Haymarket Books, 2004.

Silverman, Jacob. "Privacy Under Surveillance Capitalism." *Social Research: An International Quarterly* 84, no. 1 (Spring 2017), 147–164.

Smalls, Meredith. *Our Babies, Ourselves: How Biology and Culture Shape the Way We Parent*. New York: Anchor Press, 1994.

Sobralske, Mary, and Megan Gruber. "Risks and Benefits of Parent/Child Bed Sharing." *Journal of the American Academy of Nurse Practitioners* 21, no. 9 (2009): 474–479.

Solinger, Rickie. *Beggars and Choosers: How the Politics of Choice Shapes Adoption, Abortion, and Welfare in the United States*. New York: Hill & Wang, 2001.

———. *Pregnancy and Power: A Short History of Reproductive Politics in America*. New York: NYU Press, 2005.

Sorgi, Jay. "Barrett Starts Six Year Campaign to Drop Infant Mortality Rates." November 9, 2011. www.620wtmj.com.

Span, Christopher M. "Black Milwaukee's Challenge to the Cycle of Urban Miseducation: Milwaukee's African American Immersion Schools." *Urban Education* 37, no. 5 (2002): 610–630.

Spicuzza, Mary, and Mark Johnson. "Milwaukee Health Commissioner Bevan Baker Out After Thousands Not Contacted by City After Lead Tests." *Milwaukee Journal Sentinel*, January 12, 2018. www.jsonline.com.

Sportelli, Natalie. "Owlet's Smart Sock Makes Millions Selling Parents Peace of Mind—But Doctors Are Unconvinced." *Forbes*, October 24, 2017. www.forbes.com.

State of Wisconsin Department of Health Services. "Report on the Review of the City of Milwaukee Health Department Childhood Lead Poisoning Prevention Program." May 17, 2018. www.dhs.wisconsin.gov.

Stearns, Peter. *Anxious Parents: A History of Modern Childrearing in America*. New York: NYU Press, 2003.

Stearns, Peter N., Perrin Rowland, and Lori Giarnella. "Children's Sleep: Sketching Historical Change." *Journal of Social History* 30, no. 2 (Winter 1996): 345–366.

Stephenson, Crocker. "Safe Sleep Campaign Hits the Streets." *Milwaukee Journal Sentinel*, July 13, 2010. www.jsonline.com.

———. "Wisconsin Bill Would Make Some Co-sleeping Deaths a Felony." *Saint Paul Pioneer Press*, September 25, 2013. http://archive.jsonline.com.

———. "Milwaukee's Infant Mortality Numbers Improve, but the Racial Disparity Is Still Wide." *Milwaukee Journal Sentinel*, May 20, 2017. www.jsonline.com.

Stewart, Susan D. *Co-Sleeping: Parents, Children, and Musical Beds*. Lanham, MD: Rowman & Littlefield, 2017.

Stone, Rebecca. "Pregnant Women and Substance Use: Fear, Stigma, and Barriers to Care." *Health Justice* 3, no. 2 (December 2015): 1–15.

Swain, Geoffrey. "Co-Sleeping Deaths: Intoxication Is Not the Main Issue." *Milwaukee Wisconsin Journal Sentinel*, December 3, 2013. http://archive.jsonline.com.

———. "Birth Outcomes in Milwaukee and Wisconsin: What Can Policymakers Do?" June 30, 2016. Presentation materials shared by the author.

Swearingen, Jake. "Making My Baby a Smart Baby Was a Mistake." *New York Magazine*, May 10, 2018. http://nymag.com.

Tanabe, Kawai O., and Fern Hauck. "A United States Perspective." In *Sudden Infant and Early Childhood Death: The Past, the Present, and the Future*, edited by Jhodie R. Duncan and Roger W. Byard, 409–420. Adelaide, Australia: University of Adelaide Press, 2018.

Tankersley, Jim, and Ben Casselman. "Here's How Congress Might Replace the Extra $600 Weekly Jobless Benefit." *New York Times*, July 31, 2020. www.nytimes.com.

Tanner, Laura. "Queering Teenage Pregnancy Prevention: Temporality and Happiness Rhetoric in the Milwaukee Campaign 2006–2015." Conference paper presented at the National Women's Studies Association, 2015.

Taylor, Janelle. *The Public Life of the Fetal Sonogram: Technology, Consumption, and the Politics of Reproduction*. New Brunswick, NJ: Rutgers University Press, 2008.

Teti, Douglas M., Mina Shimizu, Brian Crosby, and Bo-Ram Kim. "Sleep Arrangements, Parent-Infant Sleep During the First Year, and Family Functioning." *Developmental Psychology* 52, no. 8 (2016): 1169–1181.

Theobold, Brianna. *Reproduction on the Reservation: Pregnancy, Childbirth, and Colonialism in the Long Twentieth Century*. Chapel Hill: University of North Carolina Press, 2019.

Thompson, Dennis. "Pediatricians Say No to Wearable Smartphone Baby Monitors." *Health Day*, January 24, 2017. https://consumer.healthday.com.

Todd, Richard. "Baby Monitors: Who's Really Watching Your Baby?" *Huffington Post*, October 5, 2015. www.huffpost.com.

Tomori, Cecília. *Nighttime Breastfeeding: An American Cultural Dilemma*. New York: Berghan Books, 2016.

Toner, Erin. "Co-Sleeping Deaths Persist in Milwaukee." Wisconsin Public Radio, December 4, 2013. http://wuwm.com.

Toompas, Shelby. "16 High Tech Baby Monitors." *Parents*. Accessed November 20, 2020. www.parents.com.

Transportation Security Administration. "TSA Releases Roadmap for Expanding Biometrics Technology." October 15, 2018. www.tsa.gov.

Tsing, Anna Lowenhaupt. "Monster Stories: Women Charged with Perinatal Endangerment." In *Uncertain Terms: Negotiating Gender in American Culture*, edited by Faye Ginsburg and Anna Lowenhaupt Tsing, 282–299. Boston: Beacon Press, 1990.

Tyko, Kelly. "Kids II Recalls 700,000 Baby Sleepers Including Ingenuity, Bright Starts, Disney Brands." *USA Today*, April 26, 2019. www.usatoday.com.

United States Census Bureau. "State and County Quick Facts." Accessed October 16, 2020. www.census.gov.

United States Congress, Senate. *Safe Sleep For Babies Act of 2019*. HR 3172, 116th Congress, 1st sess. Referred in Senate December 17, 2019. www.congress.gov.

United States Consumer Product Safety Commission. "Who We Are—What We Do For You." Accessed September 16, 2020. www.cpsc.gov.

United States Department of Health and Human Services Office of Minority Health. "Minority Population Profiles." Accessed January 8, 2020. https://minorityhealth. hhs.gov.

United States Department of Labor, Children's Bureau. *Infant Care*, edited by Max West. United States Department of Labor, 1914.

Valdez, Natali. "The Redistribution of Reproductive Responsibility: On the Epigenetics of 'Environment' in Prenatal Interventions." *Medical Anthropology Quarterly* 32, no. 3 (2018): 425–442.

Vandenberg-Daves, Jodi. *Modern Motherhood: An American History*. New Brunswick, NJ: Rutgers University Press, 2014.

Villalobos, Ana. *Motherload: Making It All Better in Insecure Times*. Berkeley: University of California Press, 2014.

Waggoner, Miranda. "Cultivating the Maternal Future: Public Health and the Prepregnant Self." *Signs* 40, no. 4 (Summer 2015): 939–962.

Waggoner, Miranda R. *The Zero Trimester: Pre-Pregnancy Care and the Politics of Reproductive Risk*. Berkeley: University of California Press, 2017.

Walker, Alissa. "Why I Don't Use a Baby Monitor." *Gizmodo*, July 1, 2016. https://gizmodo.com.

Wall, Glenda. "Mothers' Experiences with Intensive Parenting and Brain Development Discourse." *Women's Studies International Forum* 33 (2010): 253–263.

Walls, Helen, Colin Butler, Jane Dixon, and Indira Samarawickrema. "Implications of Structure Versus Agency for Addressing Health and Well-Being in Our Ecologically Constrained World." *International Journal of Feminist Approaches to Bioethics* 8, no. 2 (Fall 2015): 47–69.

Wamsley, Laurel. "Theranos, Blood-Testing Company Plagued by Scandal, Says It Will Dissolve." *National Public Radio*, September 5, 2018. www.npr.org.

Ward, Paula Reed. "Group Donates Cribs to Promote Safe Sleep for Babies." *Pittsburgh Post Gazette*, November 26, 2010. www.post-gazette.com.

Ward, Trina Salm, and Emmanuel Ngui. "Factors Associated with Bed-Sharing for African American Mothers in Wisconsin." *Maternal and Child Health Journal* 19, no. 4 (2015): 720–732.

Warner, Judith. *Perfect Madness: Motherhood in the Age of Anxiety*. New York: Riverhead Books, 2005.

Washington, Harriet. *Medical Apartheid: The Dark History of Medical Experimentation on Black Americans from Colonial Times to the Present*. New York: Harlem Moon, 2006.

Watson, John B. *Psychological Care of Infant and Child*. New York: Norton, 1928.

Weinbaum, Alys Eve. *The Afterlife of Reproductive Slavery: Biocapitalism and Black Feminism's Philosophy of History*. Durham, NC: Duke University Press, 2019.

Weiner, Lynn Y. "Reconstructing Motherhood: The La Leche League in Postwar America." In *Mothers and Motherhood: Readings in American History*, edited by Rima Apple and Janet Golden, 362–388. Columbus: Ohio State University Press, 1997.

Wendling, Patrice. "SIDS Risk Up Fourfold in Siblings of SIDS Victims." *Medscape*, March 19, 2018. www.medscape.com.

White, Shelley. "Infant Wearables: Handy Tools or Too Much Information?" *The Globe and Mail*, March 22, 2015. www.theglobeandmail.com.

Wilson, Julie A., and Emily Chivers Yochim. *Mothering Through Precarity: Women's Work and Digital Media*. Durham, NC: Duke University Press, 2017.

Wolf, Abraham W., Betsy Lozoff, Sara Latz, and Roberto Paludetto. "Parental Theories in the Management of Young Children's Sleep in Japan, Italy, and the United States." In *Parents' Cultural Belief Systems: Their Origins, Expressions, and Consequences*, edited by Sara Harkness and Charles M. Super, 364–384. New York: Guilford Press, 1996.

Wolf, Joan. *Is Breast Best? Taking on the Breastfeeding Experts and the High Stakes of Motherhood*. New York: NYU Press, 2010.

Wolf-Meyer, Matthew J. *The Slumbering Masses: Sleep, Medicine, and Modern American Life*. Minneapolis: University of Minnesota Press, 2012.

Wolford, Heather B. "Legislation Would Help Monitor Newborn Children of Drug Addicts." *Cumberland Times-News*, April 8, 2018. www.times-news.com.

Womack, Lindsay S., Lauren M. Rossen, and Joyce A. Martin. "Singleton Low Birthweight Rates, By Race and Hispanic Origin: United States, 2006–2016." *NCHS Data Brief* 306 (2018): 1–8.

World Health Organization. "COVID-19 Could Reverse Decades of Progress Toward Eliminating Preventable Child Deaths, Agencies Warn." September 9, 2020. www.who.int.

Young, Jeanine, and Rebecca Shipstone. "Shared Sleeping Surface and Dangerous Sleeping Environments." In *Sudden Infant and Early Childhood Death: The Past, The Present, and The Future*, edited by Jhodie R. Duncan and Roger W. Byard, 187–215. Adelaide, Australia: University of Adelaide Press, 2018.

Zavella, Patricia. *The Movement for Reproductive Justice: Empowering Women of Color Through Social Activism*. New York: NYU Press, 2020.

Zelizer, Viviana. *Pricing the Priceless Child: The Changing Social Value of Children*. Princeton, NJ: Princeton University Press, 1994.

INDEX

AAP. *See* American Academy of Pediatrics

ABC. *See* Alone, Back, Crib

abortion, 14–15

access, 4
 community differentiating, 37–38
 to education, 160, 165
 environment influenced by, 18–19
 to expert, 26–27
 felony limiting, 143
 intervention ensuring, 192
 to monitor, 169

Accidental Mechanical Suffocation (AMS), 56

Accidental Suffocation and Strangulation in Bed (ASSB), 6–7

accountability, 80–81

ACLU. *See* American Civil Liberties Union

Adoption and Safe Families Act, 152

advertisement, 82, 93–94, 97, 98, 99, 104–5

advice, 42–43, 206n7
 against co-sleep, 147–48
 death motivating, 28
 education reflected by, 30–31
 expert expanding, 34–35
 to mother, 26–27
 parent inundated by, 1
 by Safe Sleep Campaign, 84
 science in, 36–37
 before twentieth century, 27–35

advisory state project, 96

advocacy, 63–68

African American people, 86, 139, 142, 153–54

authority mistrusted by, 51

bed-sharing by, 92

blame on, 47

criminalization of, 131

culture of, 46

death in, 32

infant mortality in, 36, 46, 178, 217n19

intervention targeting, 82–83, 92, 131–32

in Milwaukee, 86, 117

prematurity impacting, 87–88, 193

risk associated with, 50, 193–94

SIDS in, 8

stereotype impacting, 52

stigma impacting, 113

vulnerability of, 101

Against Health (Metzl and Kirkland), 2, 172

alcohol, 59, 90, 112, 120–22, 135–44, 157
 in environment, 67
 mother using, 138

Algorithms of Oppression (Noble), 182

Almeling, Rene, 232n33

Alone, Back, Crib (ABC), 75, 110–11, 148, 176

American Academy of Pediatrics (AAP), 5, 10–11, 195
 advocacy critiquing, 65–66
 ASTM International against, 72
 against bed-sharing, 56–58
 on co-sleep, 9, 203n13
 on environment, 57, 224n45
 Fisher-Price contradicting, 74–75
 guidelines by, 55–59, 77–78, 123
 La Leche League against, 67

against bed-sharing (*cont.*)
  monitor rejected by, 175–76
  policy of, 54, 211n7
  recall and, 53–81
  Rock 'n Play Sleeper and, 55–81
  on room-sharing, 203n13
  SUID reduced by, 124
American Civil Liberties Union (ACLU), 139
AMS. *See* Accidental Mechanical Suffocation
Anders, Thomas, 64
Annie E. Casey Foundation, 113
anthropology, 63–68
anxiety, 14
  around death, 1
  exceptions heightening, 164–65
  gender and, 179–83
  market recognizing, 163
  of mother, 179–83
  of parent, 13, 161–62, 166, 179–83
  postpartum, 13
  from risk, 179–83
  in Safe Sleep Campaign, 217n17
Anxious Parents (Stearns), 164
Apple, Rima, 37–38
Archives of Pediatric and Adolescent Medicine, 211n18
Armstrong, Elizabeth, 19
asphyxia, 146, 203n11, 224n44
ASSB. *See* Accidental Suffocation and Strangulation in Bed
ASTM International (organization), 72, 79
Atkinson, V. Sue, 39
authority, 32–33, 39–40, 45, 51, 174–75
Automating Inequality (Eubanks), 141–42
autonomy, 18, 152–53

Babies Sleeping Safe, 114–16
Baby and Child Care (Spock), 41
The Baby Book (Sears, M., and Sears, W.), 48
Baby Vida (baby monitor), 169, 175

Back to Sleep Campaign, 49–51, 55, 124, 162, 218n52
Back to the Breast (Martucci), 43–44
Bad Moms (film), 182–83
A Bad Moms Christmas (film), 182–83
Baiocco, Dana, 79–81, 216n126
Baker, Bevan, 96, 117
Ball, Helen, 63–64
Baltimore, Maryland, 109–13
Baltimore City Health Department, 110
Barrett, Tom, 113, 115–17
Beck, Nancy, 77
Beck, Ulrich, 11, 12
bed-sharing, 217n16
  AAP against, 56–58
  by African American people, 92
  Baltimore City Health Department on, 110
  breastfeeding promoted by, 64
  as choice, 80, 85
  co-sleep contrasted with, 9, 66
  couch confusing, 58
  legislation on, 122
  race and, 106
  risk of, 90, 103, 109, 137–38
  safety of, 89–93, 121–22
  self-reporting of, 59
  standards resisting, 79
  UNICEF acknowledging, 59
Beltran, Alicia, 14–15, 206n63
BHCW. *See* Black Health Coalition of Wisconsin
biomedicalization, 173–74
biometrics, 162, 227n6, 227n9
birth control, 153
Black Health Coalition of Wisconsin (BHCW), 92, 114–15, 198–99
Black Mirror (television show), 161, 187
Black people. *See* African American people
Blair, Peter, 91
blame, 47, 75–76, 134
  See also mother-blame

Blaming Mothers (Fentiman), 75–76
B'More for Healthy Babies, 109–17, 148
Bolt, Richard, 39
Bonafide, Christopher, 174–75
bonding, 9–10, 42
Boston Women's Health Collective, 44
Bowlby, John, 42, 48
Brazelton, T. Berry, 45
breastfeeding, 44, 63–68, 145, 213n50
Bridges, Khiara, 46, 51, 92, 107
Briggs, Laura, 103
Britax BOB jogging stroller, 77
Buerkle, Ann Marie, 77
Byard, Robert, 127

Cadogan, William, 29
Caliban and the Witch (Federici), 31
Campbell, Nancy, 145
The Care and Feeding of Children (Holt), 33–34
CareFirst BlueCross BlueShield, 109–10
caregivers, 128–30, 199
Carrey, Jim, 165
Carroll, Aaron E., 60
case-control, 60–61
Casper, Monica, 111–12
categorization, 8, 21, 126, 128, 140, 159
    SIDS differentiated by, 6, 124–25, 129, 157
Catholic Church, 28–29
Centers for Disease Control and Prevention (CDC), 5–6, 203n11
chair, 57–59, 103, 134
"Changing Concepts of Sudden Infant Death Syndrome," 55–56
Chester, Jeff, 185
Childbirth Without Fear (Dick-Read), 45
child endangerment, 136, 138, 230n109
Children's Bureau, 38
child welfare system, 151
Chivers Yochim, Emily, 180
choice
    as bad, 2, 84–85, 122
    bed-sharing as, 80, 85

health compared with, 193
    Kerkman on, 122
    in legislation, 121
    rhetoric of, 137
    risk contrasted with, 85, 196–97
City of Milwaukee Health Department, 97, 98, 99, 116, 118
Clark, Aleia, 177
class, 39, 83, 133
    Back to Sleep Campaign impacting, 50–51
    co-sleep and, 86–89
    guilt assessed with, 132
    inequality and, 86–89
    market stratifying, 194–95
    protection stratified by, 182
    race contrasted with, 132
    social services influenced by, 141–42
    stereotypes influenced by, 14–15
    women and, 33
classification, 125–29
clergy, 27–28
coddling, 41
Colen, Shellee, 83
Collins, Caitlyn, 16
Collins, Jennifer, 132
commodity, 104
community, 96
    access differentiated by, 37–38
    BHCW in, 115, 198–99
    co-sleep in, 106
    education with, 160, 200
    individual and, 193
    leaders of, 197–200
    reproductive justice supporting, 197–98
complacency, 176
Conrad, Peter, 172
Consumer Product Safety Act, 71–72
Consumer Product Safety Commission (CPSC), 69, 71–72, 77, 79, 211n18, 214n75
Consumer Reports (nonprofit), 69, 79
The Continuum Concept (Liedloff), 48

coroner, 145
corporations, 78, 214n75
co-sleep, 1, 24, 48, 220n87, 226n104
   AAP on, 9, 203n13
   advice against, 147–48
   bed-sharing contrasted with, 9, 66
   bonding valorized by, 9–10
   breastfeeding with, 67, 145
   class and, 86–89
   in community, 106
   coroner against, 145
   couch in, 103
   counseling against, 147, 153
   in criminalization, 151
   death and, 4–10, 22–23, 122–23
   fear motivating, 150
   inequality and, 82–119
   intentional, 9, 16, 80
   legislation against, 120
   location for, 225n60
   marginalization of, 80
   in Milwaukee, 22, 86–89
   with overlay, 102–3, 146
   politics and, 82–119
   prosecution for, 159
   race and, 86–89
   as risk, 12, 105–6, 112
   safety of, 4–10, 19
   SIDS and, 4–10, 58–59
   sleep contrasted with, 102
   Spock against, 43
   stigma influencing, 12
   with substance use, 140
Cossman, Brenda, 13
Cossman, Debra, 152
cost, 104
Cott, Nancy, 30
couch, 57–59, 96–98, 126, 137, 157,
   225n60
   bed-sharing confused by, 58
   in co-sleep, 103
counseling, 146–53
courts, 152–53

COVID-19 pandemic, 23, 189–90
Cowgill, Brittany, 7, 43, 46, 155, 166, 187
CPSC. See Consumer Product Safety
   Commission
crack babies, 139
Cribs for Kids, 104, 148
criminalization, 155–56
   of African American people, 131
   co-sleep in, 151
   of mother, 139
   of parent, 134, 191
   prosecution contrasted with, 140
   of women, 139, 159
   See also prosecution
crying, 39, 43
The Cultural Contradictions of Motherhood (Hays), 16
culture, 38, 46, 64, 107, 168
Cunliffe, Emma, 133, 157

data, 188
   instincts contrasted with, 170
   monitor gathering, 169, 173–74, 184
   Owlet collecting, 170, 184–85, 227n6
   privacy of, 185, 226n96
   surveillance of, 184–85
Davis, Dána-Ain, 52, 88–89, 193
death, 128
   advice motivated by, 28
   of African American people, 32
   anxiety around, 1
   blame within, 134
   CDC tracking, 5–6
   co-sleep and, 4–10, 22–23, 122–23
   culture and, 64
   environment understanding, 124–25
   investigation of, 126–27
   location of, 134, 224n58
   monitor anticipating, 167
   mother-blame in, 134
   Rock 'n Play Sleeper linked to, 68–69
   substance use linked to, 137–38
   technology solving, 194

See also infant mortality; Sudden Infant Death Syndrome; Sudden Unexpected Infant Death
deference, 151
deficit model, 108
demographics, 86–87, 130–34
Denbow, Jennifer, 18
development, 158
device, 171–78, 181
diagnostic shift, 125–30, 191
Dick-Read, Grantly, 45
discrimination, 193–94
doctor, 44–45
documentation, 149
Doucleff, Michaeleen, 90–91
Douglas, Susan, 17, 179
Downs, Kenya, 86
drugs, 15–16, 136–41
Dubriwny, Tasha, 179, 183
Duncan, Jhodie, 127
Dunn, Halbert L., 168

education, 147
    ABC in, 148
    access to, 160, 165
    advice reflecting, 30–31
    with community, 160, 200
    environment restricted by, 197
    from expert, 75
    in hospital, 148
    individual influenced by, 36
    morality mobilized by, 109
    against parent, 150–51, 193
    as reproductive duress, 149, 152
    risk reduced by, 200
    social services mandating, 150
Ehrenreich, Barbara, 37
Elders, Joycelyn, 49
emotions, 100–101
    See also anxiety
employment, 42
empowerment, 151, 181–82
environment, 189–94, 198, 200, 230n87

AAP on, 57, 224n45
access influencing, 18–19
alcohol in, 67
for bed-sharing, 67
death understood with, 124–25
development with, 158
education restricting, 197
individual contrasted with, 36
intervention impacted by, 199
risk in, 90, 95
of safety, 99–100
SIDS impacted by, 54–55
women as, 195–96
Essay Upon Nursing and the Management of Children (Cadogan), 29
Eubanks, Virginia, 141–42
Evans, Jeff, 169
Evans, Mollie, 169
Evers, Tony, 108
expert, 21, 37, 44–45, 181
    access to, 26–27
    advice expanded by, 34–35
    education from, 75
    individual contrasted with, 12
    mother as, 49
    norms enforced by, 42
    parent accepting, 62–63
"Experts and Parenting Culture" (Lee), 63

Family League of Baltimore, 109–10
father, 112, 221n132
FDA. *See* Food and Drug Administration
fear, 143, 150
Federici, Silvia, 31
Felder, Eleanor K., 43
Feldman-Winter, Lori, 59
felony, 136, 143, 221n120
feminism, 20, 44–46, 49, 182
Fentiman, Linda, 15, 75–76, 132–33, 140
Fernandes, Leela, 3, 11
Fetal Infant Mortality Review (FIMR), 88, 113, 218n43
fetal personhood, 196

Fetherston, Catherine, 65
fetus, 140, 196
FIMR. *See* Fetal Infant Mortality Review
Fisher-Price (company)
    AAP contradicted by, 74–75
    negligence of, 71
    Peloton echoing, 214n75
    recall resisted by, 69
    responsibility of, 75
    standards manipulated by, 72–73
    testing failed by, 70–71
    trust in, 74
    See also Rock 'n Play Sleeper
Fixing Families (Reich), 151
Fixmer-Oraiz, Natalie, 14, 138
Flavin, Jeanne, 131–32, 138–40
Foley, John, 214n75
Food and Drug Administration (FDA), 174–75
FoodShare, 221n120
Fox News, 107
Fu, Linda, 83

Gamble, Vanessa, 51
Gardasil (vaccine), 177
Gathirimu, Jessica, 122
gender, 83
    anxiety and, 179–83
    Baiocco on, 216n126
    in COVID-19 pandemic, 189–90
    housekeeping implicating, 155
    in marketing, 168–71, 180
    with monitor, 164–68
    parent and, 14–20, 161–88
    race and, 14–20
    responsibility influenced by, 62, 138
    risk and, 161–88
    See also women
Geronimus, Arline, 193
Gerry Baby Safetronics Deluxe Baby Monitor, 165
Giarnella, Lori, 26
Gilbert, Pamela, 77

Golden, Janet, 38
Good Housekeeping (magazine), 42
Goodrich et al v. Fisher-Price Inc., 71
Goodwin, Michele, 132, 143
Gore, Tipper, 49
Governed Through Choice (Denbow), 18
Graco I-monitor Digital Color Video Baby Monitor, 165
guidelines, 55–59, 60–63, 77–78, 123, 126–27, 203n13
guilt, 132
Gurr, Barbara, 83, 108–9

hacking, 184–85
Harvey, David, 11
Hauck, Fern, 83
Hays, Sharon, 16, 179
health
    biomedicalization of, 173–74
    choice compared with, 193
    culture explaining, 107
    inequality and, 86–89
    as lowest common denominator, 16
    morality linked with, 172
    in neoliberalism, 1–3, 152
    Owlet promising, 170
    preconception, 101, 114
    responsibility for, 11
    weathering of, 88
    See also public health
healthcare, 190
Health Insurance Probability and Accountability Act (HIPAA), 184
heartbeat bill, 14–15
Hemphill, Katie, 32
HIPAA. *See* Health Insurance Probability and Accountability Act
history, 21, 27, 87, 154
Holmes, Elizabeth, 227n9
Holt, Luther Emmet, 33–34
home, 33
hospital, 148
Hospital Certification Initiative, 148

housekeeping, 133–34, 155
Hoyt, Waneta, 133–34
human papillomavirus (HPV), 177

incarceration, 192–93
individual
    community and, 193
    education influencing, 36
    environment contrasted with, 36
    expert contrasted with, 12
    infant mortality and, 112
    narrative intruding on, 145
    responsibility of, 1–2, 84, 145, 155, 185, 190
    risk managed by, 73, 232n33
    wellness of, 168–69
individualism, 17
industry, 2–3, 162
inequality
    class and, 86–89
    co-sleep and, 82–119
    COVID-19 pandemic exacerbating, 23
    health and, 86–89
    in Milwaukee, 86–89
    politics and, 82–119
    race and, 86–89
    See also marginalization; poverty; racial disparities
Infant Care, 38–39, 43, 208n93
"Infant Deaths in Inclined Sleepers," 78–79
infant mortality
    in African American people, 36, 46, 178, 217n19
    co-sleep and, 91
    gap in, 88, 112
    individual and, 112
    legitimacy enhanced by, 35
    marginalization impacting, 189
    in Milwaukee, 103
    parent solving, 84–85
    race stratifying, 162
    racial disparities in, 3, 8, 10, 36, 46–47, 50, 82–87, 109–14, 117, 178, 194, 199
    risk of, 178
    See also Sudden Infant Death Syndrome; Sudden Unexpected Infant Death; suffocation
influencer, 70
Instagram, 70, 173, 228n48
instincts, 170
International Classification of Diseases, 125
intervention, 21
    access ensured by, 192
    African American people targeted by, 82–83, 92, 131–32
    autonomy justifying, 18
    Beltran on, 15
    drugs involved in, 139–40
    environment impacting, 199
    Native American people impacted by, 141
    parent exposed by, 105
    surveillance threatening, 14–15
"Intimate Surveillance" (Leaver), 184
investigation, 126–27, 157–59
"Is Sleeping with Your Baby as Dangerous as Doctors Say?" (Doucleff), 90–91

Jackson, Deborah, 48
Jamison, David, 175
Johns Hopkins Center for Communication Programs, 110
Johnson, Bethany, 27
Johnston, Josée, 181–82
Journal of the American Medical Association, 169, 175
Judgment of Solomon, 25

Kemkes, Ariane, 33
Kendall-Tackett, Kathleen, 58
Kerkman, Samantha, 120–22
Kiddie Alert, 165
Killing the Black Body (Roberts, D.), 47

Kirkland, Anna, 2, 172
Kopp, Katharina, 185
Kukla, Rebecca, 29

labor, 179–80
Lamaze, Fernand, 45
law, 140, 186
Lawrence, Ruth, 66
Leach, J. Shaughn, 65
leaders, 197–200
lead poisoning, 117–19
Leaver, Tama, 173, 184
La Leche League, 44, 67
Lee, Ellie, 63
legislation, 120, 122
legitimacy, 35
liability, 68
Liedloff, Jean, 48
Lindbergh baby, 164
location, 39, 134, 224n58, 225n60
    See also bed-sharing; chair; couch
Loertscher, Tammy, 15
Luna, Zakiya, 192
Lupton, Deborah, 12, 96, 145, 183

MacKendrick, Norah, 73, 163
Macvarish, Jan, 13
Magnet, Shoshana, 162, 170–71
Making Motherhood Work (Collins, C.), 16
Mamo, Laura, 177
manufacturer, 72
marginalization, 32–33, 80, 119, 189
market, 163, 168–71, 194–95, 227n11
marketing, 70, 168–71, 180
Martucci, Jessica, 43–44
Maryland, 187, 230n109
Mashable (media platform/company), 182
maternal-fetal conflict, 19
Matthews, Dearea, 111
McKay, Mike, 187
McKenna, James, 48–49, 63, 102, 145,
    213n50
McKnight, Regina, 14, 206n63

McManus, Patricia, 92, 114, 117–18, 198
Meckel, Richard, 35–36, 46
media, 41–42
Medical Apartheid (Washington), 139
medical examiner, 157–58, 221n139
medicalization, 34–35, 52
    See also biomedicalization
Metzl, Jonathan, 2, 172
Michaels, Meredith, 179
microcelebrities, 173
Miller, Claire Cain, 60
Milwaukee, Wisconsin, 82
    African American people in, 86, 117
    Baltimore compared with, 109–13
    co-sleep in, 22, 86–89
    cost addressed by, 104
    demographics of, 86–87
    inequality in, 86–89
    infant mortality in, 103
    lead poisoning in, 117
    McManus in, 198
    poverty in, 87
    racial disparities in, 199
    See also City of Milwaukee Health
        Department; Safe Sleep Campaign
Milwaukee Journal Sentinel (newspaper),
    91–92, 217n19
Mimo (baby monitor), 169
misdemeanor, 143
Mitchell, Ed, 91
Monbaby (baby monitor), 169
monitor
    AAP rejecting, 175–76
    access to, 169
    breathing, 186
    cardiorespiratory, 167
    complacency with, 176
    contemporary, 167–68
    data gathered by, 169, 173–74, 184
    death anticipated by, 167
    gender with, 164–68
    hacking of, 184–85
    labor extended by, 179–80

marketing of, 168–71
by parent, 164–68
parent impacted by, 167
racial disparities ignored by, 178
regulation avoided by, 174–75
reliability of, 175
risk managed by, 164–68, 177–78, 187–88
SIDS and, 166–67
of sleep, 164–68
as surveillance, 177, 182
technology eclipsing, 23
wearable, 24, 168–71, 173–80, 184, 187–88
See also Owlet (baby monitor)
Montgomery, Kathryn, 185
Moon, Rachel, 83, 176
Moore, Lisa Jean, 111–12
morality, 109, 172
Moran, Rachel Lousie, 96
More Than Medicine (Nelson, J.), 46
mother
advice to, 26–27
alcohol used by, 138
anxiety of, 179–83
as bad, 138–39, 156–57, 182–83
bonding with, 42
breastfeeding empowering, 44
in child endangerment, 138
in child welfare system, 151
criminalization of, 139
with doctor, 44–45
drugs used by, 141
as expert, 49
fetus separated from, 140
as good, 159, 163, 169
housekeeping measuring, 133–34
individualism influencing, 17
as influencer, 70
neoliberalism pressuring, 180–81
pediatricians supervising, 40
responsibility of, 30, 111
rhetoric against, 217n14

risk and, 15–16, 163
room-sharing disrupting, 61
safety managed by, 27
stigma with, 219n70
surveillance of, 47–48
mother-blame, 21, 26, 28, 41, 46, 157
in death, 134
public health with, 35–36
responsibility distracted by, 103
stereotypes resulting in, 133
motherhood
intensive, 16–17, 49, 60, 163, 183
natural, 43–44
scientific, 37, 43–44, 181
Moynihan Report, 108
murder, 97–98
Murder, Medicine, and Motherhood (Cunliffe), 133
Murray, Ellie, 190

narrative, 1, 3, 107–8, 124, 145
National Infant Sleep Position, 58
National Public Radio (NPR), 86, 90–91
native advertising, 70
Native American people, 38, 135, 144
intervention impacting, 141
reproductive justice within, 83
risk associated with, 50
SIDS in, 8
negligence, 71
Nelkin, Dorothy, 12, 168
Nelson, Amber, 177
Nelson, Jennifer, 46
Nelson, Margaret, 166
neoliberalism, 163–64
health in, 1–3, 152
mother pressured in, 180–81
racialization distracted from by, 95
against regulation, 73–74
responsibility in, 137
risk and, 10–14
New York Times (newspaper), 44, 70, 140, 165, 190

Noble, Safiya, 182
norms, 4–5, 34–35, 42, 64–65
NPR. *See* National Public Radio

Oaks, Laury, 19, 83, 101, 109
Oliviero, Katie, 100
opioid epidemic, 136–37
oppression, 192
"Oscillation Between Pampering and
    Hostility" (Spitz), 42
Our Bodies, Our Crimes (Flavin), 138
Our Bodies Ourselves, 44
Ourselves and Our Children, 44
overlay, 28–29, 31, 46, 102–3, 146
Overton, Evan, 75–76
Overton, Keenan, 75–76
Owlet (baby monitor), 161, 163, 228n48
    data collected by, 184–85, 227n6
    device compared with, 175
    FDA circumvented by, 174
    health promised by, 170
    Owlet Band by, 194
    peace of mind with, 171, 173
    responsibility of, 172
    SIDS acknowledged by, 171–72
    smart sock by, 164, 169–70, 173, 177
    testimonials promoting, 176
    worry normalized by, 180

Paltrow, Lynn, 131–32, 139–40
parent, 129, 131–32, 134, 136
    accountability demanded by, 80–81
    advice inundating, 1
    Amber, 146–47, 149–50, 154
    anxiety of, 13, 161–62, 166, 179–83
    attachment, 48–49, 216n125
    as bad, 76, 121, 128
    bed-sharing by, 99, 99–100
    classification appreciated by, 125–26
    corporations compared with, 78
    counseling received by, 146–53
    Cribs for Kids contacted by, 104
    criminalization of, 134, 191

demographics of, 130–34
diagnostic shift impacting, 125–30
drugs used by, 136–37
education against, 150–51, 193
Elizabeth as, 146–47, 152, 154
expert accepted by, 62–63
gender and, 14–20, 161–88
as good, 14–20, 76, 161–88
infant mortality solved by, 84–85
intervention exposing, 105
Janet as, 135, 138
Jenna and Adam as, 136, 142–46
Leah as, 135–36, 141–44
liability of, 68
monitor impacting, 164–68
narrative about, 1
perception shaping, 31
as perpetrators, 120–60
poverty impacting, 132
prosecution of, 122–23
race and, 14–20
responsibility of, 92–93
risk and, 47, 75–76, 103, 141, 161–88
Safe Sleep Campaign misleading, 85
safety dividing, 80
SIDS motivating, 185–86
substance use by, 135–46
surveillance with, 183–88
technology utilized by, 183–88
See also father; mother
parental rights, 152
Patel, Purvi, 14, 206n63
Paul, Ian, 61
peace of mind, 161, 171, 173, 178, 188
pediatricians, 39–40
    See also American Academy of Pediat-
    rics
Pediatrics (journal), 54, 61
Peloton, 214n75
Pennsylvania, 104–5, 131, 147–48
perception, 31
perpetrators, 120–60
personality, 41

Peterson, Laci, 140
Pittsburgh, Pennsylvania, 104–5
Plant, Rebecca Jo, 41
Platt, Robert, 91
plea deal, 143
policy, 21–22, 54, 108–9, 144, 196, 211n7
politics, 77, 82–119
Popsugar (company), 182–83
position, 49, 55–56, 70–71, 124
postfeminism, 181–82
poverty
    in Milwaukee, 87
    moral construction of, 141–59
    parent impacted by, 132
    prosecution considering, 144
    risk attracted by, 145
    SIDS overlapped with, 158
PRAMS. *See* Pregnancy Risk Assessment
    Monitoring System
pregnancy, 88, 139, 144, 195, 207n46
Pregnancy Risk Assessment Monitoring
    System (PRAMS), 88
prematurity, 87–88, 116, 193–94
prenatal care, 144
Prenatal Protection Act, 140
privacy, 185, 188, 226n96
probation, 153
prosecution, 226n104
    of caregivers, 128–29
    for co-sleep, 159
    criminalization contrasted with, 140
    of parent, 122–23
    poverty considered by, 144
    pregnancy and, 139
    suffocation understanding, 124–25
prosecutors, 142–43
protection, 182
Psychological Care of Infant and Child
    (Watson), 40
public health, 35–36, 101, 119, 189

The Quantified Self (Lupton), 183
Quinlan, Margaret, 27

race, 76, 83
    bed-sharing and, 106
    class contrasted with, 132
    co-sleep and, 86–89
    gender and, 14–20
    inequality and, 86–89
    infant mortality stratified by, 162
    parent and, 14–20
    responsibility influenced by, 107
    in Safe Sleep Campaign, 113–14
    status intertwined with, 142
    See also African American people; Native American people
racial disparities
    in Back to Sleep Campaign, 50
    history reflecting, 87
    in infant mortality, 3, 8, 10, 36, 46–47, 50, 82–87, 109–14, 117, 178, 194, 199
    in Milwaukee, 199
    monitor ignoring, 178
    in prematurity, 116
    in Safe Sleep Campaign, 86
    in SIDS, 191–92
racialization, 87–88, 95, 101, 107–8
Radical Reproductive Justice (Ross and Roberts, L.), 192
Radio Nurse (baby monitor), 164
Raphael, Jody, 138
recall, 53–81, 214n75
reform, 35–36
regulation, 71–74, 164, 171, 174–75
Reich, Jennifer, 141, 151, 156
reliability, 175
Reproducing Race (Bridges), 51, 92
reproductive duress, 149, 152
Reproductive Injustice (Davis), 52
reproductive justice, 3–4, 194–95
    community supported by, 197–98
    incarceration in, 192–93
    within Native American people, 83
    public health centralizing, 119
Reproductive Justice (Gurr), 108–9

Reproductive Rights as Human Rights
   (Luna), 192
responsibility, 80–81
   of caregivers, 199
   corporation weaponizing, 214n75
   counseling and, 152
   of Fisher-Price, 75
   gender influencing, 62, 138
   for health, 11
   of individual, 1–2, 84, 145, 155, 185, 190
   of mother, 30, 111
   mother-blame distracting, 103
   in neoliberalism, 137
   of Owlet, 172
   of parent, 92–93
   politics personalized in, 95–96
   race influencing, 107
   regulation and, 71–72, 174
Rest Uneasy (Cowgill), 7, 155, 166
rhetoric, 137, 217n14
Ribble, Margaret, 44
The Rights of Infants (Ribble), 44
risk, 84
   African American people associated
      with, 50, 193–94
   anxiety from, 179–83
   of bed-sharing, 90, 103, 109, 137–38
   choice contrasted with, 85, 196–97
   co-sleep as, 12, 105–6, 112
   of drugs, 15–16
   education reducing, 200
   in environment, 90, 95
   gender and, 161–88
   individual managing, 73, 232n33
   of infant mortality, 178
   in marketing, 168–71
   monitor managing, 164–68, 177–78,
      187–88
   mother and, 15–16, 163
   Native American people associated, 50
   neoliberalism and, 10–14
   parent and, 47, 75–76, 103, 141, 161–88
   poverty attracting, 145

in pregnancy, 195
   sleep as, 180
   surveillance required by, 166, 183–84
   testimonials on, 177
Roberts, Dorothy, 33, 47
Roberts, Lynn, 192
Rock 'n Play Sleeper
   AAP and, 53–81
   death linked to, 68–69
   Instagram recommending, 70
   marketing of, 70
   recall of, 53–81
room-sharing, 24, 60–63, 123, 203n13
Rosenthal, Caitlin, 207n46
Ross, Loretta, 192
Rowland, Perrin, 26

Sacks, Alexandra, 13
Safe Sleep Campaign
   advertisement in, 82, 85
   advice by, 84
   as advisory state project, 96
   anxiety in, 217n17
   Babies Sleeping Safe contrasted with,
      114–16
   Back to Sleep Campaign incorporated
      by, 218n52
   B'More for Healthy Babies contrasted
      with, 110–11
   "Helpless" in, 100, 216n2
   "Knife" in, 93–104, 97, 98, 99, 115–16,
      218n52, 220n87
   lead poisoning and, 118–19
   marginalization with, 119
   murder in, 97–98
   "News" in, 216n2
   Outdoor Mattress Campaign in, 97–
      98, 98
   parent misled by, 85
   prematurity focusing, 116
   race in, 113–14
   racial disparities in, 86
   "Rethink Your Position" in, 102

"Rollover" in, 82, 220n87
"Tombstone" in, 93–104, *97*, *98*, *99*, 216n2, 218n52
website of, 93
Safe Sleep for Babies Act, 78
safety, 1–3, 11, 20–21, 71
  of bed-sharing, 89–93, 121–22
  as commodity, 104
  of co-sleep, 4–10, 19
  environment of, 99–100
  manufacturer influencing, 72
  market emphasizing, 227n11
  mother managing, 27
  oppression determining, 192
  parent divided on, 80
Save the Babies, 38
Schmid, John, 87
science, 36–37, 41–42
Sears, Martha, 48
Sears, William, 17, 48, 67
self-reporting, 59
self-tracking, 183
Serve Marketing, 93–94
"Should Your Baby Really Sleep in the Same Bed as You?" (Miller), 60
Shuai, Bei Bei, 14, 206n63
sibling, 156
SIDS. *See* Sudden Infant Death Syndrome
"SIDS and Other Sleep-Related Infant Deaths," 57
SIDS Task Force, 66
Silverman, Jacob, 184
sin, 28–29
slaveowner, 207n46
sleep, 55–56, 124
  consolidated, 212n39
  co-sleep contrasted with, 102
  home impacting, 33
  in *Infant Care*, 38–39
  monitor in, 164–68
  norms of, 64–65
  as risk, 180

  socialization determining, 25
  solitary, 33–34, 64
  See also bed-sharing; co-sleep
sleeper
  inclined, 68–69, 72–74, 78–79
  position in, 70–71
  recall eliminating, 76–77
  reclined, 70, 72
  regulation excluding, 72–73
  Safe Sleep for Babies Act banning, 78
  See also Rock 'n Play Sleeper
The Slumbering Masses (Wolf-Meyer), 33
smart sock, 23, 176, 180, 194
  by Owlet, 164, 169–70, 173, 177
  peace of mind with, 161
  regulation of, 174–75
smoking, 101, 109
SNAP. *See* Supplemental Nutrition Assistance Program
Snuza Hero (baby monitor), 169
socialization, 25
social services, 141–42, 150
Solinger, Rickie, 29
"Solomon's Wisdom" (Lawrence), 66
Spitz, René, 42
Spock, Benjamin, 41, 43
Sproutling (baby monitor), 169
standards, 72–73, 79
status, 3, 131–32, 142
Stearns, Peter, 26
stereotype, 14–15, 52, 133
stigma, 12, 111, 113, 219n70
stress, 88
substance use, 135–46, 187, 225n87
  See also alcohol; drugs; opioid epidemic
Sudden Infant and Early Childhood Death (Duncan and Byard), 127
Sudden Infant Death Syndrome (SIDS), 1, 123
  in African American people, 8
  AMS compared with, 56
  ASSB contrasted with, 6–7

Sudden Infant Death Syndrome (*cont.*)
breastfeeding against, 66
categorization differentiating, 6, 124–25, 129, 157
co-sleep and, 4–10, 58–59
diagnostic shift reducing, 127–28, 191
environment impacting, 54–55
monitor and, 166–67
narrative on, 124
in Native American people, 8
overlay and, 46
Owlet acknowledging, 171–72
parent motivated by, 185–86
in Pennsylvania, 131
position reducing, 55
poverty overlapping with, 158
racial disparities in, 191–92
room-sharing reducing, 60
sibling with, 156
suffocation within, 125, 156–57
SUID differentiated from, 223n28, 223n42
Triple Risk model exemplifying, 7, 126
Sudden Infant Death Syndrome Education and Prevention Program Act, 147–48
Sudden Unexpected Infant Death (SUID), 5–6, 20–21, 123–24, 191–92, 223n28, 223n42
suffocation, 6–7, 56, 146, 153
with diagnostic shift, 128
Infant Care removing, 208n93
Kerkman motivated by, 120–21
prosecution understood with, 124–25
within SIDS, 125, 156–57
See also asphyxia
SUID. *See* Sudden Unexpected Infant Death
Supplemental Nutrition Assistance Program (SNAP), 143
support, 79–80
surveillance, 194
autonomy justifying, 18

coercive, 183
of data, 184–85
intervention threatened with, 14–15
monitor as, 177, 182
of mother, 47–48
with parent, 183–88
policy reinforcing, 108–9
risk requiring, 166, 183–84
self-tracking contrasted with, 183
with technology, 162, 183–88
of women, 15
swaddling, 29
Swain, Geoffrey, 116, 121
Sweet Sleep, 67

TANF. *See* Temporary Assistance to Needy Families
Taylor, Judith, 181–82, 217n17
Taylor, Teresa, 64
technology, 227n9, 228n20
Black Mirror demonstrating, 161
death solved by, 194
in law, 186
monitor eclipsed by, 23
parent utilizing, 183–88
substance use solved with, 187
surveillance with, 162, 183–88
See also data; Owlet; smart sock
Temporary Assistance to Needy Families (TANF), 143
testimonials, 176–77
testing, 70–72
Texas, 140
Theranos, 227n9
Three in a Bed (Jackson), 48
Tread+, 214n75
Triple Risk model, 7, 126, 156
Truman Burbank (fictional character), 165
Trump, Donald, 77
trust, 51, 74
Tsing, Anna Lowenhaupt, 92
Tuskegee Syphilis Study, 51

Unborn Child Protection Act, 15
UNICEF, 59, 145, 190
Using Women (Campbell), 145

Valdez, Natali, 196, 199
Villalobos, Ana, 17
vulnerability, 100–101
Vulnerability Politics (Oliviero), 100

Wade, Willie, 98–99
Waggoner, Miranda, 18, 101–2, 114, 177–78
Walker, Scott, 108
Washington, Harriet, 139
Watson, John B., 40
weathering, 88, 193
wellness, 168–69
"Why Is Milwaukee So Bad for Black
    People?" (Downs), 86
Wight, Nancy, 65
Wilson, Julie A., 180
Wisconsin, 150–51, 159

Wolf-Meyer, Matthew, 33
women, 14
    authority suspecting, 32–33
    class and, 33
    criminalization of, 139, 159
    employment of, 42
    as environment, 195–96
    feminism and, 45–46
    law against, 140
    marginalization of, 32–33
    surveillance of, 15
    See also mother
Workman, Kurt, 161
World Health Organization, 125, 145, 190

"Your Baby After Dark" (Felder), 43
You're Doing It Wrong (Johnson and
    Quinlan), 27

Zavella, Patricia, 197
Zelizer, Viviana, 31

ABOUT THE AUTHOR

LAURA HARRISON is Associate Professor in the Department of Gender and Women's Studies at Minnesota State University, Mankato. She is the author of *Brown Bodies, White Babies: The Politics of Cross-Racial Surrogacy.*